The Work of Pierre Bourdieu

The Work of Pierre Bourdieu

Recognizing society

Derek Robbins

WESTVIEW PRESS
Boulder & San Francisco

First Published 1991 in Great Britain by

Open University Press
Celtic Court
22 Ballmoor
Buckingham
MK18 1XW

Published in 1991 in the United States by
Westview Press
5500 Central Avenue
Boulder, Colorado 80301

Library of Congress Cataloging-in-Publication Data

Robbins, Derek
    The Work of Pierre Bourdieu/Derek Robbins.
        p.   cm.
    Includes bibliographical references (p.   ) and index.
    ISBN 0–8133–1350–3 (HC)—ISBN 0–8133–1351–1 (PB)
    1. Bourdieu, Pierre. 2. Sociology—France—History.
    3. Sociology—Methodology. I. Title.
    HM22.F8B77 1991
    301′.01—dc20   91–14074
                                                          CIP

Typeset in Singapore
Printed in Great Britain

For Diana,
Oliver and Felix

Contents

Acknowledgements

The development of my work on Bourdieu was made possible by a grant under the Economic and Social Research Council/Centre National de la Recherche Scientifique Exchange Scheme for Social Scientists during 1986–7. My host institution in two visits during that year was the Institut de l'Histoire du Temps Présent, and I am grateful to Michael Pollak for introducing me to members of the Centre de Sociologie Européenne and inviting me to the inaugural meeting of the Société Française pour l'Histoire des Sciences de l'Homme. Within the Centre, it was Monique de Saint Martin and Yvette Delsaut who encouraged me, first of all, to embark on a preliminary analysis of the reception of Bourdieu's work in England before proceeding to this full study, and both were generous in their support. Since 1986, I have been greatly indebted to Yvette Delsaut who has always found time to talk with me and to provide me with up-to-date information. Since my first meeting with him in October 1986, Pierre Bourdieu himself has actively encouraged my work and I have enormously appreciated the occasions on which I have been able to discuss various projects, including this book, with him.

I have only been able to undertake the research necessary to write this book with the practical assistance of the librarians at the Polytechnic of East London and I am especially grateful to Harbans Chahal and Robin Stinson at the Livingstone House library and to Valerie Pearn at the Holbrook library. The Pro-Rector, Academic, at the Polytechnic of East London – Professor Les Allen – has offered encouragement and I have benefited from discussions with my colleagues in the Group for Research into Access and Student Programmes (GRASP) within the School for Independent Study – Phil Bradbury, John Cocking, Dr. Maggie Humm, Dave O'Reilly and Steve Brindle. I have also appreciated the interest which has been shown in my work by staff and students in the Departments of Sociology and of Cultural Studies within the

Polytechnic and, in particular, by Professor Michael Rustin, Dr. Mike Smee and Catherine Hall.

I should like, finally, to acknowledge the advice and assistance given to me by John Skelton of the Open University Press.

Preface

Vous savez, quand j'écris, je crains beaucoup de choses, c'est-à-dire beaucoup de mauvaises lectures. Ce qui explique, on me le reproche souvent, la complexité de certaines de mes phrases. J'essaie de décourager à l'avance les mauvaises lectures que je puis souvent prévoir. Mais les mises en garde que je glisse dans une parenthèse, un adjectif, des guillemets, etc., ne touchent que ceux qui n'en ont pas besoin. Et chacun retient, dans une analyse complexe, le côte qui le dérange le moins.

You know, when I write, I dread lots of things – that is lots of bad readings. This explains the thing for which I am often reproached – the complexity of some of my phrases. I try to discourage in advance the bad readings which I can often foresee. But the cautions which I slip into a parenthesis, an adjective, or in inverted commas, etc., only register with those people who don't need them. In a complex analysis, people retain the aspect which disturbs them least.

> Pierre Bourdieu. (From a conversation with Didier Eribon published in *Libération* (3 and 4 November 1979), and reproduced in *Questions de sociologie* (Paris, Éditions de Minuit, 1980), p. 14.)

The scope for misreading Bourdieu by reading him through an introduction is enormous – and fills me with dread. This is why it must be said in a preface that this book is intended to guide readers towards and through the original texts – many of which are now rapidly becoming available in translation. This introduction to Bourdieu's work tries to condense arguments which have been densely expressed in the numerous books and articles which he has written since his first main publication of 1958. I follow Bourdieu's career in chronological order and, hence, the following brief summary of that career offers a quick overview both of the career and of the structure of this book. A full bibliography is given as an appendix.

Born in the Béarn in 1930, Bourdieu studied at the École Normale Supérieure in Paris. He undertook ethnographic researches in Algeria during the War of Algerian Independence, publishing *Sociologie de l'Algérie* in 1958 and *Travail et travailleurs en Algérie* and *Le Déracinement, la crise de l'agriculture traditionelle en Algérie* in 1963 and 1964 respectively (Chapter 2). On returning to France, Bourdieu commenced a series of research projects from his initial base at the University of Lille, as well as researching into his own native Béarn. This work, culminating in the publication of *Les Héritiers, les étudiants et la culture* in 1964, is considered in Chapter 3. Whilst there was a logical development from *Les Héritiers* through to the publication of *La Reproduction. Éléments pour une théorie du système d'enseignement* in 1970, the mid-1960s also saw the publication of the findings of other projects which had been started at Lille – the analysis of the social uses of photography published as *Un Art moyen* in 1965, and the analysis of the visiting 'publics' of museums and art galleries published as *L'Amour de l'art* in 1966. Bourdieu took up a position at the École des Hautes Études en Sciences Sociales in Paris in the early 1960s and his researches continued in Paris within the Centre de Sociologie Européenne. The work which reached a climax in the publication of *La Reproduction* (1970) is discussed in Chapter 4, but, before 1970, Bourdieu had been appointed director of his own research group and *Le Métier de sociologue* (1968) – which was a practical manual for researchers – is discussed in Chapter 5. In the early 1970s, Bourdieu wrote a number of theoretical articles in which he analysed the workings of different 'fields' within society, and these are described in Chapter 6. He had already begun to reconsider his earlier interpretation of Algerian society and he made the nature of his re-interpretation explicit in *Esquisse d'une théorie de la pratique* (1972). *Algérie 60* (1977) was a very slightly re-edited version of a part of *Travail et travailleurs en Algérie* (1963), but the text of *Outline of a Theory of Practice* (1977) is much more than just a translation of the earlier *Esquisse d'une théorie de la pratique*. Chapter 7 analyses the development of Bourdieu's thinking between these two texts. Chapter 8 considers the gradual emergence of the idea of 'distinction' through Bourdieu's work and focuses on the text of *La Distinction* (1979) in which he represented the various forms of distinction adopted by different social classes to sustain their social distinction – whether in relation to the consumption of food or of works of art. The publication of *La Distinction* brought to a head the anxiety which Bourdieu had consistently felt in offering a detached analysis of experiences which were lived in an undetached way by those whom he observed. In respect of his Algerian research, this anxiety could be thought to be the normal sensation of the reluctant 'colonial' anthropologist, but Bourdieu developed a critique of the objectivism of social scientists in relation to their own societies as much as in relation to strange ones. This critique was elaborated in *Le Sens pratique* (1980) which is discussed at the end of Chapter 9. The consequence of Bourdieu's critique was that he sought to present himself as a practising social scientist with things to say and, at the same time, to present analytically the social conditions which enabled him to present himself in that way. Chapter 9 looks at the new form of presentation attempted in *Questions de sociologie* (1980) whilst Chapter 10 comments on the works which date from Bourdieu's appointment as Professor of Sociology at the Collège de France, Paris, in 1982 – *Leçon sur la leçon* (1982), *Ce que parler veut dire* (1982), *Homo academicus* (1984), *Choses dites* (1987), and *La Noblesse d'état* (1989). Chapter 11 offers, in summary, some ways of recognizing Bourdieu's work which suggest, finally, that it should be seen to be a consciously self-limiting paradigm of the process by which we should all endeavour (similarly self-limitingly) to recognize our society.

• 1 •

Introduction

I caught this morning morning's minion, king-
  dom of daylight's dauphin, dapple-dawn-drawn Falcon, in
    his riding
  Of the rolling level underneath him steady air, and striding
High there, how he rung upon the rein of a wimpling wing
In his ecstasy! then off, off forth on swing,
  As a skate's heel sweeps smooth on a bow-bend: the hurl and
    gliding
  Rebuffed the big wind. My heart in hiding
Stirred for a bird, – the achieve of, the mastery of the thing!

Gerard Manley Hopkins.[1]

Hopkins did not simply see a falcon, nor did he simply describe what he had more than seen. He 'caught' the being-in-action of the bird and sought to re-present its presence and its motion in sounds – rhymes, alliterations – and rhythms which are more than mere denotative words. Hopkins developed the technique of 'sprung rhythm' in order to re-enact the 'inscape' of the observed object. 'Mastery' – 'maîtrise' – is one of Bourdieu's favourite words. He has tried to avoid 'fixing' society, nailing it down to any limited conception or perception, and has tried to catch the practical mastery which people possess of their situations – to represent the immanent dynamics of the decisions which people actually make within society. In spite of the heavy intellectuality of much of his writing which might suggest a preoccupation with knowledge and thought, Bourdieu's main interest from his earliest work to the present has been in human relations in action.

It cannot be denied that Bourdieu is hard to read. It should be said in his defence that this is partly because he has consciously adopted a presentational strategy which resists any facile assimilation to the preconceived opinions of readers and resists being compartmented in relation to the latest fashionable '-isms', to 'movements', or to 'schools of thought'. Within his texts, he has always acknowledged indebtedness to other authors, such as, for instance, Panofsky or Cassirer or Bachelard, but he has always tried to avoid the game of 'citology' or 'quotology' which, as he suggested in 'La spécificité du champ scientifique et les conditions sociales du progrès de la raison' (1975), is a device used by authors who are seeking to raise the status of their own perceptions by association with that already accorded to 'established' thinkers. For the same kind of reason, Bourdieu has taken steps to ensure that the texts themselves should not be appropriated by any of the 'disciplines' in terms of which knowledge is socially organized. The conventional 'subject' labels which might be applied to his writing are all inadequate, and this is no accident. He has made contributions in the fields of anthropology, sociology, socio-linguistics, philosophy, economics, sociology of knowledge, sociology of science, sociology of education, art history, literary criticism and so on, but he has tried to prevent his work from reinforcing the social oppression of organized Anthropology, Sociology, Philosophy as enshrined in teaching establishments. This explains why his work resists cataloguing and why assistants in book shops have to search for his texts in different departments, guessing, perhaps, whether *La Distinction* would be likely to be found in Cultural Studies, Sociology, or Art and Aesthetics. Finally, Bourdieu has even become steadily more aware of the significance of the form of his presentations – endeavouring to act upon the argument contained within his 'L'ontologie politique de Martin Heidegger' (1975) that 'form' and 'content' are mutually reinforcing elements in any individual's insertion of a message into a public sphere. Bourdieu's earliest publications were published research reports – either of his Algerian fieldwork or, in the 1960s, of the work undertaken within the Centre de Sociologie Européenne. A major text such as *Les Héritiers* (1964) was simply the publication for a wider readership of the reports first issued as working-papers of the Centre. At this time, some of Bourdieu's research findings were summarized in articles taken by established journals such as *Les Temps modernes, Esprit*, and the *Revue française de sociologie*, but there was always an element of diversification – in small journals such as *Scolies* and *Noroit* – to defy appropriation. As Bourdieu's articles became more speculative or theoretical, there was a danger that the 'field' of sociological discourse would become the dominant context for his communication, and part of the rationale for the establishment of *Actes de la recherche en sciences sociales* must have been to resist this tendency. In his own journal, Bourdieu has now for 15 years been able to cultivate a context for publication which is a 'formal' extension of the content of his work. Nevertheless, as I argue in Chapter 8, a tension between form and content became evident in *La Distinction* (1979). Bourdieu's 'big' texts have moved into a field of production and consumption which is increasingly beyond his control. Chapters 9 and 10 discuss Bourdieu's response to this situation in his own work, but this Introduction considers the implications both of the international appropriation of Bourdieu's texts and of the fact of the production in this text of an introduction to his work which constitutes a trans-nationally vicarious representation.

'L'ontologie politique de Martin Heidegger' was published as an extended article in *Actes de la recherche en sciences sociales* (5–6 November 1975), pp. 109–56. In 1988, it was published – 'in a slightly different form'[2] – in the 'Le Sens commun' collection (directed by Bourdieu) of the Éditions de Minuit. In the formal context of *Actes*, the article was, as Bourdieu says in his notice to the reader of the book, 'an exercise in method'[3] which cross-referred thematically to a whole cluster of articles published at about the same time. The article was headed by a dictionary definition of the word 'louche'[4] which signifies grammatically a phrase in which the words seem to mean one thing whilst actually meaning something else and has come to signify people who appear to be looking one way whilst in fact looking another. The article was a case-study of a 'louche' professor, and, within the text, there was a double page of reproduced snap-shots of Heidegger in different social contexts.[5] In particular, there was a juxtaposition of one photograph in which Heidegger was 'surprised during his lecture'[6] (as the caption puts it) and in which he appears in a dark suit with collar and tie standing in front of a blackboard covered with Greek script, bright-eyed with a half-smile, and another photograph 'with his costume with lapels'[7] in which he stands in open countryside, a proud citizen of the Fatherland, a shirt buttoned to the neck without tie, in a jacket with wide, buttoned-down lapels with an oak-leaf motif, frowning sombrely. This latter was a posed, symbolically Nazi photograph – the other side of the 'louche', genial professor in front of the blackboard. It is the photograph of the sinister Fascist which appears on the cover of the book published by the Éditions de Minuit. The 'formal' context of the book is, in other words, very different from the formal context of the article. Is there something 'louche' about the relationship between the now de-contexted cover photograph of Heidegger and Bourdieu's insistence in his notice that his text was

> situated in a perspective which is not at all that of denunciation. Because scientific analysis has nothing to do with the logic of a trial and with the interrogations which it arouses (Was Heidegger a nazi? Was his philosophy nazi? Should Heidegger be taught? etc.) it cannot be certain that the unhealthy excitement which to-day surrounds the philosopher is really favourable to the good reception of this work which itself is, doubtless, always untimely.[8]

Bourdieu's willingness to authorize the new edition of his earlier article is consistent with his recent inclination to intervene strategically in current debate – to make his texts into actions – but the cover suggests that the book was marketed precisely so as to take advantage of the 'unhealthy excitement' of the 'Heidegger debate'.

The Political Ontology of Martin Heidegger is scheduled for publication in 1991. The announcement of this publication begins: 'This book is an important and timely contribution to the debate concerning the relation between Heidegger's philosophy and his political affiliations to Nazism.'⁹ The text which Bourdieu thought would be 'always untimely' has, in translation, become 'timely'. In Bourdieu's terms, this surely means that the text has become de-temporalized. In the process of double transformation from an article to a French book and then to an English book, the very text in which Bourdieu persuasively argues that philosophical texts have to be understood as integral parts of the social strategies of authors has itself become detached from the context of its production. This is not an exceptional case. Other Bourdieu texts planned for English publication in 1990 include *Choses dites* (1987), *Un Art moyen* (1965), *L'Amour de l'art* (1966), and *Le Sens pratique* (1980). The announcements make no reference to the original publication dates of these texts in France and, indeed, the translation of *Le Sens pratique* is announced as 'this new book'.¹⁰ The cluster of proposed translations seems set to produce a synchronizing effect which will encourage the reception of Bourdieu's work as a 'corpus' or, as Bourdieu would put it, in totality as an *opus operatum* – as a complete and completed body of work.

The imminent appearance of so many of Bourdieu's major texts in English is, of course, enormously welcome. The synchronizing tendency in their appearance is a manifestation of our contemporary culture in which the economics of book production contribute to an internationalization of texts and a consequent denial of the specific cultural contexts within which they are generated. If Bourdieu acquiesces in this process, it may be the case that his willingness to regard his own past work as an *opus operatum* is a strategy in his ongoing *opus operandi* (work in progress) or, perhaps more, in his ongoing *modus vivendi* (way of living). The present work considers this last possibility in its final chapters in the same way as 'L'Ontologie politique de Martin Heidegger' (1975) considers the nature of Heidegger's overt rejection of his earlier practices. This is appropriate because this study of the work of Bourdieu throughout attempts to adhere to the spirit of the analysis exemplified by Bourdieu in his account of Heidegger's philosophy – discussed in Chapter 9.

Right at the start of his article on Heidegger, Bourdieu stated the thesis that

> Learned jargon – official languages which produce and reproduce groups of specialists by a systematic alteration of ordinary language – is, like all discourse, the product of a compromise between an expressive interest and a censure constituted by the very structure of the field within which the discourse produces itself and within which it circulates.¹¹

This means that the 'form' of a production is the particular manifestation of the compromise between the 'expressive interest' of an author and the 'censure' of the 'field' within which it is located, which, in turn, means that works should not be read in 'formal' terms as if their 'form' were not an integral part of the production. It is imprecise to suggest that this book might be 'doing a Bourdieu' on Bourdieu. (It might, importantly, be more accurate to suggest that it attempts to 'do a 1975 Bourdieu' on Bourdieu.) His own interpretation and representation of his past work and of his current position in relation to it are aspects which involve his present 'expressive interest' and his present position within objective intellectual fields. Inevitably, this book presents an interpretation of Bourdieu's texts which, in form and content, is a manifestation of my strategy in reconciling my 'expressive interests' with my position in a different intellectual field.

The nature of the field operating as a 'censure' of my interest would seem to be easily defined in terms of the brief suggested by the publisher: 'Try to write for second-year students of Sociology or Cultural Studies'. The problem here, however, is that the corollary of sharing Bourdieu's perspective must be that this suggestion has to be de-simplified and, even more, the corollary of the thinking with which Bourdieu's name has been associated has been that in the last 20 years the profiles both of higher education institutions and of the students within them have actually altered substantially. On both counts, it should no longer be possible to anticipate an intellectual field within which an academic book may be received by 'students' who differentiate themselves socially by allowing themselves to be initiated into the language of 'distinctive' academic discourses. The emergence of degree courses in 'Cultural Studies' is itself a cultural phenomenon of the historical period in question. The pioneering cultural research undertaken originally in the United Kingdom in the Centre for Contemporary Cultural Studies at the University of Birmingham which was established in 1964 under the directorship of Richard Hoggart and was continued by Stuart Hall between 1968 and 1979[12] led to the institutionalization of several degree courses, mainly within polytechnics. The BA (Hons) in Cultural Studies at the Polytechnic of East London, for instance, was formally approved by the Council for National Academic Awards in 1980. The course is the product of the particular circumstances in which it emerged and, as such, expresses the interests of the staff who constructed it. To use Bourdieu's terminology, the course is itself 'culturally arbitrary'. Partly because of the expertise of the staff, the first year of the course 'is an interdisciplinary year, introducing the concerns of cultural studies, largely through an examination of aspects of seventeenth- and eighteenth-century England'.[13] The students are introduced to second-year options which include Popular Culture, Philosophy and Society, and Literary Culture. I talked with students in the second term of their second year. I spoke to Rachel, aged 22, who had left school at 19 with one A-level and five O-levels. Her parents had come to England in the late 1950s and she had spent four years in America in her teens. In sixth-form college she had run a school radio station and had then presented a multicultural programme for Radio Bristol. She was concerned about the under-representation of Blacks in the media and had joined the course after researching a programme on Black mothers for Channel 4 television. I spoke to Shelly, aged 29, who had left school at 17 with 'several CSEs'. Her parents had come to England from Ireland in the mid-1950s. After school she had worked as a computer operator in the Civil Service for four years before travelling abroad, mainly in the Middle East, for a year. She had taken evening courses at the

City Literary Institute in Psychology and World Politics and had enrolled on the polytechnic's multi-subject Diploma of Higher Education course where, in her first year, she had taken modules in Psycho-social studies, Women's studies and Popular Culture before transferring to the second year of the Cultural Studies degree. Those who had taken the first-year course mentioned that they had studied Marx, Locke, Hobbes, Defoe, Milton, Shakespeare and the English revolution, had read E.P. Thompson, Raymond Williams, Christopher Hill and had been introduced to the work of Foucault.

'Sociology' was only gradually institutionalized in English higher education in the post-Second World War period. At the Polytechnic of East London, a course leading to BA (Hons) Sociology with Professional Studies was first approved by the Council for National Academic Awards in 1973. Before the establishment of the polytechnic in 1969, staff in one of its constituent colleges had taught the BA/BSc (Hons) Sociology degree of the University of London. As the title suggests, the main feature of the new course was that it sought to integrate the vocational goals of the new institution with the academic legacy of the University of London course. I spoke to Duncan, aged 22, in the second year of the course. He had left comprehensive school in 1984 with eight O-levels and had then acquired two more O-levels at a further education college as well as A-levels in Government and Politics, and Sociology. He talked about the class divisions he had experienced at school, accentuated by the reactions to the Falklands War, and of his desire to express his political commitment in journalism. He had followed the common core of the first year in which all students take courses in Psychology, Social Philosophy, Sociological Theory, Historical and Comparative Sociology, and in which all undertake one research and one computing project. With the exception of the work on Marx, he had found the introductory year 'too historical' but was prepared to regard the content of the course as a necessary basis for developing the capacity to give intellectual substance to an already established moral and political orientation.

In so far as these profiles are homogeneous, it is because the students have become self-selectively homogenized by becoming members of the student population of the Polytechnic of East London rather than because they have become initiated into any common intellectual discourse. Higher education institutions decreasingly impose a neutral academic ethos and, increasingly, the social ethos of students and institutions are mutually reinforcing. In Bourdieu's terms, again, the 'autonomy' of the field of higher education is now very weak relative to the field of intellectual exchange within the whole of society. The receptivity of Rachel, Shelly and Duncan to ideas is a function of their sense of social position based upon their social experiences much more than of the level of potential comprehension traditionally associated with the acquisition of formal educational qualifications. The 'censure' exercised over my 'expressive interest' is, therefore, to be seen primarily as the censure attached to social groups rather than intellectual fields.

My 'expressive interest' is located within the same set of social pressures as are the interests of the students. Like Bourdieu, I would define myself as an 'oblate'[14] – someone whose dedication to the pursuit of rigorous intellectual enquiry is the manifestation of the social trajectory of a 'lower-middle-class' disposition – the manifestation of an inherited and unconsciously pursued upwardly mobile aspiration to be achieved through the accumulation of cultural rather than economic capital. The inherited 'distinctiveness' of religious non-conformist values was potentially converted into an academic 'distinction' through the process of grammar school schooling and a Cambridge undergraduate education, but the austerity of the puritan ethic – partially sustained in the traditional 'moral seriousness' of English studies at puritan Cambridge – ensured that the potential conversion would not become fully actualized. The ambivalent position of an academic 'inheritor' at the end of the 1960s at a time when the period of expansion in British 'new' universities was ending was resolved when I secured a post at the institution which was to become, first, North East London Polytechnic and, now, the Polytechnic of East London. It was in the process of designing new courses within the new institution that I first came across the work of Pierre Bourdieu. The BA/BSc (Hons) by Independent Study which was approved by the Council for National Academic Awards in 1976 was heavily influenced by the collection of essays edited by M.F.D. Young entitled *Knowledge and Control. New Directions for the Sociology of Education* which contained Bourdieu's 'Intellectual field and creative project' and 'Systems of education and systems of thought' as well as Bernstein's 'On the classification and framing of educational knowledge'. In particular, the degree course invited students to negotiate their programmes of study with staff within a framework of thinking which obliged them to articulate their own interests, or creative projects, in relation to the particular manifestation of the intellectual field which happened to be at their disposal within the intellectual and organizational structure of the institution.[15] The actual operation of this process is a continuing concern but, from the early 1980s, I have sought to understand that process better and have sought to give it wider recognition within the British higher education system. My first attempts at understanding the process involved an enquiry conducted at the London School of Economics which tried to integrate the procedures of the sociology of organizations and the sociology of knowledge in investigating higher education institutions. It was then that it became clear that the continuation of Bourdieu's work beyond the articles with which I had earlier been familiar provided the theoretical framework which could be applied to the analysis of student learning. The systematic exposition of Bourdieu's work offered in this book followed from the practical imperative to encourage the reflexivity of students and staff within higher education institutions. It was important that Bourdieu's work should be fully understood in order to be properly used.

It follows that this is not a book which is designed to enable students to make the fine distinctions which will then distinguish them. It does not compare 'structuration' in Bourdieu and Giddens, or 'codes' in Bourdieu and Bernstein – to cite some potential examination questions – but, instead, it tries to restore the logic of the whole of Bourdieu's intellectual project. The book is strictly chronological and, as far as possible, I have tried to retrace this chronological progression in the sequence of my own reading of Bourdieu's work. The attempted restitution of Bourdieu's practice, through a reading of his texts, has the effect of rendering those texts almost transparent because the aim of *his* practice has been to restore to all social agents an understanding of the logic of their practices. This book is inevitably caught up in the complexities of social communication which Bourdieu's work reveals. There is a somewhat bizarre regression at work. You, the reader, are invited to use this text produced by a member of staff in an English polytechnic to come to terms with the work undertaken over the last 30 years of a Frenchman who is now professor of sociology at one of the most prestigious academic institutions in France. This work has amounted to a concerted attempt to rescue and to celebrate the authenticity of the behaviour of ordinary people living and thinking in accordance with the dispositions which they have inherited from the group affiliations of their families. Bourdieu has taken steps to try to make sure that his work should be used by individuals in articulating their own social positions rather than to enable a small number of people to think, at leisure, about the situations of others. Arguably, his attempts to resist the academic appropriation of his work have rendered it inaccessible to those people he would want to reach. This text tries to remain faithful to his intellectual strategy whilst seeking to make it accessible. The reader is asked, therefore, to see this text as the representation of a model relationship of a social agent with social phenomena. The text will read as an intellectual representation of an intellectual relationship, but it is intended that it should offer a paradigm for everyone's cognitive commitment regardless of their preconceptions. The capacity which people possess to recognize their social position is a function of their social condition, and it would be naive to suppose that the deprived and disadvantaged of our society can be helped exclusively by rethinking their position, but, nevertheless, the condition of poverty, for instance, is, in part, constituted conceptually both by those in poverty and by those observing it:

> Mary moved into the refuge in order to escape a violent husband, after being forced to send her children to relatives in Ireland. After a while, project workers were able to support her in securing a house owned by a local Housing Association, in a tree-lined street with neat front gardens. She is delighted with it and sees her problems (despite being dependent on social assistance for the foreseeable future) as over. She said that her biggest fear had been that her choice of housing would be restricted to the run-down, unpopular housing estate where all the 'problem' families are concentrated.[16]

Mary may not read this book or any book by Bourdieu and may not ever want to reflect on the social 'distinctions' inherent in our society which determine our choices between 'tree-lined' streets and 'housing estates' and numerous other 'life-style' alternatives. But Bourdieu's work forces me, the project workers, social policy analysts, you, or Rachel, Shelly or Duncan, to consider recognizing society properly with a view to reconstituting it differently.

As Hopkins continued in 'The Windhover':

No wonder of it: sheer plod makes plough down sillion
    Shine, . . .

• 2 •

Algeria, 1957–64

Bourdieu's Algerian 'fieldwork' laid the foundations for his subsequent intellectual development and career. What are the bare facts about his researches in Algeria? The clearest statement is to be found in a footnote to 'The sentiment of honour in Kabyle society' (1965) in which Bourdieu indicates that the analyses contained in the article are based on 'information and observations gleaned in the course of several enquiries carried out in different places in Kabylia between 1957 and 1961'. He names three villages and a clan which were the principal places of enquiry; five villages about which documentary evidence was collected indirectly from informants residing in Algiers; and he also mentions that historical information had been taken from written sources but had been corroborated, as far as possible, by direct enquiry such as, for example, a conversation with a centenarian of the rural clan.[1]

Apart from the possible engagement with the four rural locations in Kabylia, it would seem that *Sociologie de l'Algérie* – published by the Presses Universitaires de France in 1958 – was mainly based on secondary material read during 1957. Clearly Bourdieu returned to Paris within the period between 1957 and 1961 since an article published in January 1961 liberally acknowledges the influence of ideas expressed by Raymond Aron in a course of lectures given at the Sorbonne in 1958.[2] It was the work carried out during 1960 which furnished the detailed empirical information which enabled Bourdieu to publish a revised and corrected edition of *Sociologie de l'Algérie* in 1961 and to embark on the analyses which were published as *Travail et travailleurs en Algérie* (1963) and *Le Déracinement, la crise de l'agriculture traditionnelle en Algérie* (1964).

Comments in these two texts[3] suggest that the researches were undertaken in a period of three months between June and September 1960. The enquiries were indebted to the official endorsement provided by the Algerian services of the Institut National de Statistique et d'Études Économiques (which provided the statistics offered in the first Part of *Travail et travailleurs en Algérie*), but the interviews were conducted by teams of mainly Algerian interviewers belonging to the Association pour la Recherche Démographique, Économique et Sociale of the École Pratique des Hautes Études, Paris.

The two texts – particularly *Travail et travailleurs en Algérie* – offer important discussions of methodology, but this level of specific information about Bourdieu's 'fieldwork' has to be offered at the outset so that it becomes possible to have some preliminary view of its relationship to what was actually happening in Algeria in the years in question. I take Alistair Horne's *A Savage War of Peace, Algeria 1954–1962*[4] as my main source for the 'facts' or 'events' which have to be remembered in considering Bourdieu's researches.

There were many complex factors which combined to generate the Algerian conflict, but the key issues can be said to have been the inequality within Algeria between the majority population of Arabs and Berbers and the minority of 'colons' (settlers) and 'pieds noirs' (Frenchmen born in Algeria); the instability and weakness of the government of the Fourth Republic; and the injured self-esteem of the French Army following its defeat in Indo-China in May 1954. The warning signs in respect of French colonial attitudes in Algeria had certainly been evident immediately after the Second World War, but policies adopted in Paris to increase the democratic representation of the Muslims were thwarted in Algeria by the dominant 'pieds noirs'. Following the impetus given to anti-colonialism by the French defeat at Dien Bien Phu (now in Vietnam), a united Front de Libération Nationale (FLN) was established in Algeria in October 1954. The first co-ordinated military action of the war took place on All Saints' Day, 1 November 1954 when uprisings took place in two rural regions – Aurès and Kabylia – and in Algiers. Initially police action was taken against the rebels but soon paratroop regiments were drafted into Algeria and reprisals were taken in the Aurès. The government policy was simultaneously to maintain peace and to push through a series of liberal reforms. Even though the premiership changed from Mendès-France to Faure in February 1955, the appointment of a new Governor-General in Algeria – Jacques Soustelle – was sustained. He argued for a programme to integrate Algeria more fully with mainland France – the policy of Algérie française. The policy of integration, however, seemed to be dependent on the suppression of rebel activities and, increasingly, atrocious rebel hostilities were even more atrociously repressed. It is thought, for instance, that in the Philippeville massacres of 20 August 1955, 123 Europeans were killed by the FLN whilst 1,273 'insurgents' were killed in reprisal. Soustelle lost sympathy with 'integration' and, when Mollet succeeded Faure in January 1956, he was withdrawn. On his early visit to Algiers in February 1956, Mollet succumbed to pied noir opposition to the proposed successor to Soustelle. This was an early sign that the French government could not retain authority over the pro-French pieds noirs. During 1956 the FLN grew in military strength and, at the Soummam conference in the middle of the year, a kind of parliament – the Conseil National de la Révolution Algérienne (CNRA) – was established which issued a statement specifying that no cease-fire would be negotiated before the recognition of independence. Towards the end of 1956 the 'exterior' wing of the FLN organization became involved in international negotiations which implicated both Tunisia and Egypt, and this diplomacy became embroiled in the Suez affair which ended abortively on 5 November 1956. The anti-climax of the retreat from military confrontation over Suez exacerbated the post Indo-China frustration of the French Army. In December 1956, Salan – who had presided over the humiliating end of the présence française in Indo-China – was made Commander-in-Chief in Algeria. The army in Algeria saw this appointment as an opportunity to overthrow civil government in Algeria – the Faure conspiracy, whilst the pieds noirs feared that Salan had been chosen to repeat his Indo-China role. Right-wing pieds noirs were probably responsible for an attempt to assassinate Salan on 16 January 1957.

1957 was the year of the Battle of Algiers. It was an FLN initiative which had been planned at Soummam. The first of the bombs was planted on 30 September 1956, and by the end of the year the violence in Algiers had reached an unprecedented level. Governor-General Lacoste brought in 4,600 'paras' and a system of 'quadrillage' was introduced in Algiers to control the town in compartments. The FLN decided to retreat from Algiers in March, but not before several leaders had been captured or committed suicide. The torture methods adopted at this time were to cause a furore in France when Henri Alleg's account of them – *La Question* – was published there a year later. Even though the FLN's cause might have been strengthened by liberal dismay at French military behaviour, the Battle of Algiers was a failure for the FLN. Rifts occurred in the interior leadership, and dominance passed from the politicians to the FLN's military colonels. The increased influence of military control within the FLN culminated in the execution of three French soldiers on 9 May 1958. Governor-General Lacoste left Algeria on 10 May and the near anarchy which followed fuelled the machinations to persuade de Gaulle to take office. On 1 June 1958, the National Assembly accepted de Gaulle's terms for accepting power. Three days later, de Gaulle gave his famous 'Je vous ai compris' speech which succeeded in commanding support from the army in Algeria and from the pieds noirs without actually specifying the nature of his policy for resolving the Algerian problem. De Gaulle took immediate steps to purge the army of its extreme ringleaders, but, in the year that followed, de Gaulle's ultimate intentions were not at all clear. In a speech given on 16 September 1959, de Gaulle argued for 'self-determination' for Algeria in terms which suggested that he favoured some form of association between France and Algeria rather than either independence for Algeria or integration with France. In a week in January 1960 – 'Aux barricades' – the pieds noirs demonstrated against de Gaulle in objecting to his speech. Although the subsequent speech of 29 January quelled the threat of right-wing uprising, de Gaulle's positive position remained ambiguous. In June, he surprisingly offered the opportunity for peace negotiations with the Gouvernement Provisoire de la République Algérienne. Meanwhile Boumédienne had become dominant in the FLN and the third meeting of the

Conseil National de la Révolution Algérienne which met in December to January 1959–60, had clearly articulated a policy which was revolutionary rather than simply liberationist. There was, therefore, no disposition to accept 'self-determination' on de Gaulle's terms. By the end of 1960, however, the military war seemed to be closing just as de Gaulle also seemed to be set on a path towards a negotiated settlement. But there was still more to come. The polarization of attitudes became acute in mainland France itself. Whilst left-wing intellectuals such as Sartre issued, on 5 September 1960, The Manifesto of the 121 which incited French conscripts to desert in Algeria, others formed in June of 1960 the comité de Vincennes which sought to sustain an Algérie française position in opposition to de Gaulle. There were comparable new right-wing manoeuvrings in Algiers so that de Gaulle was greeted with hostility when he arrived there on 9 December 1960. The hostility found tangible expression in the founding of the right-wing Organisation Armée Secrète (OAS) in early March and in the failed putsch of the generals against de Gaulle in April. The rise of the OAS was the most significant military fact of the remainder of the war. Whilst de Gaulle was making overtures for peace in May 1961, the OAS launched a terrorist offensive in Algeria and in France. The 'massacre' at the Charonne metro in Paris in which French police over-reacted to a demonstration of 10,000 against the OAS atrocities was the prelude to the final push towards a settlement. The massacre occurred in February 1962. A cease-fire was agreed on 19 March. In Algeria, an OAS–FLN truce was agreed on 17 June. A referendum on independence took place on 1 July, and on 15 September Ben Bella became president of the Algerian Republic.

To simplify grossly, it has to be remembered, therefore, that Bourdieu's fieldwork was conducted in harrowing circumstances analogous to those which might be experienced by a sociologist working today in Northern Ireland. *Sociologie de l'Algérie* was published in Paris in 1958. The work for this volume must have been undertaken at the time of the Battle of Algiers during 1957 when the political and military outcome of the conflict was far from clear, and its publication occurred when the newly installed de Gaulle was still hedging his bets about secession, integration, or association as a proposed solution to the Algerian problem. By the time of Bourdieu's empirical enquiries of June–September 1960, however, the mood was very different. The third meeting of the Conseil National had adopted a revolutionary stance whilst, in June, de Gaulle met with an Algerian delegation to discuss peace. It was beginning to be possible to assume that independence was attainable and that the more urgent issue was to shape the character of the emerging independent state. The notion of a liberal, reformed Algérie française was dead, and the idea of an Algérie française was only thereafter to be the slogan of the right-wing.[5]

Where did Bourdieu stand in relation to these developments, or, first of all, what was it that attracted Bourdieu to Algeria in 1957? What was his disposition both in relation to the events in Algeria and in relation to the range of attitudes or ideologies which were linked to those events? What was the purpose of his proposed research? What did he regard as problematic in the situation which he encountered, and what, if anything, did he want to prove?

Some of the answers to these questions are contained within the very first paragraph of *Sociologie de l'Algérie*. Bourdieu's Introduction begins:

> It is obvious that Algeria, when considered from the rest of the Maghreb, does not constitute a true cultural unit. However, I have limited my investigation to Algeria for a definite reason. Algeria is specifically the object of this study because the clash between the indigenous and the European civilizations has made itself felt here with the greatest force. Thus the problem under investigation has determined the choice of subject. This study, which is a conceptual outline of more extensive analyses, includes a description of the original social and economic structures . . . which, although not the main purpose of the book, is indispensable for an understanding of the breakdown of the social structures caused by the colonial situation and the influx of European civilization.[6]

The full force and subtlety of this opening statement is lost in translation and has to be disclosed. Bourdieu first asserts that 'Algeria' does not possess a real, objective identity or unity. But this limitation of the research to Algeria 'n'est pas arbitraire, à se placer au point de vue méthodologique' – that is to say that the limitation is not a matter of personal choice but is a consequence of a methodological logic, such that 'l'unité d'objet est fonction de l'unité de la problématique'. Bourdieu is arguing, therefore, that his sociological analysis of Algeria is not the analysis of a pre-existing reality but the analysis of a construct which is constituted from his perception of a general theme or problem. The concentration on the clash between indigenous and European civilizations is given priority but, nevertheless, the analysis of that clash can only be achieved by describing the economic and social structures of the indigenous civilization which have been affected by the European influx. Bourdieu comments that this description 'n'a pas en elle-même sa fin' – is not an end in itself – but is offered as a means of understanding the phenomena of acculturation and deculturation with which he is centrally concerned.

The thing which attracted Bourdieu to Algeria, therefore, was that it offered him a case-study of a society in transition from traditional to modern. Although this definition of the problem may have been dominant and although Bourdieu recognized that there was a reciprocal relationship between his perception of this problem and the methodological isolation of 'Algeria' as an object of study, there was, however, a basic problem of how to describe any society whatsoever which was somehow deferred by the apparent focus on cross-cultural change. In trying to describe the indigenous civilization in *Sociologie de l'Algérie* Bourdieu was, in fact, trying to apply analytical procedures which had their origins in his prior philosophical allegiance, as well as testing the validity of Durkheimian, Weberian and Marxist explanations of social organization.

Bourdieu has characterized the philosophical orientation which informed his early research. He has said that he 'undertook research on the "phenomenology of affective life" or, more precisely, on the temporal structures of affective experience'.[7] What Bourdieu means by this has to be understood, by analogy with Merleau-Ponty's *Phenomenology of Perception*[8] in relation to the articulation of a 'phenomenological ontology' advanced by Sartre in *Being and Nothingness*.[9] A reading of Sartre's Introduction – 'The pursuit of being' – is an adequate background to the problem which underlies aspects of *Sociologie de l'Algérie*. In the first section of that Introduction – 'The phenomenon' – Sartre asserts that 'The obvious conclusion is that the dualism of being and appearance is no longer entitled to any legal status within philosophy'.[10] Equally, we can reject 'the dualism of appearance and essence' so that, as Sartre continued:

> The appearance does not hide the essence, it reveals it; it is the essence. The essence of an existent is no longer a property sunk in the cavity of this existent; it is the manifest law which presides over the succession of its appearances, it is the principle of the series.[11]

Sartre proceeded to ask, of course, whether this 'manifest law' or 'principle' could itself be said to have existence. Situated within this kind of terminology, it is possible to say that Bourdieu perceived the multiplicity of Algerian social behaviours as a set of appearances for which it was philosophically not possible to find any essential cause or explanation. The problem inherent in undertaking a phenomenology of affective life was that of, first, distinguishing between 'manifest laws' of behaviour and causation and then, secondly, determining the status of any such 'laws' that might be identified.

The radical individuality of Bourdieu's research approach generated difficulties of communication. To whom, or for whom, was he writing? The second paragraph of *Sociologie de l'Algérie* conveys Bourdieu's sense, which emerges elsewhere in the text, that the mere presentation of the findings of objective research is a political act in that it constitutes a medium – highly significant in the context of the relationship between the colonized and the colonizer – for the presentation of one societal self to another. 'Any intention,' he writes, 'other than that of bringing to light the process which has led to the current situation would in no way contribute to the disinterest and impartiality which must inspire these researches' and, he insists, 'the objective and sober presentation of evidence is neither an evasion nor an abrogation'.[12] Sympathy with the rebel cause would not, in other words, be allowed to prejudice the influence of objective information which, with humanist optimism, Bourdieu believed would provoke a human reaction. Nevertheless, the book was called a 'sociology' of Algeria. Even though Bourdieu's motivation to undertake the research can be said to have been partly politically and partly philosophically inspired, and even though the text was itself thought almost to possess a symbolic power, elements of the analysis seem to be offered as 'ethnography' or 'anthropology'. The question has to be asked, therefore, how far these anticipated categories of reception were constitutive of the analysis which was offered. The answer here involves a scrutiny of the progression of Bourdieu's publications through the period of the Algerian War of Independence.

The essence of *Sociologie de l'Algérie* is that it offers, first, accounts of the social organization of four different tribal groups – the Kabyles, the Shawia, the Mozabites and the Arab-Speaking Peoples – and then, secondly, offers reflections on the consequences of the collapse of these traditional systems. This sounds a straightforward exercise but Bourdieu's attempt to represent the tribal social organizations becomes a voyage of methodological exploration, and his tentative findings here have implications for the position which he develops in relation to the process of change from traditional to modern.

In his treatment of each tribal grouping, Bourdieu adopts a similar presentational procedure. At the outset, he describes the physical environment, the habitat of the human beings. Thus: 'Settled in very heavy densities . . . in regions of hilly, rugged terrain, the Kabyles are primarily arboriculturalists';[13] and of the situation of the Shawia: 'A vast mountainous quadrilateral situated between the High Plains and the Saharan borders, the Aurès is cut by deep and parallel valleys . . . which present varying natural zones corresponding to the different climatic levels . . . ';[14] and: 'In the northern Sahara is situated the unusually desolate chebka of the Mzab . . . . This "desert within a desert" is cut by the valley of the Wadi Mzab, in which are situated the five cities of the Mozabites'.[15] In each case, Bourdieu then provides an initial summary of the basic economies. So, for instance, the Kabyle economy 'depends mainly on two trees, the olive and the fig, . . . '[16] whilst the Shawia territory 'has long existed as a closed economy, with its needs strictly measured to conform to its resources'. Following these brief introductions to the physical geography and to the economic constraints of the tribal contexts, Bourdieu proceeds to a more detailed analysis of their social structures. With the first shift of this sort – in respect of the Kabyles – we are suddenly confronted with an arresting remark:

> It becomes evident how sharp and strained is this struggle between man and his environment. By a sort of phenomenon of compensation, to the imperfection of techniques there is a corresponding exaggerated perfection of the social order – as if the precariousness of the adjustment to the natural environment were counterbalanced by the excellence of the social organ-isation; as if, to counteract his powerlessness in regard to things, man had no other recourse than to develop associations with other men in a luxuriant growth of human relationships.[17]

What is this 'sort of phenomenon' of compensation? In what ways might a social organization be an inevitable function of its physical environment or of harsh economic realities? Do these two separately condition social organization or, as it were, in a causal sequence? Are we talking about causality at all? Is there in operation some benign, natural, self-regulating mechanism whereby social organizations are not simply conditioned by their contexts but conditioned in such a way that a harmonious balance is automatically maintained? If such a process is in operation and is, in some way, the prerequisite for human survival, is it an automatic process of natural adjustment or is it the product of human agency?

These are the kinds of questions with which Bourdieu wrestles in *Sociologie de l'Algérie*. Equally, it does not escape notice that the Kabyle social organization suddenly emerges as an ideal case-study for the analysis of 'affective relations'. Not only does Bourdieu try to resolve the questions raised above, but he does so in the context of himself being methodologically sensitive to the possibility that his representation of Kabyle society is a projection of his philosophical disposition. Let us consider that representation in further detail. The 1958 text describes next the social structure of Kabyle society. The smallest unit is not the household but the agnatic family. The 'kharrouba' groups together several families descended from a common ancestor. In turn, the village groups together several 'kharroubas', whilst the tribe, as a collectivity of villages, only exists contingently in relation to external threats to security. The whole operates on the basis of concentric circles of allegiance. This exposition is then followed by an account of the judicial system. Berber law, Bourdieu says, is founded on the principle of 'private justice'.[18] He points out that extreme rigour of punishment and compassion often co-exist, and he embarks on a reflective digression which reveals some of his uncertainty. We must understand rigour and compassion

> the one by the other, the one as a function of the other: the compassion would not have to be so great if custom were not so rigorous. Thus if, in being respected to the letter, a rule risks going beyond its fundamental purpose, another principle, offered by the customary system itself, performs a mediating role.[19]

This counter-balancing function, however, is not known by the individuals involved, and Bourdieu quotes approvingly Lévi-Strauss's contention that 'the function of institutions is not necessarily – is rarely – their conscious function'. Bourdieu reinforces this point by reference to Mauss whose analyses have shown that 'magical belief is a "social judgement" which responds to a "social need"' such that the 'primary functions' of institutions (to safeguard the stability of the group, for instance) remain hidden to actors whilst they continue to act consciously within the framework of 'secondary functions'. The situation is complicated for Bourdieu by the fact that Kabyle law is not written. It may be the case that the underlying rationale for a law is hidden from its upholders, but, in practice, on the principle of private justice, all law enforcement takes place as if judicial organization has not acquired any autonomous status which is separate from the exercise of private law by the family group. However much the deep purpose of a law may be hidden, the judicial process is, in other words, one whereby external forces are made to endorse those internalized principles of justice which are deeply felt (as much, perhaps, in transgression as in adherence). Bourdieu insists that, for the Kabyles, 'private justice' means that the relation between an internal sense of justice and an external enforcement of it is not mediated by any publicly formulated laws. Since the exercise of law takes place in the context of the family, Bourdieu moves to a consideration of the Kabyle domestic organization.

The discussion of marriage in Kabyle society raises two relevant points. In describing the way in which marriages are arranged by fathers without any reference to the wishes of their daughters, Bourdieu notes that girls undergo a 'cultural apprenticeship' which ensures that they are initiated into an acceptance of a perpetually minor status. The consideration of the purpose of the dowry gives Bourdieu an opportunity to clarify his view that the apparent function – economic exchange – is only the tangible sign of an operation for which several 'secondary functions' can be identified but of which the 'primary function' is definitely to create a network of reciprocal exchanges between groups which are, or then become, mutually obligated. These two points are important because they suggest an emphasis which is a crucial component of Bourdieu's interpretation of Kabyle society. Both imply that the apparently natural stability of the social order is the result of conscious human effort or sustained social vigilance. The dowry system is a sophisticated strategy for maintaining social stability, and, equally, girls are carefully initiated into the performance of roles which also sustain that same stability. Bourdieu's main representation of Kabyle society is that all the spheres of social action which are practically focused on the family are also mutually reinforcing in order to preserve societal harmony. The 1958 text concludes with a sub-section which is entitled: 'Lived and constituted democracy' in which the position that Bourdieu had advanced in relation to Kabyle law is extended to embrace the whole of Kabyle society. The 1961 text offers this concluding exposition:

> In the Kabyle democracy, the ideal of a democracy seems to have been realized; indeed, without the intervention of any restraint other than the pressure of public opinion, the will of the individual is immediately and spontaneously made to conform to the general will. But this ideal is put into effect only in so far as it is not realized as an ideal, not objectively formulated as a formal and abstract principle, but instead felt as a sentiment, as something immediately and inwardly manifest.[20]

Bourdieu's discussion of the Kabyles manifests his personal attraction to a society which is seen to regulate itself inter-subjectively without the need for recourse to objectively formulated laws or codes. Although the structure of *Sociologie de l'Algérie* is designed to document the nature of the transition from traditional to modern social forms, there is a real sense in which Bourdieu wants to argue that the Algerian revolution should learn from the self-regulating mechanism of the Kabyles and perceive it as a paradigm by which new economic pressures might be accommodated without destroying the primacy of affective relations. Bourdieu's consideration of the other tribal organizations does not seem to be invested with such personal sympathy, and, indeed, it might be said that the foundation of Mozabite social organization is one which is inimical to Bourdieu. The representation of the Mozabites forced Bourdieu to pay serious attention to the way in which Islam had functioned in traditional Algeria and might influence the modernizing development of the new state.

The Mozabites are Kharedjite Abadhites (a heretical sect of Islam). Based on strict adherence to the Koran, they emphasize two principles: that all believers are equal and that every action is either good or bad. As Bourdieu comments, these 'egalitarian rigorists' 'appear to be the protestants and the puritans of Islam.'[21] These heretics had been forced several times to flee from persecution before they settled in their present location. The first five of the seven Mozabite cities were founded within a period of 50 years after El Ateuf (in 1011) and the other two were established in the seventeenth century. Since they were settlers, the important point of distinction from the Kabyles, therefore, is that their social organization became constituted within a different physical or economic environment. Part of the essence of Mozabite culture is that it is 'constituted' rather than 'lived' and that an element of that 'constitution' is sustained by the maintenance of conformity to a doctrinal position within Islam.

The life of the Mozabite cities is dependent on temporary emigration and commerce which provides the capital for the upkeep of a sophisticated system of irrigation which sustains the oases and the palms. Since one sixth of the male population is engaged in commercial activity within Algeria but outside Mzab, Bourdieu's interest is aroused by two queries. How, first of all, is social cohesion maintained in the face of such a level of constant dispersal, and, then, secondly, how is it that the business acumen of the Mozabites has developed without involving a denial of their devout heterodoxy? At an immediate and simple level, the answer to the first question is obvious. It is precisely the conformity to a sectarian religious position which enforces social solidarity. The presence, as Bourdieu puts it, 'in all actions and in everyone's heart of a religious law which is lived at the same time as a rule which is imposed from outside and as an inner guide to conduct'[22] implies that religious practice has the pragmatic effect of transforming 'constituted' doctrine into 'lived' experience such that Mozabite doctrine becomes as private as Kabyle justice. But this answer only begs the question which is taken up again in trying to find a solution to the second query. Does the religious doctrine itself simply offer a public endorsement of behavioral inclinations which have been differently determined? It is quite clear that Bourdieu's reflections on the Mozabites have the Weberian analysis of puritanism and capitalism very much in mind. Bourdieu comments that the Mozabite commercial success and even their doctrine could be explained in economic terms – that the poverty of the soil enforced recourse to commerce which, in turn, caused an emphasis on virtues which were then enforced by dogma. But he is not prepared to subscribe to a crude Marxist interpretation. With Weber, Bourdieu wants to consider the possibility that, with some kind of autonomous validity, the doctrines prepared the Mozabites for their economic success.

Just as the discussion of the Mozabites enables Bourdieu to express his doubts about explanations emanating from economic determinism, so the consideration of the Shawia gives rise to more general reflection about the validity of functionalist analysis. One of the characteristics of the Shawia is that the property belonging to each clan ('harfiqt') is widely dispersed in the territory and distributed amongst terrain of different kinds. There is also a similarly dispersed allocation of space for burial places. Bourdieu cites the interpretation given of this phenomenon by Jacques Berque[23] that it demonstrates a translation into practice of the requirements of an internal social equilibrium. Doubtless, Bourdieu replies, the structure of land distribution can be explained, functionally, to suggest that it offers a guarantee of social balance, but, perhaps, isn't this only a 'secondary function'? Bourdieu is more inclined to suggest that the distribution of land amongst the Shawia operates freely within strict spatial parameters. Each individual allocation of land appears random and resists a tight functionalist explanation, but the structure of the wider parameters indicates that the primary function is the preservation of the authority of the harfiqt which is the focal point for all Shawia behaviour. Bourdieu concludes, therefore, that

> Shawia culture appears then as a collection of structures constructed according to the same scheme which is applied in different domains: – techniques of labour, division of land space, organisation of festivals, the structure of the community – the centre of the system always being nothing other than the harfiqt with its political organisation, its territorial patrimony and its collective granary.[24]

Enough has been said about the 1958 text of *Sociologie de l'Algérie* to indicate that in attempting to describe traditional Algerian tribes Bourdieu was also seeking to evaluate various kinds of analytical framework. His essential position seems to have been that the primary concern of the tribes was to safeguard their internal social stability. This concern was made crucial for the tribes by the poverty of their physical environment and by the inadequacy of their technical resources. In a sense, therefore, the social structures can be understood by locating human activity within the local ecological system. However, these structures cannot be understood simply as direct responses to the environment. In each tribe, human agency constructed particular structures appropriate to the particular situation. In each case, a partially autonomous social organization was generated, containing within itself different 'secondary functions' which, often unconsciously, reinforced the primary function of preserving social solidarity. Although Bourdieu often describes tribal phenomena in terms of 'structure' and, in relation to Kabyle law, quotes Lévi-Strauss to imply the existence of a hidden structure, nevertheless the emphasis of the text is that the social structures are the product of sophisticated human creation. The structure is inherent in the perceived phenomenon much more than it is a part of the observer's perceptual disposition. In so far as the members of the tribes are themselves unconscious of the structures within which they operate, this is a sign of the strength of their processes of cultural initiation which enables regulation to be 'lived' rather than 'constituted'. In so far as the Durkheimian 'conscience collective' is present in *Sociologie de l'Algérie*, Bourdieu transforms it by arguing that it is a 'conscience' which is collectively constructed. In so far as Weberian thinking is present in relation to Puritanism and capitalism, Bourdieu transforms it by insisting that religious doctrine has secondary status since it is dependent on the willingness of individuals to accept its congruence with behaviours which fulfil the primary function of their social organization. In so far as Marxism is present, Bourdieu equally assigns economic conduct a secondary status, suggesting that economic exchanges are symbolic actions which are subordinated to the primary goals of the societies within which the transactions occur.

These explorations and tentative conclusions dominated the 1958 text. The revised edition of 1961 is slightly different and the English translation of the second edition – *The Algerians* (1962) – adds new text in different print. A detailed comparative analysis of these texts is rewarding because it exposes not only the object of analysis – Algerian society – in transition, but also the nature of the analytical and presentational activity equally in transition. There are two main kinds of alteration. The 1962 publication often adds detailed statistical information which tends to make the analysis more 'sociologically' up-to-date, whilst it also often adds anthropological elements – such as diagrammatic representations of the spatial organization of tribal villages. Small changes are indicative. Whereas the 1958 text cites and quotes from many previous writers on Algerian society, the tendency in the 1961 text is for much more unacknowledged paraphrase. In effect, the rationale for the structure of the early text was no longer tenable in 1961–2. Bourdieu had himself known in 1958 that it was tenuous since he was trying to extrapolate from present observations an 'ideal type' of traditional social organization. There had always been the danger that the extrapolation would be pure artifice, and the speed of social change in the period between the texts confirmed that danger. The reaction which is evident in the 1961–2 texts was, on the one hand, to seek to make the analysis of traditional society more authentically anthropological and, on the other, to make the analysis of the rapidly modernizing society more authentically sociological. In both cases, the consequence was that the intrinsically philosophical inspiration of the 1958 text was downgraded in 1961–2.

The most substantial difference between the two texts of *Sociologie de l'Algérie* and the text of *The Algerians* is the inclusion in the 'translation' of a completely new chapter entitled 'The revolution within the revolution'. This is a version, with very little change, of an article which appeared in *Esprit* in January 1961.[25] These were the first publications in which Bourdieu sought to adjust his position from one which was pertinent to the analysis of colonized and colonizer, to one which would be relevant to the process of revolutionary change within an independent Algerian state. The fact of the war had brought about a radical transformation:

Thus the Algerian war, by its mere existence as well as by its special form and its duration, transformed the situation in which and by which it was brought into being. The social setting in which the acts of everyday existence are carried on was radically changed and, with it, the attitude of the individual. How are we to describe and understand this complete and sudden transformation, this revolution within the revolution?[26]

Whereas the 1958 text can be said to have been written for France and for Frenchmen and still contained within it the sense that a proper understanding of traditional Algerian society might yet facilitate a harmonious cultural integration, the *Esprit* article of 1961 registers the shift towards an exclusively Algerian orientation. What now is at issue is the management of the revolution within Algeria in such a way that the traditional values which have been fractured by colonial oppression may be adapted so as to offer individuals a new kind of solidarity with an economically dominated modern society. Suddenly, Bourdieu is no longer the detached analyst of the human agency involved in constructing the kinds of social organizations exemplified in traditional ideal types. Instead, he is able to see himself, as an objective researcher, as an agent within the process of change who is contributing to Algerian social self-construction. The two books which presented the findings of the 1960 empirical research consolidate this important shift of emphasis. The lessons learnt in *Sociologie de l'Algérie* both from the social organizations which were analysed and from the methodological process of attempting to conduct that analysis were now applied in a direct engagement with the people who were experiencing the effects of physical and cultural upheaval.

The new situation was boldly announced at the beginning of a contribution which Bourdieu made in 1962 to a collection of essays devoted to the consideration of what should be the next steps in post-liberation Algeria.[27] Bourdieu's article was entitled 'De la guerre révolutionnaire à la révolution' and it argued that the challenge was precisely how to transform a revolutionary war into a social revolution. With the end of the war of liberation, the Algerian people now have to confront themselves. The issues which were abstract during the war are suddenly actual. Bourdieu makes a plea that future policies should be based on a proper recognition of the social reality. By this he means that the Algerians should guard against the myth of the 'revolutionary revolution' whereby the war might be thought magically to have transformed society. Bourdieu had already acknowledged that the fact of the war had altered the nature of the social revolution,[28] but this was not to say that the war and its completion could engineer the necessary social changes. Bourdieu's contention was that a transition from a traditional society to a modern one which would preserve the old values of 'lived democracy' would be secured only if economic changes were consciously integrated with attitudinal changes. To bring about the necessary adaptation of values, the initial pre-requisite was that the existing ambivalence of their own situation should be fully understood by the Algerian people themselves. Any tendency for an Algerian élite to attempt to operate with crude formulae in respect of the revolutionary potential of the peasantry, for instance, would be doomed to failure because it would be wilfully ignoring the complexity of the Algerian social reality. Bourdieu argued that what was needed was for help to be given to enable 'a whole people to invent for itself a system of behavioural models'[29] and, for that, 'new pedagogical techniques must be discovered at the same time as instruction must be given a new content'.[30]

Travail et travailleurs en Algérie (1963) and *Le Déracinement* (1964) were both the products of research carried out during three months in mid-1960, but the publications have to be seen in the above context as deliberate contributions to Algerian self-development and social reconstruction. Both arose out of Bourdieu's recognition that the anomie[31] of the Algerian masses which was the consequence of their only partial adaptation to modern values and behaviours meant that they were now particularly vulnerable. They might either slip into complete disaffection, marginality and despair which might be fuelled into militancy by self-seeking demagogues, or they might be encouraged positively to participate in the construction of a new society which would integrate their old values with modern, capitalist pressures. *Travail et travailleurs* presents the basis for a statistical understanding of the whole of Algerian society, but it also concentrates critically on the problems of adjustment of the numerous urban workers whose values were still partly those of the traditional rural areas. By concentrating on the effects of the colonial policy of 'regroupment' of rural communities, *Le Déracinement* offers a complementary picture of the contra-dictory attitudes towards agricultural labour of those who remained in the countryside.

There are only two translated articles which give an idea of the content of *Travail et travailleurs*, and neither does justice to the rich complexity of the full text. 'The attitude of the Algerian peasant toward time'[32] comes across as a sympathetic account of the rather bizarre traditional attitudes to time of Algerian peasants – attitudes which make adjustment to modernity very dif-ficult. Bourdieu's analysis seems anemic because it was de-politicized for an anthropological publication. 'The Algerian sub-proletariat' (1973)[33] faithfully renders a pre-publication extract from *Travail et travailleurs* which appeared in *Les Temps modernes* only shortly before the appearance of the full text.[34] The article's concentration on the reciprocal relationship between the economic and attitudinal situations of the sub-proletariat was, in French in 1962–3, immediately placed in the context of Bourdieu's wider review of a spectrum of such social reciprocities, whereas, contextually, the translation seems to suggest a preoccupation with the significance of the sub-proletariat. The extracts from *Travail et travailleurs* published in translation in *Algeria 1960* (1979) similarly convey a *post hoc* emphasis, conditioned by the orientation of a series co-published by Cambridge University Press and the Maison des Sciences de l'Homme, Paris, entitled 'Studies in modern capitalism'. What these translations fail to convey, therefore, is the way in which the whole text (567 pages) tries to offer, both statistically and sociologically, a profile of the facts and values inherent in Algerian society and a commentary on the relations between those facts and values which refuses to condone any simplistic explanatory recourse to notions of base and superstructure. The extreme selectiveness of the translations also means that there has been no recognition of the achievement of the book in integrating the substantive perceptions of the conditions and opinions of the Algerian workers with the reflexive methodological appreciation that the author, the sociological researcher, also inhabits his social space with which, too, his attitudes are solidary. Parts of the book are explicitly concerned with the nature and status of sociological enquiry, but it would be false to suppose that Bourdieu was concerned to offer any kind of obligatory research 'methodology'. There is no opposition between method and content. Bourdieu's thinking about the thoughts of Algerian workers is of precisely the same kind as his thinking about himself as thinker.

Travail et travailleurs is in two parts. The first, by Darbel, Rivet and Seibel, offers statistical data, while the second, by Bourdieu, is called a sociological study. Bourdieu provided introductory essays to both parts and it is under the surface of these discussions that it is possible to detect a latent reflexivity which has only become fully articulated in more recent work. The introduction to Part I – 'Statistics and sociology' – takes the opportunity offered by the structure of the text to reflect on the practical relationship between the two modes of analysis. Reaffirming his phenomenological orientation, Bourdieu insists that statistical data do not provide any access to 'facts'. Deliberately applying anthropological terminology to rational behaviour in a strategy which he was particularly to adopt in *Les Héritiers*, Bourdieu argues that what must be denounced is 'not the use of statistics but the fetishism of statistics',[35] and he refers to the 'superstition' of statistics and the 'magic' of figures. Once any absolute claims for statistics have been removed, Bourdieu is clear that the interaction between statistics and sociology is essential. He outlines the importance of a process of reciprocal verification. The flow of perceptions is two-way because it is equally possible that intuitive interpretations of interviews will generate questions which elicit formal statistical data, or that the emergence of unintuited patterns from statistical information will lead to further elucidation and verification in conversations.

The presentation of the argument in *Travail et travailleurs* involves a constant cross-referencing. Statistical information is juxtaposed with, and checked against, interpretations of interviews which are themselves made constantly accessible to evaluation by the presentation of extensive verbatim quotations. Indeed, an appendix also offers a full transcript of a narrative of a cook working in Algiers who is described as a 'spontaneous sociologist'.[36] This mode of presentation seeks to re-enact the inter-active process of the enquiry which is itself meticulously described in an appendix.[37] From this account of the process it emerges that the young researchers employed by Bourdieu saw themselves as engaged in 'action research'. It is crucial to understand, however, that this phrase should convey the sense that the research was undertaken as a form of action rather than that an action was undertaken in order to be written up as research. This practical distinction reinforces the intellectual position adopted by Bourdieu in the foreword to Part II where he defends himself against the charge commonly levelled against colonialist anthropologists that they collude in, or allow themselves to be the instruments of, colonialism. Bourdieu singles out for attention an article by Michel Léiris[38] in which it was argued that the anthropologist from a colonial power must bear a 'portion of responsibility' for the acts perpetrated in the name of colonialism. In response, Bourdieu accuses Léiris of trying to extrapolate a morally responsible individual from the totality of the social determinations of that individual. In Sartrean terms, Bourdieu senses that Léiris is trying to salvage an unconditioned self, and that, in spite of his disclaimers, he is trying to retain a social detachment as ethnographer in implying that the ethnographer is particularly responsible. Bourdieu wants to locate the ethnographer as much as everyone else within a determining system of social relations. Bourdieu wants to be reflexive about his researches not so as to be able to define respectably his distance from them but so as to understand fully the way in which he is inserted within them.

This understanding clarifies the meaning of what Bourdieu says about the Algerian workers who are also inserted in the same Algerian social situation. Bourdieu's analyses of the unemployment statistics on the one hand and of the stated attitudes of those interviewed towards unemployment on the other suggested some anomalies. Behaviour which was accommodated within traditional society as activity was no longer necessarily regarded as employment. Within a new context where remuneration was becoming the overriding criterion of employment, Bourdieu also describes instances in which men would work for no pay in order to retain their former sense of honour. What, therefore, Bourdieu asks, is the relationship between the 'fact' of unemployment and the consciousness of unemployment? It is too easy to argue that attitudes and opinions are simply the direct effect of economic necessity. There is a sense in which the attitude towards unemployment plays a part in constituting the objective condition, or, as Bourdieu puts it rhetorically: 'must it be admitted that economic necessity only operates through the mediation of the consciousness of it which those who suffer from it hold of it?'[39] The dilemma which follows from this conclusion is that the fact and the consciousness of unemployment are mutually constitutive and mutually reinforcing. Bourdieu proceeds to identify further structural homologies. The attitude to time is a key factor which is itself a reflection of tangibly different economic positions. Just as 'being unemployed' is partly a matter of attitude, so an individual's 'objective' future life-chances are not wholly conditioned by his current 'objective' material condition. The aspirations of individuals are dependent on material conditions through the mediation of their perceptions of the 'objective future' of the group to which they belong. Bourdieu particularly illustrates his point with reference to the sub-proletariat. Living from hand to mouth and experiencing the possibility of work as a game of chance or a lottery, the sub-proletarian existence has no stability from which to launch any future project. The economic situation of the sub-proletarian does not offer him the luxury to formulate a detached, rational plan for the future or to understand the objective basis of the economic condition in which he finds himself. As Bourdieu succinctly puts this point with reference to unemployment: 'The sub-proletariat *is* consciousness of unemployment; the proletariat *has* consciousness of unemployment.'[40] The potential for rational analysis is a function of a person's position in social space – as much for the mainland researcher as for the Algerian sub-proletarian or proletarian. Two lines of argument flow from this explication of the condition of work and workers in Algeria. First, Bourdieu argues that, unlike the employed proletariat, the sub-proletariat does not have the capacity for rational calculation which would enable it to become a revolutionary force. Secondly, he proceeds to carry out a similar analysis of the behaviour of social groups whose material existence is not so precarious. His observations here suggest that individuals within a social group which has the security to make future projections are, by virtue of that capacity, less constrained by the material conditions which enable it than are the members of the sub-proletariat. This gives rise to the general theoretical conclusions that it is only particular material conditions that make a Marxist explanation viable, and that in any historico-cultural situation it is the peculiar interactions between economic conditions and a range of cultural influences which shape an unique capitalism.

The conclusion of *Travail et travailleurs* builds upon this view that every society constructs the form of capitalism appropriate to itself, and asks whether the modern Algerian bourgeoisie will be content with the semi-revolution which it has achieved or whether it will seek to involve the proletariat in the struggle to realize a radical revolution. Bourdieu poses the question but he does not offer any blueprint. Published a year later, *Le Déracinement*, by contrast, concludes with a critique of current post-independence policies and gives a sketch of what measures are required. It is perhaps because the analysis in *Le Déracinement* is less convoluted than in *Travail et travailleurs* that a clearer recommendation emerges. *Le Déracinement* does not offer a subtle amalgamation of statistical and sociological enquiries. It first offers an account of the 'regroupment' policy which caused the enforced resettlement of millions of rural Algerians in the late 1950s, and then, on the basis of case-studies of 13 different kinds of resettlements in regions with different kinds of traditional values, it seeks to establish how far the colonial interventions could be held to be responsible for the current breakdown of traditional rural values. The conclusion is that colonialism provided a 'pathological acceleration'[41] to trends which were already latent – arising, amongst other factors, from the contact of the rural poor with urban employment in periods of economically enforced emigration to mainland France. The evidence points to the supposition that 'the rejection of agriculture is not only attributable to objective obstacles, but arises from a change of attitude towards the whole of peasant existence'. Instances of familiar indicators of this change are produced in support of statistical information. Transformations in attitudes towards unemployment and time are apparent in rural communities as much as in the conurbations. Bourdieu proceeds to discuss the demise of the previously esteemed personality type – 'the paysan accompli', as well as the effects on social cohesion of the morphological upheavals brought about by resettlement, but the climax of the book is the final chapter – 'Le sabir culturel' (the cultural lingua franca). A disinclination to choose between old and new values has been endemic in Algerian rural communities. Whilst the colonial system survived, the Algerian fellah did not need to choose. He often reached a solution by a process of 'dédoublement' whereby he would employ different kinds of agricultural techniques when partly working for a 'colon' and partly tending his own land. Footnotes suggest that this chapter was written after December 1963,[42] and Bourdieu therefore reiterates more forcibly his message of 1962. The Algerians must make choices, but must not do so by denying that their current situation is ambivalent. Bourdieu contrasts the strategies of 'libertarian socialism' and 'authoritarian socialism'. The former encourages self-development but has been organized in such a bureaucratic manner that the peasants have not been able to feel that they are re-possessing their land. The latter assumes that the peasants aspire to a secure salary and to the condition of rural industrial workers. In Bourdieu's view, authoritarian socialism assigns both urban and rural sub-proletariats to non-participating subservience as much as did the control of the 'colons'. There is a need, therefore, for the central introduction of a strategy, neither libertarian nor authoritarian, which will facilitate a process of self-determination. Bourdieu's prescription merits full quotation:

> Only educational action . . . can overcome the contradictions without magically denying them by the fictitious conciliation of opposites. This action presupposes, firstly, . . . a clear and realistic definition of the goals being pursued – in short, a systematic theory of the economic and social reality, the foundation of a methodical and progressive programme. But the task of each particular educator cannot be left to be defined by the letter of a regulation which foresees all the cases: in a revolutionary situation, the educator must day by day create the content and the form of his teaching activity . . . and his advance training must primarily offer him the means of operating this continuous creativity. The appropriate form of educational action, in its ideal form, is precisely to adapt to the aptitudes and expectations of those which it means to raise and transform – therefore to know them and to respect them, to define, in each a system of exercises gauged to their aptitudes and expectations . . . in short, to refuse to propose arbitrarily exercises defined abstractly for abstract subjects.
>
> Thus, a particularised action would be substituted for a centralising action of a rigid bureacracy, because it would be directly adapted to specific situations and to specific men. It is in the permanent confrontation between the

expectations of the peasants and the exercises of the élites (responsible for the choice and progressive realisation of rational ends) that an authentic culture can be elaborated – a system of models of economic and social behaviour which is at once coherent and compatible with objective conditions.[43]

It will become apparent that many future positions are foreshadowed in this statement. It could perhaps be said that in the process of the enquiries which led to the publication of *Travail et travailleurs* and *Le Déracinement* Bourdieu was both laying the groundwork for the necessary conceptualization of reality and demonstrating the appropriate pedagogical procedures. These two books were certainly insertions into the Algerian reality which they attempted to describe, in a way in which the first edition of *Sociologie de l'Algérie* was not. In 1960 Bourdieu returned to mainland France and was to take steps to insert his research into a reality which was authentically his own.

· 3 ·

The early research in France

In an interview first published in 1985, Bourdieu has said:

> My research on marriage in the Béarn was for me a point of transition, of connection, between ethnology and sociology. Right at the outset I had thought of this work on my own country of origin as a kind of epistemological experiment . . . [1]

It would be a mistake, however, to suppose that this chapter can represent a neat chronological transition from the Algerian fieldwork discussed in the last. The full findings of the research in the Béarn to which Bourdieu refers were published in *Études rurales* in mid-1962[2] – anticipated by a few months only by a selection of extracts released as an article for *Les Temps modernes*[3] – but the research itself was undertaken 'in 1959 and 1960'. We have already seen that the research which was undertaken in Algeria between June and September 1960 was distinctively sociological in a way in which the work for *Sociologie de l'Algérie* was not. It seems likely, therefore, that Bourdieu's 'point of transition' should be located chronologically in 1959, and that it must be assumed that the Algerian research consolidated it. It is worth making clear, in other words, that the methodological transition occurred without reference to Bourdieu's apparent career movement in 1960 from North Africa to mainland France. It is most certainly not the case that he was an 'ethnologist' in Algeria and became a 'sociologist' in France – with all that this would seem to imply in assumptions about 'developed' and 'under-developed' or 'civilized' and 'primitive' societies.

This chapter is separated from the last only on the grounds that it considers Bourdieu's earliest work in France. It could have been labelled 'From ethnology to sociology, 1960–4', but this would unjustifiably have implied a linear progression and imposed an artificial distinction. 'Célibat et condition paysanne' – researched in 1959–60 and published in 1962 – has elements of affinity with the ethnographic and social historical scholarship of *Sociologie de l'Algérie* (1958) and also indicates the use of research procedures similar to those used in Algeria in 1960 but not articulated and documented until *Travail et travailleurs* (1963). Thematically, however, the cross-references are between 'Célibat et condition paysanne' and *Le Déracinement* – researched in 1960 but not published until 1964. Similarly, *Les Étudiants et leurs études* (1964) presents the findings of research undertaken in the academic years 1961–2 and 1962–3. These 'sociological' findings were merged with the results of other enquiries to generate a presentation which, as its title – *Les Héritiers* – insisted, conveyed anthropological nuances. At the same time, it is clear from the extract from the final page of *Le Déracinement* quoted at the end of the last chapter that Bourdieu's recommendations for Algerian social reconstruction were influenced, by 1963–4, by the work which was developing at the Centre de Sociologie Européenne, Paris, in the field of education. How far, equally, was the blueprint which he had formulated for Algeria also applicable in France itself? These are the general issues which underlie this consideration of the texts which emerged out of Bourdieu's early research in France.

Bourdieu's 1985 reflection on the research which he had undertaken in the Béarn did not simply identify it as the link between ethnology and sociology. He also made the point that it was an 'epistemological experiment' in that he was seeking to analyse sociologically the region in which he had been born. 'Célibat et condition paysanne' uses frequent quotations from transcribed interviews with 12 informants. Six of these were octogenarians at the time of the enquiry, but one – 'P.C.' – was 32 years old. In 1959, Bourdieu was himself 29 years old and it is, therefore, completely possible that he may have grown up with P.C. as a child. Nowhere, however, does the text of 1962 publicize the proximity of what was being analysed to Bourdieu's own primary experience. It was clearly a 'hidden agenda' for Bourdieu personally in 1959–60 but, as we shall see, it is only in recent years that he has been prepared to give the reflexive dimension prominence. The 'self-analysis by proxy'[4] of 'Célibat et condition paysanne' was a motivating factor in the enquiry but it was not an intrinsic part of the research presentation. Instead, other motivations are articulated – with varying degrees of exposure. The first appendix, for instance – 'Bibliographical notes' – is a fascinating essay in itself. It begins with the comment that:

> The survival in the provinces of the Pyrenées – Bigorre, Lavedan, Béarn and the Pays Basque – of an original customary law whose rules could only be sustained in open defiance of the principles and legislation of the Civil Code has not failed to arouse the curiosity of historians and jurists.[5]

The impression which is given, in other words, is that the incentive for the research enquiry derived from the inherent tensions in the social organization of these provincial regions. Customary law had historically struggled for survival in the face of the central, statist impositions of the Napoleonic code in much the same way in the Pyrenées as had the customary law of the Kabyle tribe in the face of French colonialism. Bourdieu proceeds to offer a condensed historiography of the social, legal and political history of the Béarn commenting in passing, for instance, on the fact that Le Play had situated his exemplar of the ideal 'famille-souche' in the Béarn.[6] The secondary sources for the history of the Béarn are contextualized sociologically in a way in which they were not for the *Sociologie de l'Algérie*. In other respects, however, the appendix looks back to that earlier study. Bourdieu offers explanations of the characteristics of the social organization of the Béarn derived from physical and human geography in the same way as he had in describing the features of each of the Algerian tribes. The difference, of course, is that this analysis is now relegated to an appendix. In themselves these bibliographical notes offer a sketch for a region of France similar to the analyses undertaken in England which were expressed in Laslett's *The World We Have Lost*.[7] But Bourdieu was not in the process of becoming a social historian. His orientation was similar to that of the *Annales* historians,[8] but his social history is deliberately only a background to the analysis of 1959–60 events and attitudes. It was in these that Bourdieu identified the problem which he then presented as the dominant research motivation and which furnished his report with a title and a unifying theme – the problem of celibacy in contemporary Béarn.

The official motivation for the enquiry, therefore, is announced in the introductory remarks to 'Célibat et condition paysanne'. The identification of celibacy as an interesting problem is a deliberate exemplification of the research process recommended in Bourdieu's discussion of the relationship between sociological and statistical enquiry in *Travail et travailleurs*. 'By what paradox', Bourdieu asks at the outset, 'can the celibacy of men appear to the celibates themselves and to those around them as the most striking symptom of the crisis of a society which has always traditionally condemned younger sons either to emigration or to celibacy?'[9] This paradox is only apparent to the researcher because the perceptions of their own situations offered by participants have been checked against the statistical evidence. The statements of the informants are first adduced to indicate that celibacy is perceived to be a major social problem, and then Bourdieu immediately presents the results of the examination of the statistics to show that the proportion of marriages per year per head of population has not significantly diminished in the period since 1881.

The mismatch between the spontaneous sociological evidence and the statistical information establishes Bourdieu's research problem, but in presenting his solution Bourdieu at once has recourse to the form of argument used in the *Sociologie de l'Algérie*. He first tries to characterize the status quo ante in respect of the system of matrimonial exchanges in the Béarn in much the same way as he had tried to describe traditional Algerian customs. Whereas the appendix offers a social history of the region, the text attempts an historical anthropology. The analysis does not remain simply historical, of course, because the essence of Bourdieu's argument is that celibacy is perceived anomalously by social actors precisely because they still partly live within the framework of historical values which have become 'anachronistic'. Bourdieu does not use this expression and 'Célibat et condition paysanne' concentrates on documenting the mutually reinforcing phenomena of social and attitudinal change, but the text does inevitably raise the issue of causality. Even though *Le Déracinement* argued that there existed a predisposition amongst Algerian peasants to forsake traditional agricultural labour even before enforced resettlement accelerated that tendency, nevertheless, in all Bourdieu's Algerian work, the fact of French colonial intervention offered a tacit causal explanation for the process of transition from 'traditional' to 'modern'. For the first time, the early French work is not able to rely on such a causal deus ex machina. The issue is not confronted in 'Célibat et condition paysanne', but the adequacy of structuralist or phenom-enological analysis is here at stake, and we shall see that in the course of Bourdieu's educational work in the 1960s he explicitly rejected structuralism precisely so as to be able to give an account of the ways in which actors restructure their own realities.

This tension is inherent in Bourdieu's account of traditional marriage in Béarn. He begins with the statement that before 1914 'marriage was governed by very strict rules'.[10] Subsequently, Bourdieu has argued that marriage negotiations are strategic rather than regulated[11] and, indeed, an article of 1972[12] already advanced that interpretation, but, here, there is still evidence of the influence of Lévi-Strauss. Traditionally, Bourdieu implies, rules of matrimonial exchange were in force which specifically circumscribed the range of possible marriages in order to safeguard the status of contracting families and, therefore, to maintain the stability of the whole society. In several places Bourdieu enters caveats which suggest a modification of the regulatory interpretation but that interpretation is not fundamentally challenged. Having given an account, for instance, of the nature of the inheritance and dowry calculations according to the rules, concluding with the summary statement that 'the dowry was a determinate function of the value of the inheritance and of the number of the children', Bourdieu quickly adds that, for several specified reasons, the customary rules 'were never applied with mathematical rigour' and then makes the significant general comment that 'Observation of reality puts us on our guard against the temptation to construct over simple models.'[13]

Although it is qualified methodologically, the essence of Bourdieu's account of traditional Béarn practice is clear. In negotiating marriages, two basic principles were in operation – with the overall intention of preserving the family inheritance. There was, first, a clear distinction between the rights of elder and younger children, and, secondly, an equally clear distinction between marriage 'de bas en haut' and marriage 'de haut en bas' – socially ascending or socially descending marriages. It followed from the application of these two principles that every marriage was a function of, on the one hand, the birth position of each of the espoused relative to the size of their families, and, on the other, of the relative positions of each of the two families in the social hierarchy. Bourdieu proceeds to clarify the operation of these two principles and then digresses slightly to consider the extent to which the position of families within the social hierarchy was a direct function of the value of their property. In relation to the first principle, he demonstrates that the system was logically likely to favour mixed marriages between elder and younger children rather than ones in which both partners were either inheritors or younger non-inheritors. The logical application of the first principle could, however, be modified by the introduction of the second principle since it was considered to be more appropriate for girls than for boys to enter socially ascending marriages. The social distinctions were manifest in the different styles of domestic architecture, and, although they were essentially distinctions of status rather than of class – emphasizing the 'noblesse'[14] of a rural aristocracy rather than any propertied superiority – they were, Bourdieu insists, powerfully 'felt differentiations'.[15]

The important point to grasp is that matrimonial choices were family rather than individual decisions. The head of the family made calculations which paid regard to the customary rules which enforced a practice which maintained social harmony by a sophisticated balance of material and status considerations. In this system, individuals were logically consigned to social positions. It follows, therefore, that celibacy was an intrinsic component of the system rather than the consequence of any individual choice. Who then, Bourdieu asks, were the celibates? The answer is that they were mainly the youngest children of both large and poor families – individuals who could not be accommodated within the system of calculated matrimonial exchange. In addition to those in this category who drifted to the towns or who emigrated to America, there were those who remained totally content within a familial environment where their position was circumscribed but meaningful. It was meaningful because it was a fulfilment of an acknowledged logic of social relations. Yet it was not just a matter of logic. Bourdieu's caution about over-emphasizing the operation of rules causes him also to point out that the logic also had tangible consequences for the structure of affective relations. Because marriages were arranged, social life did not develop mechanisms or institutions to encourage natural relations between the sexes. Equally there was no incentive for individuals to present themselves attractively to the opposite sex. The traditional 'virtues' of the peasant which emphasized hard work and competence and could accommodate gaucherie and vulgarity were founded on the secure assumption that there was no need personally to be involved in any process of courtship. When the forms of social behaviour, Bourdieu argues, are cut loose from the logic of the system which had legitimated them because the system itself becomes, in its own terms, dysfunctional, then individuals can derive no satisfaction from performing a systemic function as celibates and, equally, find that they are actually ill-equipped to negotiate their own personal relations.

It is not surprising that the point in 'Célibat et condition paysanne' at which Bourdieu begins to elaborate on the malaise of the contemporary celibate in the light of his presentation of the past customary context, is the point at which begin those extracts which make up the article for *Les Temps modernes* entitled 'Les relations entre les sexes dans la société paysanne'. For in the remainder of Bourdieu's consideration of the condition of the peasant in Béarn he comes closer to a phenomenology of affective relations than in any of his Algerian analyses. The social psychology of inter-personal relations which is reminiscent of the work of Goffman is here firmly presented in the context of the prior exposition of the location in a socio-economic structure of behaviours which are shown still to be vestigially in force in the present. The discussion of the contemporary condition of the Béarn peasant – entitled 'Internal contradictions and anomie'[16] – begins with the introduction of statistics to suggest that the influence of the distinction between elder and younger children which was effective under the old logic has been replaced – although not destroyed – by the influence of the distinction between citizens of the town and peasants of the hamlets. The chances that a man aged between 31 and 40 living in the town will be married are seven times greater than those of a man of the same age living in the country. The figures suggest that there has been an upheaval in the system of matrimonial exchanges, and Bourdieu explores possible reasons for this before analysing the phenomenon itself in detail. First of all, the effect of inflation after the First World War destroyed the institution of the dowry which became a wasting asset rather than an investment. There was a concomitant diminution of the authority of parents since the head of the family lost what had, in the last resort, been his only authoritative sanction – the power to disinherit. The consequence was that matrimonial exchanges gradually ceased to be governed by collective regulation and became, instead, a matter of individual competition for which the country dweller was ill-equipped by his upbringing.

Bourdieu indicates the nature of the transformation of values in respect of both of the ruling principles of the old system. The statistical evidence – taken from a study of 100 marriages registered between 1949 and 1960 – shows that there are almost as many marriages between younger children as there are of the kind of mixed-age marriage favoured by the logic of the traditional system. Town dwellers, in particular, now have salaries which mean that younger children are no longer dependent for income on the economic system of the family house to which they were originally bound. In relation to the second ruling principle – discouraging marriages involving either an ascent or a descent in status – the result of the collapse of the traditional framework has been negative. Whereas the perception that a possible marriage might be socially inappropriate had in the past carried with it the social obligation to find a harmonious resolution, the principle now operates as a blockage within the new context of individual competition and is unable to deliver a compensatingly equal marriage partnership. This instance graphically illustrates Bourdieu's general contention that the anomie of the peasant is heightened by the fact that the traditional values are not completely dead. The traditional system is now caught up in a system which is structured according to different principles, but, in

Bourdieu's rhetorical question: 'Isn't it precisely because it persists in constituting a system that this system is self-destructive?'[17]

That question generates a consideration of the process of cross-cultural relations between the town and the country. On the basis of a comparative analysis of the place of origin of marriage partners between 1871–84 and 1941–60, Bourdieu demonstrates that 'social distance imposes much more rigorous limitation than spatial distance'.[18] The basis of this social distance is the inter-position of 'town' or 'peasant' stereotypes which effectively prescribe possible inter-personal relations. As Bourdieu concludes, the statistics show that 'The peasant from the hamlets of Lesquire has as little chance to-day of marrying a girl from Pau, Oloron or even the town of Lesquire as he had in the past of marrying a girl from some hamlet in the Basque country or in Gascony.'[19]

Having established the statistical position in respect of the opposition between the town and the hamlets, Bourdieu then describes its genesis and form. He offers a range of sensitive observations which document the objective separation of the town from the hamlets. These include meticulous representations of variations in domestic architecture, and the precise registering of linguistic divergence – the split between the rural use of the Béarn language and, since the period between 1919 and 1939, the dominant urban use of French. But Bourdieu is not satisfied with only establishing that his statistical and observational analyses are mutually reinforcing. If the restructuring of matrimonial exchanges has been shown to be linked to a new differentiation between town and hamlet, there are further questions which remain unanswered. Bourdieu wants to know more. He wants to know whether the phenomenon of celibacy is linked to this new opposition. He wants to know in what ways the fact of differentiated residence effects changes in matrimonial practice; why the effect of residence is different for men and women; and why it affects the behaviour of some men from the hamlets and not others. In other words, Bourdieu is not content to perceive a structure in social phenomena. He wants to know by what mechanisms a new structure of relations transplants an old. As he puts it, the final section of 'Célibat et condition paysanne' is devoted to the question whether the 'fact of being born in the town or the hamlet is a "necessary" or "permitting" condition of celibacy'.[20] Does the identified structure correspond with an objective social determinism, or are there mechanisms within the social situation which are generating the perceived changes?

Bourdieu's answer here is of the same form as it is in relation to the phenomenon of unemployment discussed in *Travail et travailleurs*. Certainly people live in conditions which are objectively differentiated, but the ways in which these conditions are perceived and subjectively internalized also constitute realities which acquire an objective status and potency. If this conclusion seems to suggest a vindication of the influence of thoughts, ideas, or attitudes in social life in opposition to a crude economic materialism, the final section, which is entitled 'The peasant and his body', attempts to show that the process of internalization is not to be thought of as a mental process alone but rather as one of incorporation

whereby the mind/body dualism is as inappropriate as the subjective/objective
dichotomy. This position is illustrated graphically by an account of the changed
structures of social encounter to be observed in the traditional dances of the
Béarn. These offer an important case-study because they represent a point of
contact between old and new social values. As the traditional values of matrimonial exchange and sexual encounter have been replaced by the individualistic
competitiveness of the modern, the dance remains an authorized institution
for providing contact between men and women but has become transformed
in such a way that the peasants are now disadvantaged in their traditional context.
As Bourdieu writes: 'The old dances which bore the mark of peasant life in
their names ("la crabe", "lou branlou", "lou mounchicou", etc.), in their rhythms,
their music and the words which accompanied them, have been replaced by
dances imported from the town'.[21] Bourdieu digresses slightly to reflect on
the fact that the peasant both is and is perceived to be physically clumsy. In
doing so, Bourdieu here introduces terminology borrowed from Latin and
Greek – 'habitus'[22] and 'hexis'[23] – which will assume greater significance in
subsequent work. The point in 'Célibat et condition paysanne' is simply that
in individual actors there is a structural affinity between physical behaviour
and attitudes or perceptions. The perceptions, therefore, which the celibates
hold of their condition – even though these are contradicted by the statistical
evidence which is available to a non-participating researcher – unite with their
bodily behaviour in such a way as actually to secure their fulfilment. There
is a mutual endorsement between the conceptual misrecognition of their situation
held by the celibates and the ensuing social and physical maladjustment.

The difficulty here, of course, is that whilst Bourdieu turned towards an
emphasis of human agency to counteract any possible suggestion that the
structural patterns observed by anthropologists or sociologists might actually
exist as determining factors in the societies which fell under their scrutiny,
his notion of the individual agent evaporates the more he identifies a solidarity
between the physical selves of participating agents and their perceptions of
the society in which they find themselves. Agents are constrained by the structures
which they themselves perceive and are, in this sense, self-determined. It is
clear that Bourdieu instinctively felt that the Béarn celibates should be thought
to be self-determined but also, crucially, self-deceived. Logically, Bourdieu
could not say that the statistical evidence invalidated the self-perceptions of
participants or that his own sociological analysis exposed the truth of what
was happening in the Béarn. Instead, Bourdieu could only authentically insert
the conclusions of his study into the situation in the Béarn and suggest that
his amalgamation of statistical and ethnographic enquiry might prove to be
perceptually congenial to the participants. In this way, Bourdieu's conceptual
analysis might itself become an instrumental agent in the recognition of Béarn
society.

The brief conclusion of 'Célibat et condition paysanne' explicitly raised
some of these questions about the social function of the sociologist, and

Bourdieu commented that sociology

> would perhaps not be worth an hour's trouble if it solely had as its end
> the intention of exposing the wires which activate the individuals it observes – if
> it forgot that it has to do with men, even those who, like puppets, play
> a game of which they do not know the rules – if, in short, it did not give
> itself the task of restoring to men the meaning of their actions.[24]

In talking to his 12 informants Bourdieu may well have 'raised' their consciousness
of their situations just as, with his team of interviewers, he may have helped
Algerian peasants to participate in the process of constructing a national identity,
but who were the readers of 'Célibat et condition paysanne' or *Travail et travailleurs*
and *Le Déracinement*? The texts could not operationalize the ideology of the
researches. As became clear at the end of the last chapter, however, the substantive recommendation of the conclusion of *Le Déracinement* that Algerian
reconstruction should be effected by the central organization of strategies to
facilitate grass-roots self-development was also, implicitly, a recommendation
that the action research which had been adopted in Bourdieu's fieldwork should
be regarded as a model for these strategies. The research itself had been
pedagogical in its context even if the textual accounts of the research had become
academic. The structure of the publication industry had transmuted engaged
social research into intellectual voyeurism. So as not to sustain this rift between
practice and text, it makes sense that Bourdieu should next have made pedagogy
itself the object of his research. There was every possibility that the conduct
of the research might modify the attitudes of the students and that they might
also find that the meaning of their actions would be restored to them in reading
the final texts.

It was logical that, from his new base at the University of Lille and under
the auspices of the Centre de Sociologie Européenne in Paris, Bourdieu should
initiate a series of enquiries which can now be labelled as 'sociology of education'
investigations. To regard the work which ensued as primarily concerned with
education itself is to miss its wider significance. The situation which Bourdieu
had observed in which the peasants from the hamlets of the Béarn had found
themselves psychologically and physically unable to participate in the dances
which were the only institutional medium available to them to move towards
a new world of values was mirrored in education. Working-class students were
the wallflowers of the educational dance. 'Célibat et condition paysanne' could
not offer any remedy for the social deprivation of the celibates other than the
vain hope that they would benefit from recognizing their situation. From within
institutionalized education Bourdieu now had the opportunity to integrate his
own practice with its textual transmission and, in doing so, both to alter the
rules of the dance and to modify the behaviour of the dancers.

Two different kinds of publication emerged out of the educational research
of the early 1960s. *Les Étudiants et leurs études* (1964) was the first working-
paper of the Centre de Sociologie Européenne. Compiled by Bourdieu and

Jean-Claude Passeron, it presents, with minimal comment, the findings of
two enquiries organized by the Sociology of Education group within the
Centre with the co-operation of professors of sociology in different French
universities – Rennes, Bordeaux, Lille, Toulouse, Dijon, Paris and Lyon. The
professors administered questionnaires to their own students in the academic
years of 1961–2 and 1962–3, which meant that the students were those who
were preparing for their *licence* in philosophy and sociology. The report was
clearly meant to be an interim presentation to sustain the momentum of a
larger programme of enquiries which was envisaged. The authors were anxious
that the findings might be specific only to the particular target group of students
and were, therefore, eager to argue in their general introduction and in their
statistical appendix that the samples for the researches were adequately representative of all students even if there were methodological shortcomings.
Subsequent enquiries would test the general validity of current findings in relation
to students working in other disciplines. *Les Étudiants et leurs études* cross-refers
to *Les Héritiers* (1964) and, in one footnote, the authors articulate the intended
relationship between the two works. 'Anxious to condense the facts as tightly
as possible', they write, 'and to restore to them their diversity and subtlety,
we have limited ourselves to a literal exposition in order to develop elsewhere,
in a systematic fashion, the context in which the results would have full meaning.'[25] In its turn, *Les Héritiers* acknowledges that it is 'mainly based on a
program of surveys carried out in the context of the work of the Centre de
Sociologie Européenne . . . the full results of which have been published
elsewhere'[26] but that this information source has been supplemented by the
use of statistics supplied by the Institut National de la Statistique et des Études
Économiques and the Bureau Universitaire de Statistique and of monographic
studies carried out by sociology students themselves at Lille and Paris. The
'scientific', 'literal' or 'factual' claims of *Les Étudiants et leurs études*, in other
words, are heightened by the overt willingness to present *Les Héritiers* as interpretative. Similarly, the zeal with which the empirical soundness of the target
group of students is defended diverts attention from the interpretative dispositions
which are already inherent in the questions contained within the research
instruments. We have seen that Bourdieu was well aware of the need for procedural reciprocity between statistical 'facts' and ethnographic 'interpretation',
but it is not clear whether the cross-referencing between *Les Étudiants et leurs
études* and *Les Héritiers* does constitute this kind of methodological cross-checking.
It is possible, instead, that together the two works offer re-interpreted interpretations. Because there can be no meaningful distinction between 'fact' and 'interpretation' within a phenomenological frame of thinking, the question then arises
whether there can be any purpose in seeking to evaluate between interpretations
and re-interpretations. In looking at the two works in more detail we must
try to retrace the process of interpretation and systematization. In doing this
we shall be wrestling for the first time with one of the crucial problems of
Bourdieu's work. In as much as his career has involved a conscious revisiting

of previous analyses and a continuous reconstruction of interpretative meaning, does this technique sustain a continuous responsiveness to, and engagement with, 'facts' or rather does it generate an esoteric detachment?

The best way to approach the facts which were at the core of the educational analyses published in 1964 is through a scrutiny of the questionnaires used in the two surveys whose findings are presented in *Les Étudiants et leurs études.*[27] The first questionnaire had 52 questions, and these can be grouped thematically in the following way. The anonymous respondents were first asked to specify personal details (nationality, marital state, sex, date of birth) and then to give information about their university, faculty and date of admission to higher education. In question 8, the respondents were asked to state the profession, the highest qualification attained, and the current place of residence of their fathers, mothers and paternal grandfathers. There followed some questions on religious allegiance, on sources of income and, if paid work was undertaken alongside study, for how many hours in each week. Respondents were next asked where they had undertaken their secondary education – both in terms of geographical region and of the nature of the institution – and then had to list the dates, subjects and grades for their first and second *baccalauréats* and to mention whatever other university qualifications they might already possess. They were asked which courses they were following at that moment and, on the grounds that the questionnaire was being administered mainly to sociology and philosophy students, it asked whether the students had already taken specific preliminary exams in those subjects. If they had failed in these exams, they were asked to what they attributed their failure. Next they were asked whether they attended classes in other subjects and then, in general, to offer a self-assessment of their prior educational results on a scale ranging from 'very weak' to 'very good'. There then followed a cluster of questions about the influences exercised on the students in making their choices of subject. Had parents, teachers, or friends influenced them in the choice of their second *baccalauréat* field of study and in their choice of university? Had they ever wanted to do anything else and, if so, what had it been and for what reasons had the alternative course been rejected? Was it, for instance, that they had been inhibited by financial obstacles or by the toughness of the competition or by their own specific inabilities? The questions were then more precise in relation to sociology and philosophy. Had the students read any sociological works, and they were asked to mention titles. Did they feel inclined to any sociological or philosophical school of thought? Why had they chosen to study sociology (or philosophy)? When had the choice been made and on whose advice or under whose influence? What did the students expect of sociology and what aspect of it (or, interestingly, of ethnology) interested them particularly – was it a field of study or a geographical area? Students were then asked to give an indication of their future intentions. Were they wanting to do research, to teach or to use their competence in a non-university profession? For what professions might a qualification in sociology (or philosophy) be a preparation? The questionnaire then offered a list of 'realities' and the students were asked to place in order those things which seemed to them to be worthy of sociological study. The list closely reflected Bourdieu's own contemporary research interests and projects: amateur photography clubs; the condition of women in Black Africa; gait; delinquent children; students; intellectuals; homeless people; mythologies; international organizations; employers; Algerian peasants; and industrial labour. There followed a group of questions which probed the extent to which students had developed for themselves routines and methods of study. These included asking whether the students possessed a box-file and, if so, used a system of classification, and whether they preferred to work in a library, a café, or at home. After these questions on study methods, the students were invited to comment on the teaching which they were receiving. Could there, for instance, be improvements in their working conditions, in the conditions in which their teaching takes place, in the techniques used in the teaching or in the teaching itself – such as its form, its content or its bias? After being asked to cite the journals or periodicals which they read regularly, the students were then asked whether they belonged to a political party, to characterize the nature of their political allegiance (between 'extreme left' and 'extreme right'), and to rate the level of their political involvement (from 'militant' to 'hostile to all participation'). Finally, the students were asked whether they belonged to a trade union and, if so, similarly to rate the nature of their commitment to it.

The second questionnaire began with a set of similar questions to the first to establish the personal details and circumstances of the respondents. An additional question in this category asked whether the students lived with their parents, in a personal flat, in a single room, with personal friends, in a hostel, in university lodgings or elsewhere. Additionally, this questionnaire asked not simply in what town the students had undertaken their secondary studies but also in what town they had spent their childhood. Whereas the main thrust of the first questionnaire was to find out the attitudes of students towards their studies, that of the second was to ascertain the nature of the culture or cultural awareness of the students. They were asked how often they had ever read 'the classics' other than set texts; whether they read a cultural review; and whether they had possessed a pass to attend lectures or to go to the theatre, the cinema, concerts or art galleries. A further question listed 17 dramatists (mainly modern, such as Beckett, Brecht, Camus, and including Shakespeare and Sophocles as major classics) and the students were asked to indicate for which authors they knew one or two works and whether this knowledge was the result of having seen them on stage or on television, of having heard them on the radio or of having read them. Students were asked whether they possessed a season ticket for any theatre and whether they had ever acted in amateur dramatics. The next group of questions related to the cinema. The titles of 26 films were listed and the students were asked in each case to specify whether they had seen the film; whether it was a silent or a talkie; and to state, if possible, the names of the director and several actors. Following the same pattern established in the questions on the theatre, the questionnaire then asked how often the students went to the cinema or to a cinema club, and whether they took photographs or made amateur movies. The next cluster of questions related to music. Ten composers (ranging from Bach to Boulez) were listed, and students were asked to indicate whose works they had heard – either on record, on the radio, on television or at a concert. The next question listed 11 jazz musicians (from Cannonball Adderley to Thelonious Monk) and students were asked to give the same indication as in relation to composers. The following question was even more specific in relation to jazz: 12 pieces were listed and the respondents were asked whether they had heard these pieces and then asked to date them. Again, the questions relating to knowledge and appreciation were followed by ones eliciting information about the musical capabilities of the students and about the accessibility of music to them. Did they play any instrument? Did they own records and a record-player? Which radio channels did they listen to most and did they have the opportunity to see television? How much television did they watch and which programmes did they find most interesting? The last category of cultural enquiry was art. Twelve painters (from Cassirer to Vinci) were listed and students were asked to indicate whose works they had seen – either in a museum, an exhibition, a private collection or in reproduction. If they had to decorate their walls with reproductions, the students were then asked, which five of 12 different painters would they choose? The students were then asked whether they owned any books on art or had any works of art at home, and, in the same way as before, whether they themselves could paint or draw. Finally, the questionnaire posed two general questions which allowed space for quite open comment – what have been the most significant events in your intellectual or artistic life, and, what new subjects would you like to see introduced at university – before leaving further space for students to offer their observations.

The first part of *Les Étudiants et leurs études* is sub-titled 'Students, school and scholastic values' and offers an analysis of the findings of the first questionnaire, whilst the second part, sub-titled 'Students and culture', analyses the results of the second survey. The dominant assumption underlying the whole report is articulated at the end of the general introduction. Here Bourdieu and Passeron state that although all of the data was the object of multivariate analysis and was, therefore, indispensable in remedying the previous scientific ignorance of the student milieu, the report only retains evidence which is relevant to their organizing principle. That principle was that the social origin of students appeared to be the main differentiating factor between their questionnaire responses. They had, therefore, wanted to catch the effects of this factor 'in different contexts – from the most manifest like living conditions to the most hidden like cultural activity and attitudes towards academic and non-academic culture'.[28] 'Specialists agree,' they continue, 'in admitting the influence of social origin on the behaviour, attitudes, and opinions of students without ever exposing the collection of mechanisms which enforce them – particularly the most subtle and devious ones.'[29] Given, in other words, that working-class students were disadvantaged in higher education in just the same way as were Béarn peasants in contexts where urban values now prevailed, the purpose of the 'educational' enquiry was, for Bourdieu, to bring out the extent to which the disadvantage of some students was the result of a nexus of mutually reinforcing attitudes, values and behaviours integrally related to objective economic and geographic factors which itself constituted a culture which was at odds with the self-fulfilling culture of the university.

Each chapter of the whole report begins with a general summary of the findings of the questionnaires in relation to an extracted theme, followed by detailed commentaries on tables of statistical information. It is only possible here to give an impression of the analysis and interpretation. The first chapter, for instance, 'The role of age', discusses the relationship between the 'absolute' age of students and their 'scholarly age' and suggests that the situation is significantly different between sociology and philosophy students: 38 per cent of the former were under 21 years of age whilst 64 per cent of the philosophy students were in that age band. The tentative interpretation offered is that philosophy, as an established subject, provides certain career prospects for young students whereas sociology, as a young subject with relatively uncertain outcomes, often attracts refugees from studies in more traditional disciplines. Within even this simple interpretation we can detect a frame of thinking which derives from Bourdieu's Algerian fieldwork. Implicitly, the interpretation is accepting that students' choices of courses of study relate to the degree of freedom which they experience to make rational future career projections, and that this degree of freedom is, for students, a function of their domestic economic circumstances in the same way as it is for Algerian workers or sub-proletarians.

A second example of the style of the report indicates the same continuity with earlier conceptualizations. The third chapter – 'Parisians and provincials' – analyses the findings of the questionnaires by extrapolating the information gained about the geographical place of origin of the respondents. There are advantages and disadvantages of Parisian student life. Parisian students tend to have higher financial support, but, on the other hand they also tend to have less contact with either their professors or their peers and may, therefore, feel isolated. The comments suggest overall that provincial students are likely to be more docile than Parisian ones: the Parisian context enables students to relativize the magisterial authority of the lecturer whereas the limited choice in the provinces enables the lecturer to monopolize cultural or intellectual transmission. Just as the attitudinal stance of the peasants in the Béarn was a function of the position which they occupied in the geographical space between town and hamlet, so the attitudes of students suggest an analogous differentiation between metropolitan Paris and provincial France.

Les Étudiants et leurs études ends with a very brief general conclusion. Bourdieu and Passeron argue that it was not possible to draw out all the practical consequences of their research findings, and this is even more true of this summary. In the event, they chose to emphasize that their research demonstrated the need for pedagogical reform to be conducted on the basis of sociological rather than psychological presuppositions. In their words, they conclude that 'The sociology of cultural inequalities is the only possible foundation for a pedagogy which does not want to cling to psychological abstractions.'[30] The emphasis of the report is on the need for sociological sensitivity to improve pedagogical performance. The analysis offered in *Les Héritiers* deliberately goes further. It places pedagogical performance itself within a social context. The notion of a 'student' becomes problematic. The self-image of students as students is a complicated social construction in the same way as were the perceptions which the Algerian peasants held of themselves as employed or unemployed or which the celibates of the Béarn held regarding their own celibacy. Clearly the findings of Bourdieu's earlier work inspired the framing of the questionnaires used in the research surveys, but the ethnographic orientation is expressed more openly in *Les Héritiers* than in *Les Étudiants et leurs études*. The extended scope of the interpretation must partly be explained by the fact that the book draws on further studies. As the preface indicates, these were on students' mutual acquaintance; examination anxiety; an attempt at integration; students' leisure; students' images of the student; and the Sorbonne Greek Drama Society and its audience. These studies, undertaken at Lille and Paris, were supervised by the authors and the titles reflect some of Bourdieu's concerns. The first project, in particular, would seem to carry across Bourdieu's interest in affective relations to the analysis of the social life of students.

The new ethnographic emphasis in the presentation of the research findings is enforced by the style of the writing. Like Mary Douglas's subsequent *Purity and Danger*,[31] *Les Héritiers* constantly maintains its anthropological perspective by employing technical terminology in arresting and unexpected contexts. The first chapter, for instance, which documents the unequal representation of the working class in French higher education is called 'Selecting the elect' and is prefaced by a quotation from Margaret Mead[32] which describes the power relations among North American Indians which cause the vision behaviour of some young men to be regarded as legitimate and not of others. Bourdieu suggests that working-class students are in a similar kind of catch-22 situation. The school system exalts a general culture which is different from the culture which it transmits. However much people become initiated into the culture transmitted in school, therefore, they are not thought to possess the kind of culture that really matters. People who are disadvantaged in relation to this 'real' culture are deceived by the school system into thinking that schooling will remove their disadvantage.

It is clear from this brief exposition of the implied significance of the Mead quotation that there is a fundamental ambiguity in the use of anthropological language in *Les Héritiers*. The use of technical terms is partly a heuristic device to encourage the readers to see their situations differently. In this way, the text of *Les Héritiers* adopts a rhetorical strategy to invite assent to its interpretations such that the analysis of pedagogical practice is itself consciously pedagogical. The text seeks to retain linguistically the interactive dimension of a research enquiry. It is more successful in this attempt than the texts which described the Algerian researches but this renders even more acute the problem of the supposed status of the analysis which is offered. There is, in other words, a strong sense in *Les Héritiers* that the account of phenomena which is presented in anthropological language is also an account of how things really are. The perception of the situation held by the researchers is not one whose potency depends on the receptivity to it of the participants. It is a perception of the actual structure of relations which is hidden from the social agents.

This ambiguous function of the use of anthropological language must be kept in mind in order to modify the impression of dogmatism which might otherwise be gained from a summary of the argument of *Les Héritiers* which inevitably suppresses the linguistic nuances. Crudely, therefore, it can be said that the first chapter asserts that students are only formally equal in their acquisition of high culture. It is a fallacy to suppose that everyone would be given equal access to the highest level of education if the same economic means were provided for all those with the requisite gifts (the 'Robbins' principle in the United Kingdom), because these gifts are not 'natural' at all but abilities which are measured by the degree of affinity between the class cultural habits of teachers and learners. The argument goes further and suggests that the more a formal equality of opportunity is achieved within a school system the more possible does it become for that system to be able to 'employ all the appearances of legitimacy in its work of legitimating privileges'.[33] This suggestion implies that within the higher education system in France there are procedures in operation which have real functions that are obscured by apparent ones, just as, in the systems of matrimonial exchange either in Algeria or in the Béarn the apparently economic function of the dowry conceals the real function which is to maintain the stability of the social organization of the tribal unit. In describing in the second chapter the 'Games students play', Bourdieu and Passeron try to identify the characteristics of studenthood – the self-image adopted by students. Like the self-image internalized by the celibates of the Béarn, that of students is the product of a range of reinforcing factors – the spatial organization of university institutions, and the attitudes of students towards time are two which indicate the continuity of this analysis with that of Bourdieu's earlier research. The educational environment is distinctive in that the tendency for there to exist a self-contained student society with its own norms and values separate from 'secular' society is reinforced by the curricula. Although Bourdieu gives no backward glance here to his Algerian work, the nearest precedent to his analysis of the differentiated character of the university lies in his account of the institutionalized transmission of Islamic laws amongst the Mozabite tribes. Part of the process of becoming a student involves the acquiescence in and imitation of the values and behaviour of professors. 'In reality, contrary to appearances,' as Bourdieu and Passeron significantly assert, 'the university always preaches to the converted.'[34]

The process by which the real function of the university is concealed by its apparent function is analysed differently in the third chapter which attempts ·to define the actual condition of students in relation to an ideal type of perfectly rational student conduct. A generally accepted definition of a student would be of someone who studies in order to prepare for an occupational future. The apparently rational function of the university which would seem to involve the allocation of qualified people to appropriate positions in the labour market is, however, a front which obscures the real function which is to perpetuate autonomous intellectual labour and to control access to this privileged occupational status. Whether they are 'exam-hounds' who concentrate exclusively on their studies or 'dilettantes' who are ostentatiously indifferent to them, students collude in the institutional self-deception because they want to deny that their present has a future orientation imposed upon it.

The notion of concealment is central to the analysis offered in both *Les Étudiants et leurs études* and *Les Héritiers*. In the former, the concentration is on the way in which the social basis for differences of student performance is concealed by an allegiance, enshrined in language, to a differentiation between supposedly innate abilities. In the latter, the concentration is on the way in which the institution entices students to participate in a process of social reproduction under the guise of offering them equitable access to occupations. Whereas the conclusion of *Les Étudiants et leurs études* recommends a reformation in pedagogic practice, *Les Héritiers* is driven to acknowledge that a transformation of the institutional context within which pedagogy occurs is an essential prerequisite for making pedagogical change possible. Bourdieu and Passeron ask at the end of *Les Héritiers* whether and how the reality of higher education which they have exposed might be changed. Given that the educational system is required to produce individuals who are selected and arranged in a hierarchy once and for all, there are two possible solutions which might follow from a recognition that achievement was not a register of individual capacity so much as a projection of differentiated social origins. As in boxing, one might, first, have competitions within social origin categories. Or, secondly, as in Kantian ethics, one might have classification in terms of social handicap – by reference to the degree of improvement in relation to one's starting point. This could theoretically lead one to regard the producers of unequal performances as equal and the producers of equal performances as unequal. Bourdieu and Passeron conclude, however, that relativizing the hierarchy in either way would only have the effect of cancelling the status of the hierarchy itself. This might sound as if they are conservatively afraid to let go of the idea that educational institutions must allocate people in accordance with judgements of capacity. Their fear, however, is not conservative and is consistent with the substance of their analysis. If the status of the judgemental hierarchy is torpedoed by the premature introduction of norm-referenced assessment, then the concealed, real function of the system will have free rein. The determinant of occupational opportunity and of extended life chances will be the nature of the prior cultural capital inherited by students from their parents and their class backgrounds. In the short term, the only way to sustain an equalizing mechanism within society is to take the apparent function of education at face value. In the long term, of course, the goal must be to ensure that the apparent function of educational institutions becomes the real and only function.

Bourdieu and Passeron believed that their exposure of the illusion of higher education would help to bring about the necessary closing of the gap of deception. They saw that opposition to their position might come as much from students as from those in positions of cultural control who would benefit from the preservation of the illusion. They attack what they call the 'populist illusion' which leads students to demand that the cultures of the disadvantaged classes should be given the status of the culture transmitted within the school system. They argue that to proceed as if the school culture is itself a 'class' culture and only that is to help it to remain so and to undermine the capacity of the educational system to facilitate the attainment of an equal society. They were eager to retain the conception of an autonomous school culture which should be separated from both 'popular' and 'privileged' cultures. They were looking for a real democratization which would mean that the techniques and habits of thought required by the school should be taught within the school so that 'the total, indivisible gifts in the charisma ideology be made available step by step through methodical teaching and learning.'[35]

Les Étudiants et leurs études pointed towards the development of a rational pedagogy as a means to bringing a proper democracy into being, but it was already clear in *Les Héritiers* that this was not alone an adequate solution. Too many of the factors which this solution presupposed were themselves problematic or variable. The 'given' nature of the relationship between the educational system and the occupational structure of a society was problematic. Popular culture did have legitimate claims and the knowledge transmitted within the school culture is itself the product of wider social construction. Finally, the 'structuralist' methodology applied in diagnosing the problem might not be appropriate. These uncertainties generated projects and enquiries throughout the 1960s which intermingled to make possible a review of the early research in France which has been the subject of this chapter. We must now turn to the process of theoretical development and empirical research which led to the publication, in 1970, of *La Reproduction. Éléments pour une théorie du système d'enseignement*, the scope of which was well expressed in its English title: *Reproduction in Education, Society and Culture.*

· 4 ·

From *Les Héritiers* to *La Reproduction*

An English analyst of French politics – Dorothy Pickles – argued in 1963 that the repercussions of the Algerian war would be most significantly felt in the subsequent course of French internal affairs.[1] Would the ideological polarization which had manifested itself in mainland France in response to Algerian events in the early 1960s lead to an explosive internal confrontation? After the resolution of the Algerian conflict in 1962, would de Gaulle retain power? As Pickles has subsequently commented:

> When General de Gaulle became the twenty-first – and last – Prime Minister of the Fourth Republic in June 1958, few people in France, even among the relatively small band of his committed supporters, would have predicted with any confidence that he would be President of the Fifth Republic for more than a decade, that is, for a period only just over a year shorter than the entire life of the previous regime.[2]

The period in which Bourdieu was undertaking his early educational research in France was the period in which de Gaulle's political authority was consolidated. By 1965 when de Gaulle was re-elected for a further seven-year period of office, considerable progress could be thought to have been made in securing French political stability and in re-structuring or modernizing French society. The six years of the premiership of Georges Pompidou – from 1962 to 1968 – saw the introduction of successive five-year plans which were negotiated and implemented with the agreement of the trade unions. De Gaulle was himself a firm advocate of social reconstruction which he saw as an essential pre-requisite in retrieving France's standing amongst the world 'super-powers'.

Gaullist social reconstruction was, however, very different from the kind of reconstruction envisaged by the Left which drew much inspiration from the revolutionary programme which had been emerging in Algeria immediately before the acquisition of independence. We have seen that there was a private logic which drew Bourdieu towards an analysis of the higher education situation within which he was working, but this was also a reflection of a general tendency amongst the French Left to look to Algerian models for suggesting ways in which political change might be effected in France by making radical changes in educational practice. In the period between 1962 and 1965, *Les Temps modernes* – the periodical still associated with Sartre – carried articles which sought to establish that Algerian experience should be paradigmatic in guiding an alternative process of reconstruction – one towards the development of a socialist and democratic state.

It is important to keep this context in mind when examining Bourdieu's work of this period – to remember that the educational research, in particular, was not conducted in a political vacuum. Some of the texts of 1966 – 'Différences et distinctions', 'La fin d'un malthusianisme?' and 'La transmission de l'héritage culturel' (all published in *Le Partage des bénéfices*) were prepared for a two-day conference, organized by Bourdieu and Alain Darbel for the Cercle Noroit, which took place at Arras in June 1965. The intention of the sponsors – as it was stated in the preface to the subsequent publication – was 'to persuade economists and sociologists to embark on a scientific discussion of one issue which both address from very different perspectives'.[3] That one issue was the transformations which had occurred in France since the Second World War, and, as the title of the publication suggests, the orientation of the debate of the two days was towards the distribution or sharing of profits or benefits. Similarly, a text of 1967 – 'La comparabilité des systèmes d'enseignement' – was the product of two conferences organized by the Centre de Sociologie Européenne in Madrid in October 1964 and in Yugoslavia in October 1965. The publication which assembled papers which had been given at these two conferences was entitled *Éducation, développement et démocratie* and was edited by Robert Castel and Jean-Claude Passeron. In their foreword the editors describe how the Madrid conference had discussed 20 contributions from ten countries on the subject of 'human and economic development' whilst the Dubrovnik conference had gathered together 23 papers from sociologists, economists and statisticians from eight countries on the topic of 'social systems in a rural milieu and systems of education in Mediterranean countries'. But they also describe the way in which the course of the discussions seemed to justify a separation of a sociology of education from one of development. It reads as if the final publication focuses upon only one component of the whole problem of socio-economic development as it had originally been represented in the conception of the two conferences. Whereas, perhaps, the Madrid conference could be seen as an extension of the work of what, in 1980, Mary Douglas called the 'new young field of Mediterranean anthropology',[4] the 1967 publication draws together articles about Algeria, Spain, France, Greece, Hungary, Italy, Arab countries and Yugoslavia specifically to 'pose some comparative questions on the relations between the scholastic system and social stratification or cultural change'.[5] There is, in short, a clear shift away from an interest in education as an instrument in the cultural adjustment to change of traditional Mediterranean societies towards an interest in the efficacy of the equalizing educational policies of the communist countries of Eastern Europe.

This shift registers the new mood of the second half of the 1960s. In 1967, Castel and Passeron were, respectively, employed in the universities of Lille and Nantes, but, by the end of the following year, they were both employed in the newly instituted university of Paris VIII at Vincennes. In 1966, Passeron had co-authored *La Réforme de l'université*,[6] in which he analysed the conservatism and the potential for innovation of the existing French universities, and the events of May 1968 shook that conservatism. For a few weeks, the revolt of the students held out the hope that changes in higher education might be the motor for a wholesale, democratized reconstruction of French society. Sartre championed the student action as an insurrection which might successfully challenge Gaullist capitalism. As he wrote in 1968:

> there is no bad Gaullism, there cannot be a good Gaullism; there is Gaullism, that's all: this means that the regime is, in itself, the expression of the dominant class which we are fighting.[7]

The events of May 1968 were well documented at the time and have been subjected to historical scrutiny, particularly in the year of the twentieth anniversary, and this is not the place for a detailed consideration. De Gaulle dissolved the National Assembly, called a general election, and was returned – although only to remain for less than a further year. A structural reorganization of the higher education system was introduced with the Loi d'Orientation which was passed by the National Assembly and the Senate in October 1968. It was under this legislation that the university of Paris VIII at Vincennes was established specifically so as to attempt to raise the level of recruitment to higher education of working-class students.

Les Héritiers (1964) had pointed to the statistical evidence which showed that working-class students were under-represented in French higher education, and had portrayed those factors which were intrinsic to university institutions which perpetuated under-representation and failure. It would seem logical, therefore, that Passeron and Castel should become involved in the establishment of a new institution which would seek to remove these adverse factors. Why, however, did Bourdieu not join them? In March 1969 *Le Monde* reported two conferences which had been held by the Société Française de Sociologie which had bearing precisely on the events of May 1968 and on the status of sociology. Of those sociologists present, Michel Crozier was represented as being amongst those who thought that the events had not profoundly modified a French society which remained structurally incapable of changing. By contrast, it was reported that Alain Touraine had repeated the argument which he had recently published in *Le Mouvement de mai et le Communisme utopique* (1968)[8] that we were now experiencing the birth of a new form of social conflict in which technocratic domination will be opposed by a new coalition of professional adversaries.

Additionally, the position adopted by Robert Castel was paraphrased. He affirmed that sociology was not capable of understanding the events of May because it is itself entirely an accomplice of technocratic capitalism. He was quoted as declaring that 'Partial sociological knowledge leads to partial action which in the end is reduced to accommodating the existing social order and to manipulating social subjects to make them adapt to it.'[9] By concentrating only on surface phenomena, sociology had become incapable of perceiving the political reality which lay behind them.

These summaries of the debate given in *Le Monde* help us to locate Bourdieu's position at this time. So does an article published by M.S. Archer in 1970 entitled 'Egalitarianism in English and French Educational Sociology'[10]. Archer there considers the responses to May, 1968, of Touraine and Bourdieu. She contends that although Touraine saw the events as a hopeful sign for the production of new social forms whilst Bourdieu was inclined to see the events as a kind of demonstrative self-deception which concealed processes of social reproduction which remained unaltered, nevertheless both interpretations emerge from the same tradition of educational research. This tradition was characterized as one which concentrated excessively upon the differential chances of students according to social class. Archer's presentation of Bourdieu's position, however, is mainly derived from a reading of *Les Héritiers* and the subsequent pedagogical research conducted within the Centre de Sociologie Européenne. Archer's argument pre-dates the publication of *La Reproduction*. The purpose of this chapter is to show the development of Bourdieu's thinking between *Les Héritiers* and *La Reproduction* and so to show that this development meant that he became less and less able to regard the educational system as itself an agent for social change. The chapter shows, therefore, that Bourdieu tacitly resisted the tendency evidenced in *Éducation, développement et démocratie* to elevate the potential of educational reform for securing a democratic society. It charts the complex interactions in his thinking which led him to regard the politicized appropriation of sociological research as dangerously simplistic. The following chapter will also consider the steps which Bourdieu took to argue that the methodological position assigned to Castel in the report in *Le Monde* could be counteracted both by articulating fully an understanding of the natures of research and participation, and by developing a notion of the profession of being a sociologist.

The contexts of Bourdieu's work in Algeria and in the Béarn had allowed him to perceive the social phenomena in both cases in terms of a process of transition from traditional to modern culture. The Algerian tribes had possessed their own sophisticated forms of social organization. Diverse kinds of social behaviour including warfare, property rights, customary law, matrimonial exchange, economic activity and patrimony – each of which possessed discrete rules – were, nevertheless, harmoniously united and balanced by virtue of their subordination to the over-riding principle that the purpose of the integrated social organization was to safeguard the survival of the tribal group in its constant struggle against adverse geographical or climatic conditions. Traditional societies were presented as being closed systems in which rigid hierarchies guaranteed harmony and in which the whole culture was so self-validating that individuals were automatically socialized to perform valuable and valued functions. There was no possibility that individuals might conceptualize their situations as deprived or unequal. Once this charmed circle was broken, however, the edifice of mutually supporting and mutually validating functions had to crumble in its entirety. Bourdieu did not isolate any one factor which could be said to have caused the general collapse of traditional society. It was enough for him that it was patently happening before his eyes. He meticulously documented what he observed – that people whose actions had possessed meaning within the old closed system found that those same actions were dispossessed of meaning within the new system. There was no going back to the traditional ways, but Bourdieu had been sufficiently attracted to the socially constructed harmony of the closed system to want to direct his efforts towards facilitating the construction of a harmonious society based upon individualism and equality rather than on unequal hierarchy. His exposure of the situation of individuals caught between two cultures was designed to enable those individuals to understand the way in which their predicament had been socially constrained and might, for that very reason, be altered by them as reflexive social agents. Tribal organization had been a sophisticated construction in response to physical conditions, and the best human aspects of that organization could still be preserved by constructing a response to the new conditions of modernization. The important thing was that the individuals who were suffering from a kind of culture shock should not internalize an interpretation of their malaise which might suggest that they were essentially – in themselves as individuals – inadequate. An enlightened educational policy would help here because it would begin by recognizing the situation in which the culturally displaced persons found themselves and would set itself the task of encouraging creative cultural adjustment. It would not seek to confirm that the people were personally deficient by setting tests which they would be bound to fail precisely because of the nature of their prior cultural situation.

The form of Bourdieu's analysis was the same in relation to the celibates of the Béarn. Celibacy had now lost the meaning which it had possessed within the closed system of traditional peasant society. At some point this century there had been some fracture of the self-validating structure of peasant society, such that there were now individuals in mainland France who were unhappily trying to reconcile two worlds of values. The malaise manifested itself in a growing rift between the country and the town, and, at the inter-personal level, in increasing difficulties in relations between the sexes. Bourdieu's response in the Béarn was the same as in Algeria. An educational strategy was necessary which would ease the process of transition from rural to urban values in such a way that urban values would themselves be forced to assimilate the traditional. There was no sense in which the individualism of urban life could now be denied, but an educational strategy which would allow for a mutually enriching communication between traditional and modern values, might mean that individualism would gain a new strength by being located within a socially constructed collectivism adapted from traditionalism.

This thinking clearly persisted into the educational research which commenced at Lille in the early 1960s. A rational pedagogy was needed which would start from the cultural situation of working-class students. It was assumed that 'working-class' students were the same as peasants and that the function of an educational strategy was to give these students an opportunity simultaneously to insert themselves within a modernizing society and to participate in constituting the nature of that society. *Les Étudiants et leurs études* summarized investigations which satisfactorily demonstrated that working-class students were disadvantaged within higher education because they had not already been initiated into the culture which the educational system upheld, but the jump from this demonstration to the conclusion that a rational pedagogy should be introduced was much less convincing. There were two main problems. The first was apparent in the discussion of *Les Héritiers*. There was an important sense in which the higher education system in France was itself an instrument of a traditional society. The rules of that system were discrete and self-contained in the same way as were the rules of matrimonial exchange in traditional Algeria. Staff and, importantly, also students colluded in practices which perpetuated the closure and the autonomy of the system. Just as the apparent function of the dowry may have been financial whilst the real function was to sustain a social equilibrium, so the apparent rationale of the university – to enable students to acquire knowledge and skills so as to find appropriate places in the occupational structure of society according to their tested merit – was a front to conceal the reality which was that the system was an elaborate mechanism simply to reinforce a pre-existing social hierarchy. Whereas it had been possible in newly independent Algeria to suppose that an educational strategy might be the means by which a socialist state would enable its population to construct its own new collective consciousness, it appeared in France that a 'state' education system was already in the grip of an entrenched traditionalism. How could, therefore, the introduction of a 'rational pedagogy' within the higher education system have the desired social effects when the covert purpose of that system within society was plainly to counteract the achievement of those effects?

The second problem relates specifically to the students. The model derived from Algeria and the Béarn was that a rational pedagogy would be the point of encounter between the representatives of modern and traditional cultures and that the encounter would facilitate a new kind of modernism – one sensitive to collective values. Not only was it possible that lecturers were in fact, often unwittingly, the representatives of traditionalism, but also that students had already acquired a culture with which they were satisfied. Perhaps the function of higher education should be to endorse the 'popular' culture already constructed by working-class students rather than to force them to negotiate a pedagogical experience which would remedy their putative deficiency in cultural capital.

The simplest way to represent Bourdieu's dilemma in the early 1960s is in terms of a tension between three kinds of culture – what might be called an 'aristocratic' culture reinforcing traditional social hierarchy, a 'rational' culture committed to harmonizing society on equal, democratic foundations, and a 'popular' culture which might either be harnessed for rational purposes or be a comforter patronizingly proffered by the aristocracy. It was crucial that the rational culture should not be reduced to either of the other two, and, particularly, that the content of studies should be shown to possess some intellectual autonomy. It was all very well to prove that a student who had never heard a symphony of Beethoven at the concert hall or had never seen a performance of Shakespeare in the theatre would be disadvantaged when assessed by staff for whom familiarity with Beethoven and Shakespeare was an indication of the requisite cultural and aristocratic qualifications; but it was quite different to establish whether, rationally, familiarity with Beethoven and Shakespeare ought to be transmitted.

To put the problem in these terms is to summarize the concerns of Bourdieu's work in the period leading to the publication of *La Reproduction*. The pedagogical research which had been inaugurated with the investigations reported in *Les Étudiants et leurs études* continued within the Centre de Sociologie Européenne throughout the decade. These continued to demonstrate the need for a rational pedagogy which would be grounded in an awareness of the social background of those who were expected to receive the messages which lecturers were transmitting. At the same time, however, Bourdieu was involved in empirical research which can be called 'cultural analysis'. In analysing the social function of photography, Bourdieu was explicitly reflecting on the status of an emergent 'popular' culture, whilst his analysis of the social function of museums and art galleries involved an assessment of the process of transmitting high culture outside the framework of the higher education system – it involved, in other words, the exploration of the possibility of rationally transmitting aristocratic culture within institutional contexts which might not be reinforcing a social hierarchy.

I have suggested earlier in this chapter that by the mid-1960s the force of the argument that no rational pedagogy could be introduced within the existing institutional ethos of French higher education was pushing some of Bourdieu's colleagues and collaborators within the Centre de Sociologie Européenne towards overt political action. For Bourdieu, however, it was necessary to clarify the relationship between the structure of knowledge and the structure of institutions. Both were socially constructed but both also acquired some objective status. De-constructing either the curriculum or the institution or both did not, in the end, mean that an absolutely de-constructed society would be achieved. Whereas the educational and cultural work of the first half of the decade was empirical, the second half is characterized by an increasing degree of theoretical and speculative thought. Bourdieu was developing an approach to the sociology of knowledge which did justice to the view that knowledge was operative within society rather than in some mysterious way transcendent. This approach entailed a clean break with structuralism in favour of a position which could explore the mechanisms by which societies construct their structures. It began to emerge most clearly that there was a reciprocal relationship between the structures of thought within a society and the institutional structures which both reflect and generate the thought. It was as if – and here the linguistic analogy deliberately anticipates some of Bourdieu's later work – the educational system constituted a societal generative grammar which was not innate but which the society created for itself in order to make it possible for it to talk to itself. The educational system was intrinsically conservative – not in the sense that it conveyed aristocratic or traditional values but in the sense that it was established by society in order to provide a neutral sphere within which its identity could be conserved and modified. The educational system operated for society in the same way as a diary might for an individual. It offered clean sheets on which might be written both accounts of what has happened and projections of what might occur. It structurally guaranteed a continuity between the past and the future and sustained the individual's sense of personal identity and was, therefore, conservative, but it embodied no predisposition in favour of either the past recollection or the future aspiration.

Bourdieu took the view that to identify the implementation of a rational pedagogy with the development of a new, radical university was to fix the nature of the institution as if it possessed an institutional essence and to lose sight of the important recognition that the ethos of an institution is a variable factor in the logic of all pedagogical communication. It was more fundamentally radical to continue to argue that people have within themselves the capacity to recognize and radicalize their own situations than prematurely to insist that one institutional innovation embodied the essence of radicalism. More importantly, the 'radicals' of 1968 were forfeiting any commitment to a rational culture which might act as a change agent to harmonize the whole of society. The post-1968 innovations were overtly partisan as much as, covertly, was the aristocratic system which it sought to overthrow. Neither institutions nor curricula constituted meta-narratives through which society might converse with itself. It is significant that Paris VIII at Vincennes became the institutional base for post-modernism, and, as far as Bourdieu's position at the time is concerned, equally significant that it is now possible to suggest in retrospect that the new institution within the French higher education system has become steadily more and more marginalized. What we see in Bourdieu's attitude at the end of the 1960s is the foreshadowing of his modernist opposition to post-modernism. The process of his research and thinking which culminated in *La Reproduction* laid the foundations for that subsequent opposition.

To communicate the nature of that process this account superimposes a matrical pattern on the reality and pauses at key intersections. It follows separately the chronological sequence of Bourdieu's educational, cultural and theoretical work in the 1960s, but tries to articulate the cross-references at about 1965–6 and, again, in 1970. This representational artifice should not only clarify the background to *La Reproduction* but should also give an insight into Bourdieu's originality – his capacity to avoid asking self-fulfilling questions within 'autonomous' discourses by refusing to recognize their autonomy.

The second of the reports of the Centre de Sociologie Européenne – *Rapport pédagogique et communication* – followed naturally from the emphasis on the need to develop a 'rational pedagogy' which was outlined at the end of *Les Héritiers*. The introduction – written by Bourdieu and Passeron – was called 'Langage et rapport au langage dans la situation pédagogique' and was the same as an article of that title which appeared in *Les Temps modernes* in September 1965. It is an introduction to four chapters which summarize the findings of enquiries carried out in the first few years of the decade. Of these, Bourdieu was joint author of two: 'Les étudiants et la langue d'enseignement' and 'Les utilisateurs de la Bibliothèque universitaire de Lille'. The first reports the findings of an investigation undertaken in 1962–3 with the same participating institutions as for *Les Étudiants et leurs études*. A pre-enquiry had been carried out in 1960–1 which had already established the importance of linguistic misunderstanding in the process of communication between staff and students. There had been two intentions in pursuing the enquiry further: to evaluate the knowledge which students have of the language commonly used by professors, and to establish the relation between different levels of comprehension and the social characteristics of the students. In short, the enquiry reported in 'Les étudiants et la langue d'enseignement' ran in parallel with that reported in *Les Étudiants et leurs études*. The assumptions behind the two enquiries were the same, the method was similar, and the finding that there existed a prior stock of linguistic capital which advantaged middle-class students mirrored the finding that the possession of a prior cultural capital had a differentiating effect. Some of the findings of the second contribution to *Rapport pédagogique et communication* with which Bourdieu was specifically associated – based on a questionnaire issued to a total of 880 students who entered the library at the university of Lille at least once in one week in March 1964 – were used in *Les Héritiers* to indicate the attitudes of students towards intellectual work and towards libraries as places of work, but the essence of the 1965 report from the Centre de Sociologie Européenne is that it concentrates on the use of language within educational institutions. Viewing education as a process for transmitting information from teachers to learners, Bourdieu and Passeron contend in the introductory 'Langage et rapport au langage dans la situation pédagogique' that the French higher education system of 1965 was intolerably inefficient. In a fashion which is familiar from the argument of *Les Héritiers*, the authors suggest that the intolerable is tolerated precisely because the apparent function of transmitting information is not the real function. A degree of linguistic misunderstanding sustains the superiority of the teacher and this is often a superiority which students wish to endorse in order themselves to become initiates of the system. Bourdieu and Passeron propose a formula for measuring the degree of communication achieved, but they recognize that the efficacy of this quantitative instrument is undermined by the social forces which impinge on the communicative process.

Although the form of this discussion seems familiar, the analysis of language raises questions which, for Bourdieu, generated reflections in sociolinguistics and in the sociology of knowledge. In this 1965 text, the eagerness with which the hidden structural function of the institution was adopted as an explanation for the interference which contaminated pure rational communication blinded the authors to the intrinsic sociolinguistic problems of knowledge communication. Bourdieu and Passeron concluded that 'it is only a matter of making explicit all the presuppositions of the scholarly manipulation of language for it to become possible to make transmission explicit'[11] but noted, equally, that staff and students are trapped within a system which makes this kind of rationalization unlikely because the stability of the whole system is at stake.

It was too easy, however, to imply that the system alone inhibited the straightforward transmission of information. There are two weaknesses in this view of an ideal rational pedagogy. First, the view seems to assume that there are bodies of static information to be transmitted and that, therefore, education can be improved by improving the mechanisms of transmissions. Secondly, and related, it seems to assume that there is a pedagogical use of language which is the means of explicating the language adopted in specialized fields. To put the problem in the terms of McLuhan – whose theories of mass communication were then becoming popular – Bourdieu and Passeron do not here countenance the possibility that the medium might be the message. Put differently, this discussion of rational pedagogy takes insufficient account of phenomenological epistemology.

For Bourdieu the resolution of this problem had to come from an acceptance that the social and institutional contexts of a communicative process are constitutive and are not alien interferences – that the knowledge which is transmitted has an intellectual autonomy as a 'field' possessing its own rules and language which, however, can only be transmitted at all if it suspends its autonomy in order to be actualized within a habitus, a social setting which facilitates the internalization or the incorporation of abstract ideas. For the moment, though, let us assume that the educational strand of Bourdieu's thinking is frozen at 1965. Other empirical work was already challenging the notion that the meaning of a message was exclusively defined by the intention of the transmitter.

Bourdieu had been a keen photographer in Algeria. *Travail et travailleurs* contains photographs taken by Bourdieu which offer a powerful visual supplement to the written text. We have seen that sociology students were asked in the first questionnaire analysed in *Les Étudiants et leurs études* how they would rate the importance of an investigation of amateur photography clubs. Just such an investigation, carried out in the Lille region under the direction of Raymonde Moulin, was one of a cluster of 22 projects undertaken in the academic years 1961–2, 1962–3 and 1963–4, which are listed in an appendix to *Un Art moyen* which was published in 1965. This text gathers together the work of a team of collaborators within the Centre de Sociologie Européenne, but the introduction and first part, written by Bourdieu, furnish the controlling framework for the whole study.

Understanding 'the social uses of photography', as *Un Art moyen* is sub-titled, was a major preoccupation of the Centre alongside its educational research and, indeed, Bourdieu's monograph on the function of photography for peasants was a by-product of his work in the Béarn which pre-dated the research in Lille. The initial attraction of the study of photography can be readily appreciated in the context of Bourdieu's other concerns, but involvement in the study influenced the development of Bourdieu's general outlook. The text provides the following summary of the argument of the introduction:

> The study of photographic practice and of the meaning of the photographic image is a privileged opportunity to put into operation an original methodology which attempts to grasp a complete understanding both of the objective regularities of behaviour and of the lived experience of this behaviour.[12]

This was thought to be the case because a photograph of a group of people constitutes a fixed, objective representation of a set of relations in which those people have themselves colluded or participated by virtue of being prepared to be photographed. Bourdieu seemed, at first, to be content to leave it at that. He takes time in his introduction to defend the analysis of photography as a legitimate field of sociological enquiry, and his defence is that it is a particularly appropriate means of uniting the strands of sociological enquiry which, in the past, have been in opposition – strands which, on the one hand, have wanted to analyse social phenomena only as objective facts, and strands which, on the other hand, have wanted to emphasize only the meaning of phenomena articulated by participants.

If the first attraction of the study of photography was, for Bourdieu, that it enabled him to think through some of the methodological problems which had troubled him in his work in Algeria and the Béarn, there were also attractions which cross-referred to the substance of his analysis in other fields. In the first chapter of *Un Art moyen* he launched an attack on the explanation of photographic activity which argued that it fulfilled a psychological need for people. He insisted, instead, that photographic practice could only be fully understood in its social setting. The formal wedding photo, for instance, had become current in the Béarn because there had been pre-existing social conditions which were fulfilled in the new technology. The wedding ceremony was already a ritual event which consecrated familial alliances and an official photograph served to consolidate that consecration. Photographs taken officially at weddings and baptisms helped to sustain traditional values, but Bourdieu's analysis suggested that the attitudes of peasants towards themselves taking photographs was a register of their general attitudinal stance in relation to the town. Equally, Bourdieu showed from his research that unmarried men were more likely to adopt an 'aesthetic' attitude to their photographic practice because, as celibates who had lost their meaningful position within a traditional system of values, that practice had no communal frame of reference.

Much of the detailed analysis of photographic practice which is given in *Un Art moyen* is more comprehensively interpreted in *La Distinction* (1979) and will be considered again in a later chapter, but there was a third attraction of the study of photography which still places *Un Art moyen* as a product of the thinking of the early 1960s. This was that photography could be seen as an unconsecrated culture. The analysis of photography and of photographic practitioners provided Bourdieu with the opportunity to explore cultural practice which was apparently independent of the domination of schooling. Photography was an emergent popular culture. There were no judgements about photography to be transmitted by any rational pedagogy and there was no pre-existent hierarchy of aristocratic values masquerading as aesthetic evaluations. The discussion of photography, therefore, constantly had a point of contact with the contemporary reflection on the nature of educational institutions.

In the same years as Bourdieu was pursuing his analysis of photography and photographic practitioners, he was also engaged with a massive survey of European museums and art galleries. This began as an analysis of the museum at Lille and of visitors to the museum which was similar to the contemporary analysis of the users of the university library also at Lille, but the enquiry expanded to embrace, first of all, a total of 22 French museums and, finally, a total of 123 museums in France, Spain, Greece, Holland and Poland. The analysis of the attitudes of visitors to museums for France alone was based upon a national sample of 9,226 people. The findings were briefly summarized in two articles – 'Les musées et leurs publics' (1964) and 'Le musée et son public' (1965) – and then published in full in *L'Amour de l'art, les musées d'art et leur public* (1966) and in the expanded edition of 1969. Whereas the framework of *Les Héritiers* had concentrated on the extent to which prior familiarity with cultural institutions such as museums advantaged students within higher education, *L'Amour de l'art* confronts directly the nature of that prior experience. What emerges is that familiarity with aristocratic culture is almost as independent of schooling as is the development of the new popular culture of photography. Bourdieu argued that educational practice was not providing pupils rationally with the conceptual tools necessary to appreciate the culture on display in museums. Middle-class children imbibed a formal affinity with museum culture because it reinforced their class identity. A corollary of this formal affinity was that aesthetic appreciation acquired a mystique similar to the mystique of 'talent' or 'innate ability' which was current within higher education practice. Museums and visitors to museums colluded in creating a myth of natural 'taste' which concealed the reality which was that all taste had been socially acquired in the past and had been handed down within the family context. What had been learnt in the past and was now presented as 'natural' could be learned in the present, and Bourdieu's analysis exposed a deplorable unconcern on the part of schools.

Aesthetic appreciation and photographic activity both, in different ways, fulfilled social rather than psychological functions. This was the clear message from *L'Amour de l'art* and *Un Art moyen*. Photographic practice was in the course of generating its own rules and social conventions independent of educational practice whilst the educational system had failed to break the circle of appreciation whereby, within museums, cultural providers covertly sustained a social alliance with those people who chose to make visits. Both pieces of work seemed to confirm, therefore, that rational pedagogy was not performing its ideal function of mediating between 'aristocratic' and 'popular' culture. Although this seems, at first sight, to be a conclusion which corresponds with the findings from the educational research – for museums, for instance, substitute universities – the two cultural enquiries of the early 1960s raised in more acute form the incipient problem of *Rapport pédagogique et communication*. How far does a commitment to the need to reform pedagogical practice itself reinforce the notion that there exist objective values or verities which ought to be transmitted to people who have not been socialized at home to possess the equipment to receive the transmissions? Once the real, but hidden, function of museums and universities – to preserve social differentiation – has been exposed and removed, are there any grounds for supposing that their apparent function – to make objectively valuable knowledge and culture equally accessible to all members of society – will have any substance? Might it not emerge that the culture of museums and universities is integrally related to the ethos of those institutions and cannot be de-contextualized and packaged for democratic consumption? Might it not prove to be the case that the practice of photography is intrinsically democratic because it is an ordinary activity, a 'grass-roots' culture, whereas museums are doomed to be the morgues of culture and universities to be the museums of knowledge?

L'Amour de l'art manifests a tacit attachment to the cultural contents of museums and art galleries. The school system is failing society because it is not enabling the whole society to appreciate what is displayed. Similarly, there is in *Un Art moyen* some attachment to the view that official photographs reflect and confirm pre-existing social relationships. One of the social uses of photographs, in other words, is that family photograph albums and collections become domestic museums. The important consequence of Bourdieu's investigation of photography was that it enabled him to articulate the view that we all generate the artefacts which we then appreciate. This meant, of course, that the working distinction between 'aristocratic' and 'popular' culture evaporated. The researches presented in *Un Art moyen* all suggested that photography was rapidly establishing its own artistic conventions – of, for instance, what was legitimately photographable or not – and that, equally, photographers were creating the institutional framework in clubs and competitions for the exercise of aesthetic judgement. Popular culture did not remain permanently in an idealized, de-regulated realm. The construction of rules was a necessary condition for its development. Popular culture was not, therefore, a different kind of culture from museum culture. It was simply developing, rather than developed.

Some of the articles published by Bourdieu in 1966 seem to suggest that he had not himself fully assimilated the implications of his studies of photography. *L'Amour de l'art*, 'La transmission de l'héritage culturel' and 'L' école conservatrice, les inégalités devant l'école et devant la culture' constitute a cluster of texts which cross-refer and jointly reinforce the view that the school system is offering a false cultural neutrality and is perpetuating rather than removing the unequal access of the working-class to the benefits of the whole society. Part of the problem, certainly, is that the deprived are inhibited by their adoption of group values which enable them to acquiesce in their deprivation. All that this means, however, is that educational practice has to accept that it is a key part of the educational task to tackle these restraining attitudes at source. There is no sense at all that the practice of learning might be analogous to the practice of taking photos and that both sets of practitioners might comparably be involved in the process of constructing their own institutional settings.

Instead, the other articles of 1966 explore in abstract and in different contexts the phenomenon which is thought to keep the working class in a subservient role. Just as the aspirations of deprived people are repressed by their internal representation of what appears to be objectively possible, so, historically, the pure expression of an artist is constrained by his anticipation of the way in which critics will receive his work of art. 'Champ intellectuel et projet créateur' (1966) which became well known in the United Kingdom because of the inclusion of a translation in M.F.D. Young's collection of essays entitled *Knowledge and Control* (1971)[13] was originally published in a number of *Les Temps modernes* devoted to a consideration of the problems of structuralism.[14] The article argued that the production of a work of art is the meeting point, for the artist, between the 'intrinsic necessity of the work of art', what it is he or she feels internally compelled to express, and 'social pressures which direct the work from outside'.[15] There is a high degree of reciprocity and self-fulfilment about this transaction. Creative projects are modified at inception by the artist's perception of the field of receptivity to which the work will be assigned, but, equally, each new project modifies the nature of the field. The successful artist is one who optimally combines what he wants to say with a sufficient element of what he anticipates that critics will be predisposed to esteem. For the sociologist of art or literature, observing this process, the implication of Bourdieu's article was that it was not appropriate to attempt to understand a work of art in its own terms without reference to social context, and, more importantly, that it was foolish to seek to identify structural patterns amongst the expressive arts as if these various expressions had existences which were totally divorced from the creative strategies adopted consciously by the artists. What Raymond Williams was at that time calling 'the structure of feeling' of an age or what had traditionally in German *Geistesgeschichte* been called the *Zeitgeist*, or spirit of the age, was not something which had an ideal or objective existence. It was itself a social construct which had a constantly transitory, because continuously functional, character.

Another article of 1966 – 'Condition de classe et position de classe' – wrestled with the same kind of problem. It follows up a hint that Bourdieu had already made in *Travail et travailleurs* to the effect that the appropriateness of 'class' analysis was a function of the kind of class to which it was applied, but now the hint is transformed into a full theoretical discussion of what sociologists and anthropologists might mean by the word structure when they talk about social structures. It is possible to identify general patterns of class behaviour, such as the behaviour of peasants, which are linked to intrinsic conditions like the physical environment, but these conditions constitute only one factor in defining the class position of any specific class within any society. The notion of a class with which individuals choose to identify themselves is a construct created by those individuals in the same way as the notion of an intellectual field is the creation of artists who wish to predetermine the way in which their creativity is publicly endorsed. The appropriateness of the structuralist analysis which was dependent on the identification of patterns of material conditions was always bound to be relative to the extent to which the particular classes under consideration had managed to acquire positional self-determination or relative autonomy.

Both 'Champ intellectuel et projet créateur' and 'Condition de classe et position de classe' were indications that Bourdieu was theoretically taking stock of his position. They were almost the first of his publications which were not explicitly linked to findings from empirical research. This same trend continued with the publication, in 1967, of his translation of Panofsky's *Gothic Architecture and Scholastic Thought* with an important 'postface', and the associated paper on 'Systèmes d'enseignement et systémes de pensée'. 'Champ intellectuel et projet créateur' had already anticipated the more detailed discussion of Panofsky's work, and all three texts can be taken together to indicate Bourdieu's emerging position. The attraction of Panofsky's work was that he had not been content merely to observe patterns of similarity in Gothic architecture, but had gone further to suggest that these patterns were the direct result of the common internalization of modes of scholastic thinking in the period between about 1130 and 1270. The structural patterns were not an expression of the conceptual disposition of the analyst but were inherent in the historical situation. Equally, Gothic architecture was not the embodiment of an abstract intellectual system as such but of a system which had achieved common currency by the 'habit-forming' affects of an educational system which 'held the virtual monopoly of education'[16] in the environs of Paris. 'Systems of education and systems of thought' re-stated the view that the modes of thinking which are peculiar to nations or to 'schools of thought' are not automatically homologous but are the products of educational systems.

If the early educational and cultural work of the 1960s had, simultaneously, argued the need for a rational pedagogy which would counteract disadvantage, and demonstrated that the desired effects of such a rational pedagogy in seeking to generate a common culture through the mediation of neutral schooling were far from being attained, Bourdieu's writing of 1966 and 1967 nevertheless confirmed that educational systems perform a necessary logical function within societies. The actual existence of educational systems had offered a way out of the problems of structuralism because they showed the way in which social structures could be tangibly structured by social participants. Bourdieu now had to incorporate the reflections on 'habitus' which were inspired by his reading of Panofsky and which seemed to justify the social function of educational systems into his thinking about the educational process itself. *La Reproduction* provides a framework for thinking about the pedagogic process in a way which does not presuppose the methods of institutionalized schooling, but that framework is predicated on the view that some form of organized educational communication within society is a necessary pre-requisite for securing societal harmony and equality.

The discussion of this chapter has tried to indicate the cross-fertilization between ideas developed in contexts each of which possessed their own autonomous logics – concentrating on the work published in 1966–7. There was no slowing down of momentum in activity on each of the three fronts in the last few years of the decade. The continuing pedagogical research was reflected in 'Les fonctions du système d'enseignement: classes préparatoires et facultés' (1969) – a mimeographed paper of the Centre – and in 'L'excellence scolaire et les valeurs du système d'enseignement français' (1970). In the cultural field, Bourdieu was developing a sociology of artistic or aesthetic perception to which we shall return in examining *La Distinction*, whilst two articles published first in English ('Sociology and philosophy in France since 1945' (1967) and 'Structuralism and theory of sociological knowledge' (1968)) both assessed the status of the sociological analysis undertaken within the Centre and will be considered in the next chapter. Whilst the separate strands of work still persisted, Bourdieu and Passeron themselves produced – in *La Reproduction* (1970) – their own brilliant synthesis of the various components of the research of the 1960s. Briefly, I have suggested that the early pedagogical research operated with naive views of communication and of epistemology and that these were refined as a result of analyses of non-pedagogical cultural transmission and of theoretical reflection on the place of knowledge within society. What seemed to be emerging was a sense that, as it were from within, the educational system needed a more sophisticated conception of its pedagogical activity whilst, simultaneously from a societal perspective, there was a need for the educational system itself to become a forum for democratic discourse – a 'public sphere'. At both the macro and the micro levels, there was a similar need to recognize that authority was socially constructed and was not the automatic preserve of either the teacher or the educational system. These emerging emphases were summarized in *La Reproduction*.

The English translation of the text – *Reproduction in Education, Society and Culture* (1977) – gave the English public its first glimpse of the full complexity of Bourdieu's research and thought. We have followed the progression through the 1960s from research which had originated in a problematic – the lack of success in higher education of working-class students – which was familiar to English readers brought up on the educational sociology of Floud and Halsey to the formulation of findings contained in *La Reproduction*. What was inscrutable in *Reproduction* in 1977 should now be clearer. Most accessible in 1977 was the second part of the text in which the authors discursively gathered together conclusions derived from the earlier empirical researches. But it was the first part which caused more difficulty and now still requires detailed exposition. Just as *Les Héritiers* had shocked by using anthropological language about French phenomena, *La Reproduction* secured a comparable rupture with commonplace thinking by deliberately advancing a set of logical propositions as a means of understanding social relations.

The grouping of the propositions into four categories concerned with Pedagogic Action (PA), Pedagogic Authority (PAu), Pedagogic Work (PW) and the Educational System (ES) indicates that *La Reproduction* seeks schematically to suggest a way of approaching the relations between pedagogy and educational systems. Starting with the 'Twofold arbitrariness of pedagogic action' the text offers a series of accumulating propositions. The initiating proposition is that 'All pedagogic action (PA) is, objectively, symbolic violence insofar as it is the imposition of a cultural arbitrary by an arbitrary power.'[17] The starting-point for the propositions, in other words, is the view that the knowledge which is transmitted from one person to another (or, equally, the culture which is passed on from one person to another) has no absolute validity. From the outset, the proposition denies what seemed to be the assumption of both *Rapport pédagogique et communication* and *L'Amour de l'art* that there existed intellectual or cultural absolutes which had to be transmitted rationally. Both the content of what is transmitted pedagogically and the social context within which the transmission takes place are arbitrary. As the gloss which follows immediately points out, this general principle applies whether the pedagogic action occurs within a social group, a family or within institutionalized education, and, similarly, applies whether the cultural arbitrary is an imposition of the dominant or the dominated classes. The arbitrariness of pedagogic action is twofold simply because (proposition 1.1) the context within which transmission occurs is arbitrarily determined by the power relations between groups within society (arbitrary power) and because (proposition 1.2) the content of what is transmitted has no absolute reference but is only a reflection of the interests of the group controlling the context. However, it is important to retain the sense that pedagogic action has a twofold arbitrariness because Bourdieu and Passeron want to retain the tension of the two conflicting dimensions. They insist that what happens in a pedagogic communication is not to be seen purely as a manifestation of power relations nor, equally, as the communication of contents which have no relations with socio-economic bases, in the same way as Bourdieu had argued in 'Champ intellectuel et projet créateur' that an artefact should not be perceived either as wholly a free-standing 'work of art' or as a simple, mechanistic manifestation of underlying economic relations.

The crucial implication of the propositions concerning pedagogic action is that it always tends to reproduce the interests of the groups imposing arbitrary power. Pedagogic action cannot, by definition, generate products which possess a cultural capital which is transferable or convertible. Pedagogic action is only self-affirming and self-fulfilling. Nevertheless, it can only have that effect if the real nature of this circularity remains hidden. As the second main proposition therefore states:

> PA necessarily implies, as a social condition of its exercise, pedagogic authority (PAu) and the relative autonomy of the agency commissioned to exercise it.[18]

Pedagogic action logically needs the trappings of pedagogic authority to conceal the arbitrariness of its procedures, but the precise character of pedagogic authority is socially constructed in ways which are independent of the logical requirements of pedagogic action. In other words, pedagogic authority can be bestowed on a teacher for reasons which are extraneous to the demands of the pedagogic relationship (as, for instance, in the case of the authority of the Church). At the same time, the fact that pedagogic action does necessarily entail some kind of pedagogic authority, derived from whatever source, means that those in receipt of the pedagogic action are predisposed not to question it because it is an expression of the authority which they already accept before entering the pedagogical relationship. Hence, for instance, students did not question the validity of ideas communicated to them by their professors because they already colluded in the social values of the institution which bestowed authority on those professors.

Since pedagogic action can no longer be transformed into a rational pedagogy which attempts to deny the extraneous influence of socially constructed pedagogic authority, it is unavoidable that the reception of information is embedded socially as much as its transmission. This leads to the third main proposition which states that:

> PA entails pedagogic work (PW), a process of inculcation which must last long enough to produce a durable training, i.e. a habitus, the product of internalization of the principles of a cultural arbitrary capable of perpetuating itself after PA has ceased and thereby of perpetuating in practices the principles of the internalized arbitrary.[19]

The degree to which pedagogic work can be thought to be successful can be measured by the extent of the durability and transposability of the dispositions established under pedagogic conditions. The extent to which, for instance, homologies can be detected in Gothic architecture is a measure of the completeness of the pedagogic work practised within medieval schools. This measure is applicable at the same time that it can be fully recognized that within the full context of medieval society this pedagogic work instilled an attachment to an arbitrary system of ideas arbitrarily enforced within monastic institutions whose power was arbitrarily established by the arbitrary and pedagogically extraneous authority of the Catholic Church. To put this more provocatively, the degree to which pedagogic work can be thought to be successful can be measured by the extent to which members of society who have inherited traditional values internalize, instead, values which have been arbitrarily transmitted within schools which derive their authority equally arbitrarily from that arbitrary substitute for the Catholic Church – the 'State'.

The consequence here, of course, is that the propositions necessarily shift from the micro to the macro levels. It is not just that pedagogical processes are riddled with arbitrariness but also that the educational system is itself arbitrary. It has a fixed logical character in the same way as PA, PAu and PW, but the actualization of that logic is similarly dependent on socio-economic and socio-historical conditions. The logic of the educational system is that it is intrinsically conservative:

> Every institutionalized educational system (ES) owes the specific characteristics of its structure and functioning to the fact that, by the means proper to the institution, it has to produce and reproduce the institutional conditions whose existence and persistence . . . are necessary both to the exercise of its essential function of inculcation and to the fulfilment of its function of reproducing a cultural arbitrary which it does not produce . . .[20]

Logically, that is to say, every ES performs the function assigned to it within Panofsky's schema, but the exact nature of that performance varies in different cultural contexts. This insistence on variability reflects both Bourdieu's argument in articles such as 'La comparabilité des systèmes d'enseignement' (1967) and 'Le système des fonctions du système d'enseignement' (1969) and his awareness, expressed in 'Champ intellectuel et projet créateur' (1966), that the ideology of autonomous art, or art for art's sake, was the product of particular social and historical conditions in the nineteenth century.

The achievement of the propositional formulation of Part I of *La Reproduction* was that it dramatically shifted the emphasis of the analysis which had been offered in *Les Héritiers*. The earlier text was written as if the researchers had uncovered a clandestine conspiracy. Nasty institutions like universities, and, then, in other research, museums, were pretending to offer an universal culture universally whilst, in fact, consolidating a particular culture by the particularity of their ethos and their practices. *La Reproduction* showed that these nasty practices were completely normal and that, therefore, the appropriate response was not to try to impose a favoured 'universal' position by means of a refined pedagogy but, instead, to recognize every different particularity and to analyse the different interconnections in the PA, PAu and PW nexus. Hence, to return to the points made at the beginning of this chapter, there could be, for Bourdieu, no magic route to social change in throwing in his lot with Paris VIII at Vincennes since that institution would rapidly establish its own customs and regulations according to the logic of pedagogic relations. Vincennes would generate its own institutional ethos in the same way as the research for *Un Art moyen* had shown that photography tended to mimic or adopt the conventional practices of consecrated art.

La Reproduction began with one proposition which was the premiss of all the others:

> Every power to exert symbolic violence, i.e. every power which manages to impose meanings and to impose them as legitimate by concealing the power relations which are the basis of its force, adds its own specifically symbolic force to those power relations.[21]

Bourdieu and Passeron suggest that this axiom is 'the principle of the theory of sociological knowledge'. Everything contained within *La Reproduction* had to be seen, in other words, as an expression of an imposed meaning derived from a social position which had its own symbolic force and its own power location. This introductory proposition was fundamentally reflexive. Bourdieu was seeing his own sociological activity within the framework of his own social analysis. If he was located in an institution which embodied aristocratic culture, he could, nevertheless, create a sociological workshop, an artistic atelier within the walls of the museum, and establish procedures for himself and his team of researchers which would be analogous to those developing in the ordinary art of photography. The publication of *Le Métier de sociologue* (1968) and of *Esquisse d'une théorie de la pratique* (1972) were attempts to institutionalize sociological practice and to clarify how different was such practice from the academic transmission of sociological knowledge which would have been such an incongruous corollary of his previous educational research.

· 5 ·

On practising sociology

In a Foreword to the English edition of *La Reproduction*, dated 1976, Tom Bottomore wrote that

> The first important characteristic of this work, then, can be seen in the continuous interplay between theory and research; the overcoming in an ongoing collective enterprise of that division between the construction of theoretical models by 'thinkers' and the use of such models, in a derivative way, by 'researchers', which has so often been criticized as a major failing of sociology as a science. It may well be that the division can only be transcended effectively by this kind of long-term involvement in the exploration of a particular broad domain of social life, by a group of researchers who acquire to some extent the qualities of a 'school' of thought. In the present case this characteristic is evident not only in the books that Bourdieu and his colleagues have published, but especially in the recently established journal Actes de la recherche en sciences sociales which seems to convey even in its title the notion of a continuing process of theoretical-empirical investigation.[1]

Bottomore meant by the 'particular broad domain' the research on what he called 'cultural reproduction' which had seemed to be the focus of the work undertaken at the Centre de Sociologie Européenne for more than a decade and which was summarized in *Reproduction*. It is important to remember, however, that this was a perception of 1976 and it is unclear how well Bottomore was aware of the work in French which had not yet been translated at that date. This is important because it is the intention of this chapter and the one which follows to show that Bourdieu adopted different strategies before and after 1975 in seeking to sustain a 'school' of thought and an associated group of researchers. This chapter looks at the period between 1967 and the publication of *Esquisse d'une théorie de la pratique* (1972). As we shall see, Bourdieu tried to argue in this period that the foundation of sociological practice had to be a willingness to ask fundamental epistemological questions, and the intention was that *Le Métier de sociologue* (1968) would be a handbook of good epistemological practice. The unifying principle of the group was, therefore, not at all that it had identified a 'particular broad domain' but that it had sought to emphasize a structural approach which would underpin any particularity and be sceptical about any possible autonomization of a domain. *Le Métier de sociologue* was not fully successful. It tried to offer examples of paradigmatic practice, but the mode of presentation was almost logically incompatible with the intended message. *Esquisse* offered, instead, Bourdieu's own explicit reflections on his theoretical–empirical practice in his Algerian fieldwork. There is a sense, therefore, in which, between these two texts, Bourdieu retreated from abstract prescription to personal retrospection. Chapter 7 will look at the development in the second half of the 1970s in which Bourdieu was able to move towards the presentation of a methodical prescription which was based on, but not reflecting on, his past practice and which was reinforced by his involvement in the active researches communicated in his journal.

Bottomore's comment conflated several strategies which were historically distinct, but his general point was sound that the Centre de Sociologie Européenne had acquired an identity which was almost that of a 'school' of thought. This, of course, did not just happen. Analysing the process by which the identity was acquired or achieved involves the use of the conceptual tools which Bourdieu was himself developing contemporaneously. There were, that is to say, socio-economic factors which can be cited as objective influences operating within the field in which the Centre was situated, but, equally, the nature both of that field and of the Centre were the products of Bourdieu's reflexive creative project. In the terms discussed in the last chapter, Bourdieu's response to the events of May 1968 – which was not strictly a response at all because the lines of his thinking had all been prefigured much earlier – was self-consciously to institutionalize sociological practice. The sustained production of empirical researches entailed a process of reproduction as much as did the transmission of cultural arbitraries within the educational system. Bourdieu was showing both that practice was the logical conclusion of his demolition of the assumptions of pedagogical transmission and also that practice itself was not exempt from those same assumptions. Practice was the culmination of pedagogy but, at the same time, the implementation of a programme of practice involved the creative construction of institutional conditions for practical action, authority and work. The framework of logical principles provided in *La Reproduction* became the blueprint for the creation of a research team.

In an article published in 1982 on the development of the social sciences in France from 1945 until the end of the 1960s, Alain Drouard provided an outline of the objective conditions which influenced the nature of French sociology.[2] He suggested that until the end of the 1950s the growth of the social sciences was mainly the result of the initiative of individuals. Outside the universities, new research and teaching institutions were established but, typical amongst these were the Institut Français d'Opinion Publique associated with Jean Stoetzel and the Centre d'Études Sociologiques associated with Georges Gurvitch. The governmental awareness of a need for social scientific support in introducing policies of reconstruction in the late 1940s; the encouragement provided by international organizations – particularly UNESCO; and the sense that French social science and research were falling behind in comparison with other advanced countries were all factors which generated new initiatives. At first, according to Drouard, these initiatives were fostered by comparative reference to the development of the natural sciences and to the development of American social science. Nevertheless, growth was on a small scale. Drouard cites the information offered in the Rapport Longchambon of 1957 which revealed that there were at that time only four chairs in sociology in the whole of France. Outside the universities in the scientific establishments like the Collège de France or the École Pratique des Hautes Études (the former pre-dating the university teaching reforms of the nineteenth century and the latter a by-product of those reforms as a research institute), the social sciences still had a low priority. Only in the Section VI of the École – of economic and social science, founded in 1947 – was there any significant presence – 48 directors of studies in 1956. In most of the new centres established in the decade after the war there were rarely more than a dozen researchers. In the main, therefore, social science in France was not reproduced within teaching institutions. The first two terms of reference of the Centre d'Études Sociologiques, founded in 1946, were to 'promote and direct researches in different branches of sociology' and 'to train researchers', but the activities of the various research groups were so fragmentary that they could not challenge intellectually the supremacy of the university system within which the social or human sciences were often subsumed under the faculties of Letters and Law. Drouard's view is that this all changed in the early 1960s. A social and political demand for social science emerged which is partly to be explained by the favourable climate offered by Gaullism for making contributions to the reconstruction and modernization of France after the Algerian war. There was a pressure for social scientists to sell themselves as social engineering technicians. Drouard argues that the other major factor which led to a sudden acceleration of the development of social science in the early 1960s was the governmental decision, following the Colloque de Caen of 1956, to institutionalize social science teaching within the higher education system. 1958 was the crucial year here. For the first time, formal, nationally recognized sociology qualifications were established (the licence and the doctorate of the third cycle) and Faculties of Letters were re-named Faculties of Letters and Human Sciences. The expansion in the number of sociologists in France in the 1960s was dramatic and, as Drouard points out, was backed by the growth of professional status, supported by an explosion in book production and publishing initiatives. It was his conclusion, taking the story only as far as the aftermath of the events of 1968, that the expansion of university sociology meant that the danger that social science would be subordinated to the interests of bureaucrats and technocrats had been averted. Drouard's hope was that a sociological orientation might have become an intrinsic part of a modern self-image, a part of modern culture, with the result that the main challenge for the next decade would be to ensure that this culture would be disseminated within the whole society.

Drouard's is one account of the transformations in French sociology between 1945 and 1968. We need to insert Bourdieu's career into that account. He was a first generation sociologist of the early 1960s, having received a philosophical education at the École Normale Supérieure in the 1950s. On returning from Algeria in 1960, he had taught at the Sorbonne for two years (where Aron had been appointed to a Chair in 1955 in a move which can be seen to have been a preparation for the professionalization nationally of university sociology teaching). In 1960, the Centre de Sociologie Européenne was founded with Aron as its director and it is not surprising, therefore, that Bourdieu's research was conducted within this context. (Aron wrote a preface to the 1962 translation of *Sociologie de l'Algérie* and *Un Art moyen* is dedicated to him.) This remained the institutional context for Bourdieu's research during the two years which he then spent as a lecturer at the University of Lille, and it continued to be so after he joined, in 1964, the swelling ranks of the directors of studies in the École Pratique des Hautes Études. For four years, therefore, Bourdieu combined undergraduate teaching for the new licence with personal research undertaken in collaboration with other members of the Centre. His post at the École was formally most likely to involve research supervision which ran parallel with the research projects of the Centre. In 1967, Bourdieu's work within the Centre was recognized by the establishment of a separate Centre de Sociologie de l'Éducation et de la Culture under his direction. This summary suggests that in the 1960s Bourdieu gradually situated himself objectively within an institutional context which sustained the post-war ethos of French social science research. He seems to have resisted both the attractions of bureaucratically sponsored research and of institutionalized university sociology.

This historical attempt to insert Bourdieu into the context of the institutional progress of French social science tentatively provides a background to the objective conditions within which he tried himself to institutionalize a research group with its own peculiar ideological rationale. The tantalizing thing in writing historically about Bourdieu, of course, is that he has himself already articulated an analysis of precisely this contextual situation of the late 1960s – in articles which were simultaneously about and within that situation, 'Sociology and philosophy in France since 1945: death and resurrection of a philosophy without subject' (1967) and 'Structuralism and theory of sociological knowledge' (1968). Although these texts were produced historically within the situation of the establishment of Bourdieu's new group and of the May events of 1968, it is, however, clear that he did not want them to be parts of that situation. Both texts were published in the United States in English in the journal *Social*

Research and neither has ever been published in French. There is a double explanation, at least, for this phenomenon. Both texts sought to challenge the intellectual basis of the dominant American sociology of the day by indicating the inadequacy of the historical intervention of American sociology in the development of French sociology during the early 1960s. The articles were targeted at American sociologists, but, equally, Bourdieu would have known that a French readership would have seen the extent to which the account of French sociology offered to the Americans was also a personal history. Bourdieu was too familiar with the integrated medium of the Parisian intellectual field which he describes in the earlier article to be prepared to consign his reflexive analyses to the local sphere within which they might constitute significant statements. Although the articles indicate the nature of his thinking, he did not want the thoughts yet to have the weight of actions. This is in accord with the suppression of the self-involvement in 'Célibat et condition paysanne', but not with his subsequent willingness, in *Homo academicus*, to come clean and to name names. Taking as an analogy one which must have been present to Bourdieu's mind, it was as if the organizer of a club photographic competition only felt able to attack styles of photography within his own club derived from the practice of a rival club by analysing for the rival club the nature of its influence on his own members – for fear that by openly exposing his own position to his own members he might endanger both his criteria of photographic value and the sense of professionalism within the club which was associated with his preferred kind of practice.

The first thing to note about 'Sociology and philosophy in France since 1945' is that Bourdieu and Passeron immediately assert that they are seeking to provide

> a sociology of the main trends of sociology which, in order to restore their full meaning to works and doctrines, tries to relate them to their cultural context, in other words, tries to show how positions and oppositions in the intellectual field are connected with explicitly or implicitly philosophical attitudes.[3]

The cross-reference is made at once to Bourdieu's 'Champ intellectuel et project créateur' and it would seem therefore that the article is set to analyse analogously both the objective structure of the 'sociological field' and the processes by which that structure has been structured by practising sociologists whose analyses have partially created the field but, also, whose analyses have been partially created by it. Not so, however. The main trends of sociology seem, instead, to be functions of the different philosophical attitudes which underpin them. We are alerted to the possibility that philosophy is thought to possess some fundamental status or primacy not possessed by sociology. Since the article seeks to analyse sociologically the relationship between sociology and philosophy within the post-war period, it is crucial to observe the development of the argument to establish whether or not philosophy is assumed to have a privileged status. Moving straight into their discussion, Bourdieu and Passeron begin:

Whether they deplore or welcome it, French and foreign observers are agreed
in recognizing the close link which has always existed between French
sociology and philosophy. The exception proves the rule: those who date
the appearance of a truly scientific sociology in the post-war period (i.e.
from the moment when certain sociologists openly repudiated any philosophical motivation) unconsciously express by that very fact a philosophy
of science and at the same time reveal their place in the French intellectual
field . . .[4]

Again, the same uncertainty. Which is the more important determinant of a
contemporary observer's social history of sociology? Is it the unconscious
disposition only to recognize as sociology in history that which corresponds
with the sociological assumptions which he brings to bear upon that historical
analysis? Or is it, rather, the place which the observer occupies within or in
relation to the French intellectual field? The butt of these comments, the person
who specifically exemplified the exception which proved the rule, was T.N.
Clark who conducted research in Paris in the late 1960s which led to the
publication, in 1973, of *Prophets and Patrons. The French University and the
Emergence of the Social Sciences.*[5] Clark argued that Durkheimianism gained the
ascendancy within French higher education as a result of an internal patronage
which operated by means of 'clusters' of influence. His interpretation, for
Bourdieu and Passeron, showed every sign of being a superficial organizational
sociology which imposed its own limitations on the phenomena which it observed.
It follows that their refutation of Clark was operating simultaneously on two
fronts. They were intent on retrieving the complexity of the historical factors
which shaped the progress of Durkheimianism whilst simultaneously condemning
the contemporary sociology which was incapable of appreciating that complexity.
To put the position positively, Bourdieu and Passeron wanted to retrieve a
full comprehension of the institutionalization of Durkheimianism precisely
because, properly understood, it offered a model to be imitated and issued
warnings of pitfalls to be avoided in relation to their own task of counteracting
the positions of those who were now misrepresenting the past.

   The flaw in the position advanced by Bourdieu and Passeron, however, would
seem to be that their case against Clark could just as easily be turned against
themselves. They could be said to be finding in a particular kind of interpretation
of the past an endorsement of their present position – without which present
position that interpretation would be unthinkable and that past would have
no existence as objective authority. Bourdieu and Passeron are rescued from
this apparent impasse by the fact that they refer to philosophy in two crucially
different senses. We shall have to consider whether this distinction is legitimate
and, indeed, we shall also see that Bourdieu's later analysis of the political
ontology of Heidegger is a vehicle for his own consideration of this issue. The
point is that Bourdieu and Passeron distinguished between institutionalized
Philosophy and philosophy of science or epistemology which they regarded

as the ground of all knowing. For them, Philosophy and Sociology both stood in the same relation to the basic epistemological imperative. Philosophy and Sociology were both socially contingent forms of the undivided epistemological necessity. One way of describing Bourdieu's endeavour at this date is to say that he was trying to create an institutional framework within which the epistemological necessity might be actualized. Arguably, *La Reproduction* offered the possibility that the epistemological endeavour might be preserved from social contingency within a context which self-consciously and systematically recognized it as such. But this is to move on too soon because the publication of *La Reproduction* in 1970 was, perhaps, already an admission that, like 'rational pedagogy', epistemology too was an evanescent absolute. For the sake of a clearer understanding of 'Sociology and philosophy in France', let us revert to 1967 and assume the validity of a notion of a non-contingent epistemological activity. In essence, the purpose of Bourdieu and Passeron's article was that it sought to outline the emergence of their brand of positivist phenomenology and to suggest that it was different both from contemporary positivism and from contemporary structuralism – which was really an embodiment of phenomenological philosophy masquerading as social science. The authors suggested that their position was like Durkheim's original position. The continuation of this argument is of interest both as a historical account and as a reflexion on the force of contingent institutional interference.

Historically, Durkheim's real position came to be identified with a misrepresentation from opposite sides – that he was a positivist and, therefore, anti-clerical and that he introduced metaphysical explanations. He was identified after his death with a sterile, institutionalized position by the post-war generation of phenomenological/existentialist philosophers – like Sartre – who sought to emphasize subjective freedom, assisted in this by conditions in the resistance which fostered liberationism.

There were then two developments. Philosophers like Merleau-Ponty seemed to hand over their 'authority' to the ethnologists and, therefore, seemed to endorse empirical enquiry. It was existentialist thinking which held back the development of social science for nearly 15 years. What could be said for existentialism in this context was that its commitment to total 'engagement' with politics and social issues did encourage a phenomenological method which would be prepared to tackle any problem by contrast with structuralism which sustained an élitist philosophical phenomenology. In the early 1960s American neo-positivism caught on and empirical sociology established itself as a 'new beginning'. It was epistemologically ignorant, however, and spawned sociologies 'of' things. Because American neo-positivism had no fundamental view of science, the sociologies of x, y and z which were developed were uncritical responses to the demands of society. The structuralism which, in 1949, had seemed, for Simone de Beauvoir, itself to be a new empirical awakening had, by 1963, become the successor to existentialism in offering a philosophical alternative to American empirical sociology. But structuralism only offered a superficial opposition to neo-positivism, in the view of Bourdieu and Passeron, because, like its opponent – although for different reasons – it autonomized the object of study and kept it at a distance. Anthropological structuralism avoided the challenge of confronting unmediated experience as much as did the developing 'sociologies of' education, crime, literature or whatever.

The argument which was advanced through an historical dissertation in 'Sociology and philosophy in France' was continued philosophically in 'Structuralism and theory of sociological knowledge'. It was Bourdieu's view that, historically, structuralism had only offered a partially satisfactory alternative to neo-positivism. It had properly attempted to make sense of social phenomena by looking for patterns other than those spontaneously known by social actors, but it had failed to acknowledge that these patterns were themselves human constructs – that they were the expressions of the structuralists' introspective or intuitive sense of what it might mean to be human and were, therefore, incorrigibly ethnocentric. For Bourdieu, the structuralists had failed to be sufficiently positivist in respect of phenomena. This is straightforward, but the next step in his reasoning is more unexpected and is important for a clear understanding of his subsequent work. The problem of ethnocentricity cannot simply be offset by a routinized recognition of the 'value-orientation' of the observer. There must, instead, be a fundamental epistemological rupture such that phenomena are appreciated as internally and intrinsically structured without reference either to an underlying reality or to any anthropomorphic imposition. It would seem, again, that Bourdieu was overstating the possibility of a socially unconditioned epistemology were it not for the fact that 'Structuralism and theory of sociological knowledge' makes it clear – for the first time in Bourdieu's work – that this humanist way of thinking about thinking is itself not appropriate. The essay makes explicit reference to Gilbert Ryle and Bourdieu's argument throughout is based on the view articulated in *The Concept of Mind* that the mind is not an entity but a process. It follows that the mind is intrinsically 'value-free' and able to process data neutrally and automatically, and that, as we shall now see, the sociologist should aspire to be – or recognize that he naturally is – an embodied 'artificial intelligence'.

At the beginning of the essay, Bourdieu argues that a proper appraisal of structuralism can only be made by first recognizing a clear-cut distinction between 'theory of sociological knowledge' and 'theory of the social system':

> The *theory of sociological knowledge*, as the system of principles and rules governing the production of all sociological propositions scientifically grounded, and of them alone, is the generating principle of all partial theories of the social and, therefore, the unifying principle of a properly sociological discourse which must not be confused with a unitary theory of the social.[6]

There are, in other words, three stages in the acquisition of a scientific knowledge of society. There is, first of all, the primary apperception of phenomena, but Bourdieu here concentrates on the distinction between the second and third stages. The second stage involves the delimitation of primary apperception and the consequent construction of 'sociological' knowledge. This socially constructed sociological orientation is unified precisely because its instrumental *raison d'être* is to generate 'sociological' accounts of particular phenomena, but this is completely different from the 'theoretical' unification achieved by making connections between these generated accounts as if they possessed some primary reality. Bourdieu is interested in the unity of orientation shared by Marx, Weber and Durkheim even though that unity resulted in the generation of different theories of society. The mistake of Parsons was to attempt to construct a systematic summa derived from previous theories of the social rather than to attempt to derive from previous sociological practice a refined articulation of the sociological orientation which might then function as an improved research instrument. The ideal refinement would be the recognition that sociological discourse is as relational as the discourses of modern mathematics or physics. In mathematics, for instance,

> it has been possible to discover that any geometry is nothing but a pure system of relations determined by the principles governing them and not by the intrinsic nature of the figures entering those relations.[7]

but the problem for sociology and anthropology has been that the equivalent 'figures' entering relations are human beings. Hallowed assumptions have to be challenged if sociological discourse is to make the kind of progress achieved this century by mathematics and physics. Closely following an argument advanced by Ernst Cassirer, Bourdieu recognizes that the capacity to see language, culture and social relations as internally coherent systems requires a break with the classical rationalism which posited an opposition between 'formal eternal truths of logic and mathematics and contingent empirical truths of history'.[8] Similarly, it requires a willingness to renounce the everyday experience of freedom in favour of an acceptance, for scientific purposes, that 'social reality may be dealt with as a system that has immanent necessity'.[9]

As we have already seen, Bourdieu had, in his postface to Panofsky, developed a view of the role of 'habitus' and of schooling systems as institutionalized contexts of 'habitus' as the interfaces between constructive human agency and constraining social structures. There is no sense, therefore, in which Bourdieu is actually a determinist. Nevertheless, he argues that a pre-condition for the refinement of sociological science must be an acceptance of a model of social relations which facilitates only a relational understanding of phenomena. Social psychology is abhorrent to Bourdieu because it fatally confuses knowledge derived from primary experience with knowledge which aspires to be scientific. Scientific discourse has an important social function even though our everyday experience of living may seem to be best reflected in the analysis offered by social psychology. Science has an important role in offering practical choices to human agents whereas primary experience and social psychological knowledge are mutually reinforcing such that alternatives for living cannot be exposed and deployed.

Bourdieu recognized that scientific fallacies – such as the notion of the autonomous self or the free agent – are deeply embedded in the social life which is the object of scientific analysis. Errors have a social function and also have institutional support and reinforcement. The only solution is to be epistemologically ruthless in taking as 'given' any aspect of a situation without first understanding the social conditions of that givenness. 'Structuralism and theory of sociological knowledge' takes juvenile delinquency as an example of a situation in which intellectual interpretations of the problem have become incorporated within it and Bourdieu also cites Goffman's achievement in *Asylums* as an example of the way in which socially reinforced attitudes can be scientifically challenged. The article concludes, however, with some general suggestions for constructing a system in any situation 'which alone can reveal the hidden truth of the case considered because it contains the principle of its own interpretation'.[10] Here Bourdieu discusses the use of analogies, of 'ideal-types' and of comparisons as devices for generating interpretations of situations which can be different from the interpretations already inherent in those situations. His comments incidentally confirm the functional status of these devices in his own earlier work – the use, for instance, of analogical models in *La Reproduction*, of 'ideal-typical' students in *Les Héritiers* and of comparison in the second edition of *L'Amour de l'art* – but the overall intention is to recommend structuralism as a method – a 'structural approach' – and to regard a sociologist as someone who should have a large number of intellectual tricks up his sleeve.

Taken together, these two English articles indicate that by 1968 Bourdieu had fully developed his own view of what it meant to be a sociological practitioner and had consciously situated the research activity of the Centre within the institutional field of French sociological research. He had developed a rationale for the philosophical and institutional autonomy of scientific research which enabled him to be neither 'academic' nor 'populist'. He now attempted to consolidate the orientation of his research team – and to proselytize – by producing a tradesman's manual – *Le Métier de sociologue*. By deliberately de-mystifying the professional activity of the sociologist, Bourdieu was sustaining a democratic commitment to the view that a form of scientific thinking is accessible to all. The path on which Bourdieu was embarked in this apparently technical and specialized work was to lead, a decade later, to the full formulation in *Le Sens pratique* of a social democratic theory founded on an everyday exercise of practical science.

Le Métier de sociologue was ambitiously conceived. It was due to appear in three books which would elaborate the approach to sociological theory and practice briefly sketched in 'Structuralism and theory of sociological knowledge'. Only the first of these three books appeared, entitled *Epistemological Preliminaries*. This itself is a text of just over 100 pages which cross-refers to over 70 'illustrative texts' which take up more than a further 200 pages. The table of contents for the first book provides a three-page outline of the content of the proposed second book which was to be devoted to *The Problematic* and a few lines indicating the subject-matter of the proposed third book which was to be entitled *The Tools*. The essence of the venture was that all aspects of sociological enquiry were to be represented – having regard to technical as much as conceptual elements of research procedures – in such a way that the essential inter-connectedness of theoretical and practical activities would be communicated. 'Theoretical' was here understood to refer to the theory of sociological knowledge rather than to the theory of the social, and it followed that texts could be adduced to illustrate sociological practices in conformity with Bourdieu's epistemological fundamentalism without reference to the particular social contexts within which they had possessed meaning.

Quite apart from the practical problems associated with the scheme of *Le Métier de sociologue* which must have been enormous, the failure of the grand design poses two critical questions: was the failure of the endeavour the result of an incompatibility between the content and the form of presentation or, more seriously, does the failure expose weaknesses in the philosophical position which Bourdieu was articulating at the time?

The foreword to the published text was the intended foreword to the three books. It began by approvingly quoting Comte to the effect that 'method' cannot be studied separately from the researches in which it is used, and it argued that there was a need for the proposed project because so many textbooks in sociology were appearing which contrived either to emphasize empirical practice at the expense of theory or to construct a theoretical canon without reference to practice. If 'methodology' was acquiring a spurious detachment from 'theory', there was also a false tendency to suppose that operational research 'techniques' were independent of both theory and method. There was an urgent need to reinsert all three separating components into one research process. The first book would try to 'give specific precepts for epistemological vigilance'[11] and it was proposed that the second book would explore strategies to be adopted in order to isolate and develop a specifically sociological knowledge. The intention here would be to refine a distinctively sociological orientation without creating a tradition of sociological thought or a 'capital of concepts'.[12] Hence these concepts would act as tools for the advancement of further provisional knowledge in exactly the same way as would techniques of, for instance, statistical measurement, and it was proposed that the third book would concentrate on instrumentation.

Within this overall schema, the only published text focused on the primary epistemological activity which had seemed, in 'Sociology and philosophy in France since 1945', to have been assigned an absolute status, and which had been passed over in silence in 'Structuralism and theory of sociological knowledge'. Closely following the ideas of Gaston Bachelard, Bourdieu insisted that the primary epistemological activity was itself a process involving the 'constant polemical action of Reason'.[13] That process was characterized by Bachelard as one which entailed the winning, the constructing and the proving of scientific 'facts', and Bourdieu's discussion follows this formula. Facts are, first of all, conquered in opposition to the illusion of immediate knowledge. Bourdieu emphasizes here that techniques of rupture must be employed systematically and deliberately to counteract what he calls the fallacies of 'transparency', 'spontaneous' knowledge and 'artificialism'[14] all of which conspire to sustain the 'pre-notions' or pre-suppositions which are already inherent in social phenomena. A principle of 'non-knowledge' has to be adopted which has to work on the assumption that humans have no privileged capacity to understand social relations by virtue of being human. It has to be accepted that ordinary language embodies human self-deception, with the result that the epistemologist must neither be trapped into forgetting to be sceptical about the linguistic formulations of social actors nor into forgetting that the language which he will use in his analysis also transmits the very social deceptions which it is seeking to expose.

Having conquered facts, epistemological activity involves next the construction of objects. Bourdieu quotes Saussure's view that 'the point of view creates the object' which means that 'scientific research is in fact organised around constructed objects which no longer have anything in common with the unities carved out by naive perception'.[15] All scientific researchers construct for themselves an autonomy which is a function of their social position rather than of any imperative emanating from 'reality'. It is through not realizing this that boundary disputes arise, for instance, between sociologists and psychologists as if there were a squabble about reality rather than about the social organization of their differentiation. Bourdieu outlines a series of strategies adopted in all science for the construction of objects, such as the use of models, analogies and hypotheses. These strategies lead into the third phase of epistemological activity which involves the exercise of 'applied rationalism' to contest the facts which have been conquered and constructed.

It will be clear from this account that Bourdieu's description of 'epistemological preliminaries' which were meant to be the prolegomena to all knowledge turns out to be remarkably similar to his account of the theory of sociological knowledge in 'Structuralism and theory of sociological knowledge'. All knowledge acquisition requires the construction of fields within which objects are located and this process of construction is conditioned by the social position of those making the construction. The isolation of chemical or biological knowledge is, therefore, conditioned sociologically, but the situation seems more incestuous when it is recognized that sociological knowledge is sociologically conditioned. This means, in effect, that Bourdieu's fundamentalist epistemology was nothing other than a sociology of knowledge reflexively applied. He considered this in the conclusion to the first book of *Le Métier de sociologue* – 'Sociology of Knowledge and Epistemology' – and commented:

> It is in the sociology of sociological knowledge that the sociologist can find the instrument which gives full force and specific form to the epistemological critique.[16]

Bourdieu then proceeded to offer suggestions as to how this reflexivity might be practised. In a discussion which is reminiscent of the comparison between French and American sociology in 'Sociology and philosophy in France since 1945', for instance, Bourdieu recommends that sociological researchers should systematically become conscious of the constraints on their practice imposed by socio-economic conditions. Bourdieu prescribes here the kind of self-awareness for a sociologist in respect of his position within institutional and intellectual fields which, as we shall see, he was himself to offer in *Homo academicus* on the basis of analysis undertaken in 1968. The prescription is not intended to alert the researcher to the fact that his practice is 'determined', but, on the contrary, to enable the researcher to adopt intellectual strategies which will enable him to maximize his influence within a system of objective constraints that are understood. As we shall also see, Bourdieu was beginning to articulate his view that the intellectual is a strategist as much as is an Algerian peasant, but, for the moment, the main strategic imperative was for him to establish the social conditions which would sustain the formal exercise of epistemological vigilance. At the end of the final section of *Le Métier de sociologue* – 'Learned community and epistemological vigilance' – Bourdieu quoted sympathetically the words used by Durkheim towards the end of *The Rules of Sociological Method*:

> We believe that the moment has come for sociology to turn its back on worldly success and to take the esoteric character appropriate to every science. It will win in dignity and authority in this way what it will perhaps lose in popularity.[17]

This can be taken to be a cri de coeur or a credo on Bourdieu's part. It is doubtful, however, whether *Le Métier de sociologue*, as envisaged in three books, could perform the required function in helping to actualize the esoteric stance which Bourdieu was seeking. The conception of the books was flawed. As it became clearer that the illustrative texts which were meant to be exemplars of pre-sociological, epistemological practice should logically be themselves understood sociologically, their presence as an assembly of de-contextualized extracts seemed unsatisfactory because it seemed both arbitrary and dogmatic. The collapse of the philosophical distinction between primary epistemology and secondary sociological knowledge entailed the collapse of the proposed structure of the books within which it was supposed that extracts from scientific writings could be presented unsociologically in order to demonstrate epistemo-logical processes. There might seem to have been two possible solutions to the problem which seems to have been articulated in the process of constructing the books. *Le Métier de sociologue* is, first, full of suggestive analyses of the work of other scientists, particularly Durkheim. Bourdieu's personal sociological orientation might, therefore, have been clarified through a rigorous sociological analysis of Durkheim's sociological practice. This would, however, have entailed a social history of Durkheim's research and thinking which could only be conducted by artificially reifying the social context within which Durkheim could be said to have operated. Perhaps Bourdieu's subsequent analysis of the work of Martin Heidegger should be seen as just such an attempt to explicate the social conditions for the emergence of ontological thinking, but, in the late 1960s, he does not appear to have wanted to undertake what he has recently called an 'exercise in method'.[18] Instead, he was driven to only one solution. *Le Métier de sociologue* could only logically be salvaged if Bourdieu were to make explicit the ways in which the illustrative texts had impinged upon his own research practice. Only by inserting these texts into an account of his own research processes might he exemplify the conjunction of theory and practice which he was recommending.

Le Métier de sociologue had to die or to be killed, but, for reasons something like those suggested above, the death led to the birth of *Esquisse d'une théorie de la pratique* which was published in 1972. This text is significantly different from the 'translation' which was published in the United Kingdom as *Outline of a Theory of Practice* in 1977. The discussion which follows in this chapter presents *Esquisse* as Bourdieu's attempt to communicate differently the message of *Le Métier de sociologue*, whereas a subsequent chapter will look at the changes made for *Outline* in the context of developments in Bourdieu's thinking in the 1970s and, in particular, will see the English text in relation to the rethinking of the Algerian fieldwork which culminated in the publication of *Le Sens pratique* in 1980.

Esquisse was itself an uneasy mixture of the two emphases which were more clearly exposed in the differences between it and *Outline*. The full title of the first edition of 1972 was *Esquisse d'une théorie de la pratique, précédé de trois études d'ethnologie Kabyle* and the text was partitioned in the way that the title suggests. The first part offered three old texts which had emerged out of the Algerian fieldwork. The first, dated January 1960, had never been published in French but had been published in English in 1965 in a collection of anthropological essays devoted to 'Honour and Shame' under the title: 'The sentiment of honour in Kabyle society'.[19] The second essay – 'La maison kabyle ou le monde renversé' – had recently been published in French in 1970 in a collection of essays offered on the occasion of the sixtieth birthday of Lévi-Strauss,[20] but had been written in 1963–4. The third essay – 'Stratégie et rituel dans le mariage kabyle' – was also published in the same year as *Esquisse* in a further collection of Mediterranean anthropological studies edited by J. Peristiany,[21] but, although it is not dated, it is clear from a footnote that in this case the article had been recently written on the basis of work undertaken during the period since 1960.[22] The dates of these studies are important because the extent to which *Esquisse* can be shown to be a strategically different presentation of the ideas of *Le Métier de sociologue* depends on the kind of 'epistemological vigilance' exercised by Bourdieu in relation to his own past research.

The inside page of *Esquisse* offered the factual information about the Kabyle studies provided above, and then the three studies were themselves preceded by a foreword in which Bourdieu briefly situated them historically. Here Bourdieu admits that, in the context of the Algerian war, he had been partisan in favour of the social organization of the Algerian tribes in opposition to 'inhumane ideologies',[23] but his reflexion does not go so far as fundamentally to explore the nature and implications of that partisanship. Instead, Bourdieu's retrospection is primarily the prelude to the explication of a revised theory – a proper theory of practice – which will interpret more adequately his original research findings rather than an attempt to reflect historically and sociologically on the origins of those findings. Bourdieu was, in other words, as reluctant to undertake a social historical analysis of his own research practice as he might have been of Durkheim's. *Le Métier de sociologue* had begun to advance the idea of the sociologist as a strategic intellectual practitioner who deploys a range of techniques to ensure that his research findings do not simply endorse his pre-notions. Bourdieu's reflexion in *Esquisse* on his earlier Algerian fieldwork revises it so that he develops a notion of the Algerian peasant as strategic agent which is consistent with his view of the practical sociologist, but the procedure which he follows does not in itself exemplify what he recommends.

In reviewing his earlier texts, Bourdieu was saying, in 1972, that he had originally assumed that symbolic systems, such as that associated with 'honour', had developed as strategies which were intended to reinforce pre-conceived 'rules' of social, economic and political organization. He now wanted to say, however, in respect of the same social phenomena, that there were no pre-existent rules inherent in organized societies such that, for instance, religious practice satisfied the demands of economic necessity, but instead a series of strategies or fields which interact. The focus of analysis, therefore, could no longer be on the ways in which agents adapted themselves to the requirements of objective structures and regulations in any society but on the ways in which agents strategically worked the system of temporarily dominant structures in order to construct a new, and constantly adapting, social balance. Bourdieu's presentation in Part I of *Esquisse* was designed to clarify the implications for his interpretation of traditional Algerian society of his rejection of structuralism. Whereas the structuralist emphasis of the first two studies is faithfully reproduced, the third article makes it clear that the kind of imposed genealogical pattern or regulation typically adopted as explanation by Lévi-Strauss is an inadequate basis for understanding the factors involved in marriage strategies. Historically, the perspective of the third study and of the total text of *Esquisse* merge, and Bourdieu is able resolutely to write of his current analysis that, referring to Lévi-Strauss, 'we find ourselves a long way from the pure – because infinitely impoverished – universe of the "rules of marriage" and of the "elementary structures of parenthood".'[24]

The second part of *Esquisse* still endeavours to suggest that its presentation of a revised theory is an example of proper scientific practice.

The foreword to this part reproduces almost word for word a sentence of *Le Métier de sociologue* when it begins:

> This reflection on a scientific practice is made to disconcert as much those who reflect on human sciences without practising them as those who practise without reflecting.[25]

Nevertheless, Bourdieu was well aware of the practical difficulties involved in attempting to present a paradigmatic reproduction of the process of reciprocity between practice and reflection in his work. The second part of *Esquisse* was written in 1972 'from notes written between 1960 and 1965'[26] and Bourdieu had wanted, as he says, to 'retain in this discourse of work or, if you prefer, of work in process, the double character which it owes to the conditions of its construction',[27] but this presentation could only have had full value if he had been able to offer an integral publication including his notes with his findings. In spite of his intention, then, the second part of *Esquisse* offers a systematic discussion of a theory of practice which is based on his own practice but which does not analytically make cross-references to it.

Whereas *Le Métier de sociologue* had primarily been concerned to expose the inadequacy of 'spontaneous knowledge' and of 'spontaneous sociology', *Esquisse*, by contrast, first continues the rejection of structuralism outlined in the first part by introducing a critique of the kind of 'objectivism' of which structuralism is one example. Bourdieu argues that the tendency to identify 'objective rules' in operation within observed societies followed from the social relationship between the observers and the observed. This point is powerfully made by analogy with the use of street maps. People who know the geography of the area within which they live do not use street plans to organize their routes from place to place. It is only the outside observer who feels the need to construct a map. The fallacy of structuralist anthropology arises from the fact that observers have supposed that local people have regulated their journeys in accordance with an abstract map which, in fact, only has existence because observers imposed an order on phenomena which was in accordance with their own needs. Bourdieu realized, however, that his argument was hazardous. To push his analogy further than he does himself, the problem of Western European traditional thinking is that its dualistic structure only allows it to countenance an opposition between the spontaneous, subjective and instinctive cartographic sense of the locals and the abstract, objective and rational knowledge of detached observers. Bourdieu recognized that in rejecting 'objectivism' he might open the floodgates of 'subjectivism'. He was hostile to the view that the only alternative to the 'objectivist' account of phenomena is one which accepts that local agents alone have access to the map which directs their actions. His argument is that agents make strategic plans of routes in the context of 'objective' maps and guidelines which have been generated and developed within their own localities but which may not have been formulated or articulated. An external observer can perceive the totality of the actions of local agents in a way which is not accessible to the agent himself, and if the external observer rigorously assesses the extent to which his observation derives from his particular, external position, there is a chance that the account of the agent's actions provided by the external might coincide with the structure of the possible routes which are open to the agent and amongst which he makes his choice of journey. The map devised by the anthropologist has no existence for the agent and does not, therefore, regulate his behaviour, but it may make explicit the implicit parameters within which agents make their strategic choices.

This protracted extension of Bourdieu's analogy illustrates what he means by the 'three modes of theoretical knowledge' which he proceeds to detail. There is, first, the primary, phenomenological knowledge of the social world, and then there is the second, 'objectivist' knowledge which attempts to impose a structure on the primary and unarticulated knowledge. The second knowledge requires a break or a detachment from primary experience, but the important emphasis of Bourdieu's position is that there must be a second epistemological break so as to reach a third kind of knowledge. This second break requires that the observation of the observer should be observed or, preferably, be reflexively undertaken. The difficulty which is experienced with Bourdieu's account arises from the fact that he is simultaneously referring, in identical terms, to the researcher and to the subject of researches. *Le Métier de sociologue* had concentrated on the strategies which should be adopted by a sociologist to attain a scientificity which did not simply endorse the primary experiences of subjects or manifest the presuppositions of researchers. *Esquisse* seems, at first, to be wanting to exemplify Bourdieu's own historical progression through the three modes of knowledge in respect of his Algerian studies (from the spontaneous knowledge of *Sociologie de l'Algérie* to the objectivist structuralism of 'The sentiment of honour' to the third mode of knowledge enshrined in the revisions of *Esquisse*), but, at that point in the text of *Esquisse*, the emphasis shifts. The reason for this is that the third mode of knowledge suggests to Bourdieu that the primary experience of the Algerian tribes possessed exactly the same form as the apparently sophisticated intellectual behaviour of the sociologist. Both were and are involved in generating new worlds of thought and experience from those they have inherited, and, in both cases, the new worlds are legacies out of which further new worlds are constructed. In moving towards an explication of the sophistication of traditional Algerian behaviour, however, the problem of *Esquisse* is that it increasingly seems to present itself as an anthropological account rather than one which applies with as much force to contemporary Western European society.

After a theoretical digression in which, anticipating *Ce que parler veut dire* (1982), Bourdieu exposes the objectivist structuralism of Saussurean linguistics, *Esquisse* concentrates on the social processes which enable a continuous reciprocity between structure and structuration. A section devoted to 'Structures, habitus and practices' explores the modus operandi of 'habitus', which is defined as 'the durably installed generative principle of regulated improvisations'.[28] As we have seen, *La Reproduction* had already outlined the function of 'habitus' within the educational context and by means of an almost algebraic mode of presentation. *Esquisse* embellishes the concept by setting it in a social context, where it becomes clear that Bourdieu means by 'habitus' a process of socialization whereby the dominant modes of thought and experience inherent in the social and physical world (both of which are symbolically constructed) are internalized by social agents. It is not just a matter of cognitive understanding. The following section, entitled 'The incorporation of the structures', explores in detail the ways in which the structure of the physical world which is itself produced in mythico-ritualistic symbolisms and oppositions, such as right/left, and male/female 'leads to the incorporation of a space structured according to mythico-ritual oppositions'.[29] The argument here reinforces Bourdieu's revision of the structuralist interpretation of oppositions, comparable to Lévi-Strauss's cooked/raw, offered in the second chapter of the first part – 'The Berber house or the world reversed'. It does so, however, in a way which conveys the impression that these patterns of reinforcing internal and external symbols are peculiar to a pre-logical, pre-rational or, dare I say it, a 'primitive' society and mentality.

The problem of *Esquisse*, therefore, was that it autonomized anthropological behaviour in the production of a book which was situated primarily in an anthropological rather than a sociological 'field'. The intention to re-visit old anthropological texts in order to demonstrate the processes of sociological practice back-fired. Bourdieu was already engaged on a reflexive analysis of his own social situation as a researcher, but that emphasis does not prevail in the text of *Esquisse*. It was now Bourdieu's task to bring together the various strands of his thinking in order adequately to communicate his conception of the inter-relationship between his sociological practice and the practice of social agents – both operating alongside each other within the same society.

'Field'-studies, 1970–5

Imagine a large hall in which chairs and tables are laid out in clusters and in which, in groups, people are playing board games. You watch the games being played in each of the clusters and you observe that there are patterns between corresponding games in each cluster. You know yourself that when you play a game like chess you have to make your moves in accordance with a set of prescribed rules and you therefore decide that in the games which seem to correspond with others in different clusters the players must be adhering to common rules. Your analysis of the rules which seem to be held in common will, you think, tell you something about the personalities of all the players in the hall.

As we have seen, this account encapsulates, for Bourdieu, the fallacy of structuralism. In his own observations of the separate components of the social organization of each of four Algerian tribes (separate games within four different clusters), Bourdieu had noticed that there were there common forms. It was as if each game had an apparently distinct character but that, in fact, all had the hidden function of ensuring satisfactory performance in the game of the cluster which was never openly played – the game which constantly safeguarded the coherence and the survival of the cluster itself. Bourdieu had at least three kinds of objection to structuralist analysis. He thought, first, that it was a mistake to extract corresponding games from their clusters – to extrapolate, for instance, patterns of matrimonial exchange from their specific social contexts – in order to try to establish the basis of universal human nature. He thought, secondly, that the general interpretation offered by structuralists was an expression of assumptions which derived from their own social position and experience – that, for instance, the view that similarities in performance in observed games suggested adherence to stated rules simply imposed on all games the model of games playing available to the observer through his knowledge of chess. By wilfully ignoring this imposition of the experience of the observer on the experience of the observed, structuralism was wrong, thirdly, in suggesting that universal rules are embedded in particular societies and that humans are not, therefore, free agents.

Bourdieu was most eager to adopt an interpretative framework which would preserve the possibility of free human action. Although he resisted the universalistic tendencies of structuralism, his early work seemed to be based on a compromise version of structuralism. Within traditional Algerian society there were a range of social behaviours or practices – religious, legal, matrimonial, patrimonial, commercial, agricultural – which were all inter-locking and were all designed to reinforce the social organization within which they functioned. Bourdieu wanted to insist that this functional structuralism took different forms in different societies because it had been differently constructed by human agents as a creative response, normally, to different kinds of physical condition – climate, terrain and natural resources, for instance. Traditional societies gave the impression of regulation because they were socially undifferentiated and because the social organization had been so well constructed and so well reproduced that individuals behaved naturally and automatically in a well-regulated fashion. The particular characteristic of traditional Algerian society meant, in other words, that Bourdieu's attitude towards structuralism was not at first fully exposed. The important point is that, for Bourdieu, people could be thought to be following rules in their behaviour because they were unconsciously adhering to practices which had been consciously constructed for their own particular society, and not because they were following patterns of behaviour which are intrinsic to universal human nature.

It was precisely because Bourdieu held this view of the sophisticated construction of 'primitive' tribal organization that its collapse offered such a challenge. There was a sense in which individuals had been able to rest on their laurels as their society had functioned coherently and harmoniously. The fracture of the traditional fabric meant that individuals had to bring into play in new circumstances the creativity which had produced the old order. It was the purpose of *Travail et travailleurs* and *Le Déracinement* to stimulate inventiveness, to encourage Algerian self-development. Although Bourdieu resisted the notion that human nature was everywhere intrinsically the same, he did, however, seem to operate with an unarticulated assumption that there are structural affinities between all societies – that the mutually reinforcing inter-relationships between the games played in each cluster are the same for each cluster. Hence, Bourdieu's recommendations for the development of a radical pedagogy in independent Algeria were posited on an assumed function for the educational system which would help to constitute a new social organization in alliance with developments in the economic system. There was a tacit assumption that every society needs a mechanism by which its members can participate in its construction and, equally, learn to internalize the meaning and to implement the behavioural implications of the structure which is constructed. Using a hint taken from Panofsky, Bourdieu in effect strengthened in the mid-1960s his adherence to a functional structuralism in order to oppose the kind of structuralism associated with Lévi-Strauss. Working from Panofsky's contention that the structural patterns in Gothic architecture were not to be explained by any mystical *Zeitgeist* but simply as the actualizations of a shared scholastic learning, Bourdieu adopted the view that in every society the educational system is the mechanism which facilitates societal self-knowledge and which secures the allegiance of all individuals to this collective consciousness.

What seemed a neat explanatory solution in relation to the relatively homogeneous and uncomplicated society of twelfth-century France was, however, inadequate in relation to the France of the 1960s. Bourdieu had envisaged an educational system which would adopt a pedagogical approach which would enable it to generate systems of thinking which were based on the experiences of the learners – however socially disadvantaged – on the grounds that only in this way could these people become incorporated into the society to which they belonged. The educational research of the early 1960s showed Bourdieu that far from accepting and building on the experiences of deprived students, the French higher education system was ensuring that these students remained excluded from any position in a society whose structure had been constructed and was now sustained by those members of society who were in control of the educational system. Bourdieu struggled to advocate an ideal 'rational pedagogy' which would secure a functional neutrality for the educational system within the totality of French sub-systems. He hoped, for instance, that the social status which seemed to be bestowed by familiarity with high culture might be made accessible to disadvantaged people if schools would inculcate the necessary aesthetic competence scientifically. Increasingly, however, he realized that, internally, the educational system did not work in this way. *La Reproduction* documented the way in which cultural arbitrariness was inculcated peda-gogically – not, sadly, the way in which enabling competences were transmitted.

Even though the ideal of a functional neutrality for the educational system had faded by the early 1970s, there remained the sense that the system retained an actual and determinate place within society. The educational system was failing to equalize opportunities within society, but it definitely had a fixed function in allocating people to occupational positions and in affecting their cultural assumptions. This chapter traces the way in which Bourdieu dismantled that certitude. He did so by linking the idea of 'strategic' as opposed to 'regulated' action – the new stance which was the substance of his revision of the early Algerian research offered in *Esquisse* – with the idea of 'fields' which he developed dramatically from the original formulation in 'Intellectual field and creative project' in 1966.

Imagine, again, the large hall. You now realize that it was foolish to suppose that some games being played within different clusters were being played in accordance with the same rules. This time you decide to focus on what seems to be happening in all the games within one cluster. You originally thought that the same types of game were being played in each cluster and that the relationship between these games was fixed and was the same in each cluster, but you have become uncertain about this and you want to examine this point in detail. Each game is certainly distinct in the sense that it has its own discrete set of rules, but it also seems as if all the games are in some way inter-dependent: performance in one game seems to relate to performance in another. For the sake of clarification, let us suppose that you know some of the games. Ignore, for the moment, the possibility that you might be imposing your prior knowledge of these games on what you are observing. You recognize, shall we say, 'Block-busters' (a quiz game), 'Monopoly' (a game about property development), 'The Game of Life' (a game about careers), and 'Poleconomy' (a game about politics and finance). You realize, perhaps, that the games are structurally similar even though they must have had to distinguish themselves initially in order to be marketable. At first, you assume that the correspondence between the perfor-mance of the same player in different games (for the players move around) is a consequence of the structural relations between the games or, even, of the fact that performance in all games is a reflection of a system of handicaps allocated to players in one fundamental game that you are not able to observe.

Suddenly it occurs to you that you are still trapped in the frame of thinking which assumes that every player is only playing one game at a time in accordance only with the rules of that game. You realize that what is really happening is that all the players are playing all the games simultaneously with a view to winning the game of games. When, for instance, a player lands on a square in 'The Game of Life' which allocates to him the educational qualification on which his progress in the game will depend, the player can call in his level of performance in 'Blockbusters' as a substitute token. Or when, for instance, a player requires money to purchase 'Park Lane' in 'Monopoly' he can transfer the finance he has accumulated within 'Poleconomy' for that purpose. In short, all players seem to be strategists. They transfer performance tokens from one game to another in order to maximize their chances of performing well altogether. This second stage of your observation, however, is overtaken by a third. You realize that the performance of some players seems to corroborate your perception that they are strategically deploying their tokens, but you also notice that other players seem to hold significant 'trump cards'. Whilst the performances of the strategists are not determined by their success or failure in any one game, nevertheless their strategies are dependent on the stability or predictability of each of the games. But there do seem to be other players who have the capacity to make strategic moves which consistently bend or break the rules of the games. If success in 'The Game of Life' seems to depend on the allocation of a good educational qualification – assigned on a square on the board – these strategists can, for instance, write their own quiz questions in 'Blockbusters' to maximize the tokens which they transfer, or they can simply down-grade the importance of the educational qualification within 'The Game of Life', or they can down-grade the weighting of 'The Game of Life' in relation to the total of games and substitute for it, instead, a new game which they create and which they are equipped to win and to which they are able to allocate maximum points in relation to other games. This flagrant disregard not just for rules of behaviour in playing (which, anyway, you had discounted as an explanation of behaviour) but for the rules of the games without which the devising of strategies seems meaningless, seems inexplicable until, finally, you remember that you have ignored the temporal dimension of the games you have been observing. It becomes clear that the players were playing long before you started to watch and that previous winners carried forward their tokens to new games. In the face of this revelation of a historical process in which generations of dominant players constantly adapt and change the rules to maintain their domination, dismayed you try to withdraw from the hall. Of course, it cannot be done. You have been playing along with the players all the time. Your perception of the game is part of your strategy within it.

This rather Kafkaesque scenario does, I think, accurately represent the accumulated sense of the many articles which Bourdieu wrote in the first half of the 1970s. For 'games', substitute 'fields'. This account will try to describe the common structural features of different fields – their genesis, structure and reproduction – and also to describe the distinctive 'specificity' which Bourdieu identified in each of the fields which he analysed. It will follow the conceptual development outlined analogically above whereby Bourdieu moved from the analysis of the relations between fields to the analysis of the processes of conversion and reconversion of capital between fields (viewed continually from slightly different perspectives – from outside in or from inside out in relation, for instance, to the fields of education and economics) and, finally, to the analysis of the historical masterminding of the deployment of fields themselves achievable by the possessors of inherited power.

Bourdieu had already introduced the concept of 'field' in 'Champ intellectuel et projet créateur' in 1966. In that article, his main intention was to counter the version of structuralism that was becoming current in literary criticism. For Bourdieu it was not satisfactory simply to perceive structural relations between cultural products and the social conditions within which they were produced. Bourdieu's article sought to emphasize the agency of the artist. It is the artist who is actively engaged in creating the homology between project and 'field' which is subsequently perceived by structuralist critics. Bourdieu had concentrated on elaborating the view that artists take positions within a cultural field which is hierarchized between the sphere of 'legitimacy claiming universality', the sphere of 'what is in process of legitimation' and the sphere of 'the arbitrary as regards legitimacy',[1] but he had made two other factors completely clear. The first point to be remembered was that the extent to which the production of art could be interpreted in terms of position-taking within a cultural field depended on the extent to which, historically, the cultural field had itself secured autonomy from other social fields. The second point to remember was that the achievement of autonomy and the generation of an ideology of autonomy were mutually supporting processes which, in turn, entailed the generation of the theory and practice of the autonomous criticism of autonomous art. This meant, in other words, that we have to be aware in the present that the frame of thinking which we adopt in relation to past works of art is itself a legacy of the intellectual field which artists created in order to facilitate the reception of those works. In short, there were, in 'Champ intellectuel et projet créateur', certainly three kinds of problems which can be differentiated. There was the historical problem of how a field might establish its autonomy within 'society' or in the context of other fields. There was the historical problem of how individuals might produce artefacts within a field which had achieved some degree of relative autonomy, and, finally, there was the present problem of how contemporary individuals might, or should, respond to products which had been historically generated.

This last problem was the epistemological one which had been at the heart of *Le Métier de sociologue*. Just as our understanding of the social world is constituted out of language formulations within which prior understandings or 'pre-notions' are inherent, so our present responses to art are constituted out of the processes of its past production. In both cases, the effect is that we delude ourselves into thinking that we have a natural or spontaneous relationship with the world or with artefacts and, in consequence, we unconsciously reduce the difference or the objectivity of those things which impose themselves on us. Paradoxically, therefore, Bourdieu sought to dissect the processes of social explanation and of artistic creation in the past so as, simultaneously, to be able to represent that dissection as a mode of scientific analysis which held out against the reduction of all responses to the level of spontaneous experience. The analysis of fields of production was, therefore, partly a means by which Bourdieu could explore the relationship between agents and structures, and, partly, a continuing exemplification of the practice of scientific sociology.

'Outline of a sociological theory of art perception' (1968) showed the need for scientific perceptions of art. The capacity to say of a picture: 'that's a Cézanne' involves an acquired acquaintance with the range of possible styles of painting available to a painter, whereas to say of the same picture: 'that's a forest' involves only a recourse to a world of experience which is other than that of the painting itself.[2] The article suggested that a scientific perception would involve an understanding of the situation of the artist which would be similar to the understanding of his own position within his artistic field possessed by the artist himself, but this point was still overshadowed by the concern with 'cultural capital' which dominated *Les Héritiers* and *L'Amour de l'art*. Without formal introduction in schools to the codes of scientific art perception, the cultural legacy of previous centuries, displayed in museums and art galleries, would not be democratically available to all.

By contrast, 'Champ du pouvoir, champ intellectuel et habitus de classe' (1971) focused on the dimension of cultural production rather more than of reception. Here the epistemological break with pre-notions in responding to literary texts is not explored, in a way which would be analogous with the response to paintings, in terms of the texts themselves but, instead, in relation to the presumption – which is historically a legacy of Romanticism – that the process of creation is a process of self-expression. This is an important shift. By analogy with 'Outline of a sociological theory of art perception', Bourdieu should have sought to advance a sociology of literary criticism, and should have argued that proper instruction in schools would lead to the acquisition of the competence necessary to read great works of literature. Rather than seek to ask what might be necessary to be able to say of a passage of prose: 'that's Flaubert', Bourdieu instead concentrated on an analysis of the relations between the field of power and the intellectual field within which, for example, the works of Flaubert were produced. This suggests, in other words, that Bourdieu was beginning to disengage his analysis of 'fields' from the functionalist frame of thinking which assumed that it was the function of the educational system to initiate the population as a whole into a proper appreciation of those fields and their products which it had inherited. The fields were no longer mainly of interest as potential objects of schooled knowledge – curriculum fodder – but were of interest for themselves as social phenomena. As Bourdieu lost faith in the disposition of the educational system to inculcate the scientificity necessary in all kinds of enquiry, it became possible for him to locate the educational system as a 'field' alongside all other fields. It also followed that the action of 'habitus' which had been demonstrated in *La Reproduction* specifically within the context of a series of pedagogical propositions was effective within all fields in securing the reproduction of arbitrary power. By virtue of the line of enquiry which it did not take, therefore, 'Champ du pouvoir, champ intellectuel et habitus de classe' marked a significant moment in which Bourdieu began to concentrate on the structures of fields and on the nature of the relations between fields.

What Bourdieu described as 'a rigorous science of intellectual and artistic facts'[3] which was necessary to put in opposition to the biographism which was the literary critical equivalent of spontaneous sociology and spontaneous art perception, required three stages of analysis: first, 'an analysis of the position of the intellectuals and the artists in the structure of the ruling class (or in relation to this structure when they do not belong to this class either by their origin or by their condition)'; secondly, 'an analysis of the structure of objective relations between the positions which the groups placed in a situation of competition for intellectual or artistic legitimacy occupy at a given moment in the structure of the intellectual field';[4] and, thirdly, the construction from these two variable contexts of the social trajectory of an individual or of a group and, further, the construction of the 'habitus' which transforms an actual trajectory into future possible trajectories for other individuals. By taking the career of Flaubert as his main case-study, Bourdieu proceeds to argue that his analysis of the structural relations – both of the intellectual field in relation to the field of power and also internally – explains the life of the novelist more satisfactorily than did the small biographical details supplied by Sartre in his analysis of Flaubert's life and work.[5] Flaubert's social trajectory is to be explained not, as Sartre implied, by his self-inflicted and self-inhibiting feeling 'in himself and outside himself, that the bourgeoisie was his class of origin',[6] but with reference to the objective position within which Flaubert was situated as a dominated member of the dominant class which enabled him to adopt circumscribed strategies both inside and outside his intellectual field.

To express Flaubert's career in these terms is already to import the language of 'strategies' which Bourdieu was employing within the context of anthropological discourse to his cultural analysis. This conjunction was effected in two articles of 1971 which were clearly inspired by a detailed consideration of Weber's sociology of religion. 'Une interprétation de la théorie de la religion selon Max Weber' (1971) follows *Le Métier de sociologue* in exemplifying the proper attitude that should be adopted by a practising sociologist to a classic sociological text – in this case, Weber's *Wirtschaft und Gesellschaft*.[7] Bourdieu argues that Weber over-reacted against Marx in exalting the charismatic powers of religious leaders in an attempt to defend the potency of religious belief against Marxist reductionism, but that, nevertheless, there are hints in Weber's sociology of religion which, as a sociological tradesman, Bourdieu can now deploy to his own advantage. Notice that Bourdieu is as eager to discredit the Weberian notion of 'charisma' as he was to discredit Sartre's representation of Flaubert's autonomous self. The reason for this is the same in both cases. Bourdieu wants to show that the title of the 'charismatic' leader and the title of the 'creative' artist are both bestowed in particular social circumstances and are devices or strategies adopted in their respective 'fields' by those people within those fields who wish to legitimize their power or authority in the eyes of those who have neither power nor authority. According to Bourdieu, then, Marx and Weber both neglected

> the religious work which agents and the specialised spokesmen undertake, invested with power, institutional or not, by responding, by a determined type of practice or discourse, to a particular category of the needs appropriate to determined social groups.[8]

The article concentrates on an analysis of 'religious work' in terms which are similar to the analysis of 'pedagogic work' offered in *La Reproduction* – mainly, that is, in terms of the competition within an autonomous field. The difference, however, is that *La Reproduction* took the 'cultural arbitrariness' of educational content as a given and the legitimacy of 'educational systems' as universal and unproblematic, whereas the above sentence posits religious work as non-arbitrary because it responds to the non-universal 'religious needs' of particular social groups. 'Une interprétation de la théorie de la religion selon Max Weber' described the differentiation of religion from magic in logical, almost tautological, terms: 'religious interests' can be defined as such precisely when they function ideologically in supporting social positions. In a series of propositions reminiscent of those of *La Reproduction* it exposed the by now familiar pattern in the operation of the religious field. The success of religious agents, in other words, is dependent both on their positions within the field of power and on their positions within the relatively autonomous religious field. Bourdieu's exploration of the specificity of the religious field here enabled him to articulate clearly the constant tension between the producers of world-views – the prophets and the sustainers or institutionalizers of world-views – the priests. The success of a prophetic vision in becoming institutionalized within a Church is a function of the extent to which the prophet can mobilize the 'extra-religious' force of the laity situated within society in such a way as to cause the priests to accommodate the new vision in order to retain their own internal power. Just as the bourgeois artist in nineteenth-century France had to achieve recognition by satisfying both the dominant classes in control of the intellectual field and the 'public' of the popular classes outside the field, so the revolutionary visions of the prophets could only become 'successful' if they worked the system of the field which they ostensibly were overturning.

'Genèse et structure du champ religieux' (1971) raised the much more fundamental question begged by the analysis of competition within an established religious field. As in 'Une interprétation de la théorie de la religion selon Max Weber', the discussion of 'Genèse et structure du champ religieux' was rooted in the recommended practice of Le Métier de sociologue. Theories of religion had become so embedded and naturalized that they now inhibited the scientific construction of religious facts. The purpose of Bourdieu's article, therefore, was to get behind the theoretical pre-notions and to make religious experience and practice problematic. He explains that Durkheim quite explicitly tried to find in a sociological theory of knowledge, and, also, of religion, a positivist foundation for Kantian apriorism.[9] It was this endeavour which led to the kind of structuralism which was concerned to identify universal human characteristics. By contrast, Bourdieu clarifies again that his intention is to use the Durkheimian approach as an end in itself which allows for the description of relational structures without seeking to reach universal conclusions. Bourdieu claims that symbolic systems have been only partially understood because there has been an analytical polarity between those who are interested in the forms of symbolism without reference to their power contexts and those who are interested in power without recognizing the potency of symbolism. 'Genèse et structure' reproduces the opening sentences of 'Une interprétation' which argued that Bourdieu's development of hints within Weber's work had enabled him systematically to make the necessary connections between symbolic discourses and material power. Whereas 'Champ du pouvoir, champ intellectuel et habitus de classe' had offered a detailed revision of 'Champ intellectuel et projet créateur' by suggesting that the social trajectories of individuals arise actually from the intersection of different 'fields' rather more than from the artist's perception of his relationship with his audience within the intellectual field, nevertheless it had not explored the intrinsic relationship between power and symbolic expression. Bourdieu's sociological consideration of religion led him to bring together both the

Durkheimian hypothesis of the social genesis of schemes of thought and the Marxist commitment to the facts of class divisions to suggest that:

> religion contributes to the (concealed) imposition of the principles of structuration of the perception and thought of the world and, in particular, of the social world in proportion as it imposes a system of practices and representations whose structure, objectively founded on a principle of political division, presents itself as the natural/supernatural structure of the cosmos.[10]

The first part of the article embellishes this formulation. Bourdieu quotes Marx to substantiate the view that changes in material conditions, notably the transition from country to town habitation, were crucial in opening up the possibility of abstract thinking. The kinds of 'modernizing' economic and technical changes which had been unanalysed in Bourdieu's consideration of the attitudinal adaptations of Algerian or Béarn peasants are here introduced to give a stable point of reference for the establishment of the religious field. As we shall see, the 'objectivity' of 'political' division (as opposed to power division) was shortly to be questioned as Bourdieu analysed the genesis and structure of the political field, and, similarly, the 'objectivity' of class division was to be challenged in 'Classes et classement' (1973). There are two possible explanations for Bourdieu's willingness in this article to make his own amalgamation of Marx and Durkheim. It could either be that his thinking still needed some sense that intellectual fields are reflections of objective realities. Having cancelled the privileged status of the field of education as a point of pedagogical reference for intellectual fields, the commitment to the facts of class divisions provided, perhaps, a temporary alternative objective correlative. The second explanation is a matter of presentation. It could be that in order to convey the relations between constantly variable fields, Bourdieu felt the need heuristically to hold one variable constant in order fully to explore the others. We shall see that there is an element of truth in both. It is almost as if the process of exploring the specificity of different fields reinforced Bourdieu in his rejection of structural functionalism and in his rejection of the absolute primacy which Marxism would accord to class division.

One element in the subsequent rejection of class divisions became clear in 'Genèse et structure'. Having acquiesced in the principle that religious practice covertly and purposefully sustained class divisions, Bourdieu proceeded to show that religious work involved the imposition and consecration of dualistic thinking. Religious power depended on a series of homologous divisions – between good and evil, sacred and profane, ordained and lay. Bourdieu was beginning to say something much more fundamental than that religious practice reflects class position. He was beginning to say that the construction of a religious field, with agents, practices and beliefs, was in itself a formal attempt to impose an ideology of social division. The establishment of a religious field should be seen as a power strategy by which those with dominant power covertly legitimated a distinction between those possessing religious competence and those who were religiously dispossessed. Bourdieu's view of the function of religious establishments was, therefore, analogous with that of the function of museums or universities. These kinds of institutions needed to generate sophisticated ideological distinctions within their fields in order to reinforce a social separation – which they had themselves created in the first place in order to establish themselves at all – from a 'public' which possessed practical mastery of social behaviour but which had not been initiated into the nuances of intellectual debate associated with a range of fields.

The distinction between the 'practical mastery' exercised by the politically impotent and the intellectual distinctions made by those holding political power was to be a crucial one leading, respectively, to *Le Sens pratique* (1980) and *La Distinction* (1979). In 'Genèse et structure', Bourdieu argued that the nature of religious influence within any society could be plotted by reference to two extreme poles – what he called, on the one hand, 'religious self-consumption'[11] and, on the other, the 'complete monopoly'[12] of religious production by specialists. Within any society 'self-consumption' could be achieved either by a process of socialization within families whereby 'practical mastery' might be almost unconsciously acquired by a population, or by a conscious process of instruction which would enable the whole population to be introduced through 'learned mastery' to a corpus of shared norms and values. By contrast, 'complete monopoly' involved the construction of self-fulfilling religious ideologies, such as systematic theologies, which might partly be responsive to the needs of particular societies but which often had pretensions to universality.[13] This clarification in respect of religious ideologies has a much wider significance. In the early 1970s, Bourdieu was involved in characterizing a range of different 'fields' and in defining their features. We shall see how he viewed fields other than the religious field in terms of the substitution of 'learned mastery' for 'practical mastery', and perceived the ways in which 'learned mastery' always tends to depreciate 'practical mastery' and always tends to strive towards 'complete monopoly'. These tendencies could be understood and, to some extent, accommodated within one society, but we shall see that Bourdieu's reservations about 'world religions' are mirrored in the 1980s by his reservations about the internationalization of knowledge and, in particular, the international appropriation of his own context-specific sociological work.[14]

Just as art perception raised problems about art production and art reception, so Bourdieu's analyses of historical religious production and practices registered the importance of the contemporary French religious field from which the past was viewed. *En passant*, Bourdieu makes several illuminating asides which offer sociological accounts of the nature of adherence to the theological views of Teilhard de Chardin and Reinhold Niebuhr,[15] but the engagement of his thinking with contemporary issues was, perhaps, most evident in the articles which explored the relationship between the field of power and the field of political science – 'L'opinion publique n'existe pas' (1971) and 'Les Doxosophes'

(1972). The title of neither article would suggest that they both pursue the form of enquiry adopted in relation to the fields of religion, art, and literature, but they are actually studies of the field of politics. In 'L'opinion publique n'existe pas', Bourdieu develops his argument from a simply stated set of reservations about the status of opinion polls. The first supposition of opinion polls which Bourdieu challenges is that

> everyone can have an opinion; or, stated otherwise, that the production of an opinion is within everyone's range of possibility. At the risk of offending a naively democratic sentiment, I contest this.[16]

Bourdieu's contention is that the production of 'public opinion' by the dominant classes serves to legitimize their exercise of power. The political scientists – identified particularly in 'Les Doxosophes' as the products of the Sciences-Po[17] in Paris – are the agents of the new field of politics as much as, historically, there have been agents of religious ideology. In 'Genèse et structure' Bourdieu had argued, in the face of the pre-notions of centuries of belief reinforced by 100 years of analytical sociology of religion, that no attitudes or opinions are intrinsically religious. Discretely or 'properly' religious interests emerged historically as a way of differentiating a ruling social group from the magical practices associated with 'inferior' social groups. In the same way, more recently, political agents have found it necessary to constitute a discourse of political explanation and understanding which excludes those who do not possess the intellectual competence to think about their social behaviour in political terms. Bourdieu draws attention here most of all to the effect in political analysis of ignoring the significance of the 'no responses' to questionnaires. Opinion surveys suggest problems and pose questions which are conceptualized in political terms which ensure no responses from the conceptually uninitiated and then proceed to construct a 'public opinion' from the responses which were pre-selectively unrepresentative. The ruling classes compete for supremacy within the autonomous fields which they have constructed – whether of religion, culture or politics. They interpose an ideology of shared or common doctrinal, cultural or political assumptions or allegiances, such as, perhaps, belief in God, deference to the merit of Shakespeare or adherence to 'democratic' values, which accommodates the pretension of the popular classes to become involved in these artificial discourses. The basis of people's behaviour, however, is that it is ethical in the sense that it is a manifestation of their 'ethos'. In 'L'opinion publique n'existe pas', Bourdieu argues that the analyses of political science are inadequate and incapable of offering predictive results precisely because they try to treat respondents as absolute individuals without reference to their sense of class allegiance. A sociological political science would want to pay attention to the problems which people might formulate rather than to their responses to posed, dominant problems, and it would want to acknowledge that people adopt political opinions by reference to those of the group to which they feel that they are attached – often on non-political grounds. Other than rendering political science sociological in this way, Bourdieu saw two possible ways in which the imposition of the dominant political ideology by means of opinion polls might be counteracted. Just as in relation to aesthetic competence, Bourdieu still hoped that schooling might fulfil a socially egalitarian purpose effectively. The necessary political competence might be inculcated in the same way as the necessary aesthetic competence should be communicated in schools to enable the whole population to appreciate the art displayed in museums. However, Bourdieu's interest in an alternative solution seemed to be much greater at this time. Those politically disempowered by the conceptualisms of politicological enquiry should strive to formulate their own counter-problematics. The mistake of the popular classes had been to collude in their intellectual exclusion by acquiescing in the legitimacy of the 'political' questions to which they responded inadequately. 'Les Doxosophes' makes it much clearer than 'L' opinion publique n'existe pas' that Bourdieu was not at all adhering to the notion that the working class should universally realize its potential as a revolutionary force. Bourdieu was explicit in 'Les Doxosophes' that such a conceptualization of the potential of a class was as much an imposition of a dominant political discourse as any other 'political' ideology. What was needed, rather, was the capacity to problematize 'politics' itself, to remove the pre-notions of the field of politics which were almost as deeply 'naturalized' in society as the pre-notions of religion.

Both 'The thinkable and the unthinkable' (1971) and 'Classes et classement' (1973) are evidence that Bourdieu was grappling with a fundamental problem which had been exposed by his consideration of the structures of fields. If fields are the arenas within which internal competition for authority occurs and within which systems of reproduction are adopted to sustain the authority of those who already possess it, and if, as we shall see, it was becoming increasingly clear that those people with social power were in a position to juggle with the status of the various fields which might underpin that power, how could those without power begin to think thoughts other than those which held them subject, begin to re-classify their situation in terms other than those by which they were already classed or classified, begin, in short, to re-cognize their society? The final paragraph of 'Genèse et structure' offered a brief consideration of the general problem. Bourdieu was convinced that no political revolution could logically secure a political transformation unless it were accompanied by a radical, political re-conceptualization. Whilst a political crisis has no prophet 'the schemes with which one thinks about the world reversed are the product of the world to be reversed'.[18] In a passage which is all the more telling for being coded within an academic analysis of the function of religious prophets, Bourdieu continues:

> The prophet is the person who can contribute to bringing about the coincidence of the revolution with itself in effecting the symbolic revolution which labels the political revolution. But if it is true that the political revolution only finds full expression in the symbolic revolution which makes it exist fully in giving it the means to think about itself in its truth, i.e. as

unprecedented, unthinkable and unnameable according to former codes, instead of taking itself for one or another of the revolutions of the past; if it is true therefore that every political revolution calls for this revolution of symbolic systems which the metaphysical tradition calls metanoia, it remains the case that the conversion of minds as a revolution in thinking is only a revolution in the minds of already converted religious prophets who, as a result of an inability to think about the limits of their power, i.e. of their thinking about power, cannot give the means of thinking this unthinkable thing which is the crisis without at the same time imposing this unthought thing which is the political meaning of the crisis, thus making themselves culpable, without knowing or wishing it, for the deception which has been played on them.[19]

In identifying the need for radical re-conceptualization Bourdieu does not take refuge in recommending the role of a charismatic prophet, revolutionary or innovator. Clearly reflecting tacitly on his own Algerian experiences, Bourdieu is here saying, for instance, that a socialist revolution has to be conceptualized as such if it is not simply to mimic the performance and adopt the ideology of stereotypical independence movements.[20] Equally, however, those effecting the symbolic revolution – involved, that is, in constituting it by naming it – can only avoid imposing their predispositions if they make explicit the social and political base which gives them the power to generate symbolic representations. Bourdieu had sought to articulate the truth of the social phenomena which he observed in Algeria and had sought to recommend pedagogical procedures which, through sociological sensitivity, would allow the Algerians to construct their own symbolic naming of their political actions. The distinction in the above passage between the 'unthinkable' ('impensable') and the 'unthought' ('impensée') is crucial. The 'unthinkable' is a situation for which there do not exist the tools for re-cognition, whereas the 'unthought' is a position-taking where the position-holder is unaware of its power base. Bourdieu's contention is that it is a deception to suppose that anything 'unthinkable' can actually be thought. Instead, the 'unthought' basis of thinking has to be constantly thought in order to understand the ways in which re-thinking functions as a thinking of the previously 'unthinkable'.

Bourdieu's analysis of 'fields', therefore, exposed the powerlessness of people who were excluded from those fields, but did so in such a way that it reinforced the commitment to a reflexive sociology as being the only way in which the structures of domination might gradually be modified. Whereas *Le Métier de sociologue* had seemed to be a work in which Bourdieu had sought to define a role for the practise of sociological research which was separate from the transmission of sociological knowledge within the higher education system where he was located, the consequence of the analysis of 'fields' was that reflexive practice acquired a function for all social agents. Bourdieu's analyses of the subtleties of the strategies of reconversion of capital practised by the dominant classes to maintain their superiority to which we must now turn are not to be understood as attempts to construct a social theory or to pin down precise relations between different fields but, instead, as guidelines to enable social agents to think what might be 'unthought' in their position-taking. They are to be understood as exercises in vicarious or paradigmatic reflexivity rather than as building blocks of a social system.

In the terms set by the long analogy which introduced this chapter, Bourdieu's 'field'-studies of the early 1970s had observed performances in cultural games and had correlated those performances with attainment in educational games. It was an extension of the educational and cultural research of the 1960s to suppose initially that cultural competence was a reflection of acquired educational competence and then to realize that the educational system seemed only to be able to endorse the cultural competence already possessed by students. It became possible to observe that those people who were in possession of economic capital were able to manipulate the educational and cultural games to ensure that they remained dominant. 'Reproduction culturelle et reproduction sociale' (1971), for instance, noted that the members of the dominant class who held their position by virtue of their wealth and economic achievement did not necessarily invest in higher education for their children as heavily as those members who owed their membership of that class to their own educational achievement. Equally, the status of educational institutions was as important as the nature of the education offered within them. The sense that the connection between educational, cultural and economic fields was not at all mechanical but, rather, infinitely variable, was confirmed in 'La défense du corps' (1971) where Bourdieu described the influence of two markets – internal or 'restricted' and external or 'large-scale' in the language of economic metaphor elaborated in 'Le marché des biens symboliques' (1971) – on the trajectory of teaching staff in contemporary French universities.[21] These were, however, still observed variations. It was only after the clear announcement of a commitment to strategies rather than to rules of action – made in *Esquisse* (1972) and confirmed in 'Les stratégies matrimoniales dans le système de reproduction' (1972) – and after the realization, therefore, that not only were there not any rules of games or between games but that the games themselves were strategies, that Bourdieu was able overtly to present the relations between fields no longer as observations of relationships but as the manifestations of the strategic choices made by social agents. Hence, the title of 'Les stratégies de reconversion. Les classes sociales et le système d'enseignement' (1973) is significant in marking a convergence of the work which had separately culminated in *Esquisse* (1972) and *La Repro-duction* (1970). The first paragraph of the English version of 'Les stratégies de reconversion' – 'Changes in social structure and changes in the demand for education' (1977) – confirms that the analysis presented stands in opposition to the functionalism which would want to see the growth in demand for education as a response to technological need, emphasizing, instead, the dialectical relations between the two kinds of changes. In effect, Bourdieu was positing a strategic functionalist – a social agent who might develop strategies on the understanding himself that the functional relations between fields were fluctuating and contingent – and inserting such an agent within his own perception of society. Although 'Classes et classement' had made it clear that class divisions themselves were contingent social constructs, the first paragraph of 'Les stratégies de reconversion' (which was not reproduced in the English version) strategically deployed the notion of 'class' to clarify that perception of society and, importantly, of social history. Bourdieu wrote:

> The strategies of reproduction by which the members of the classes or parts of classes in possession of capital tend unconsciously and consciously to maintain or improve their position in the structure of class relations by safeguarding or increasing their capital, constitutes a system which functions and transforms itself as such – their being the product of the same unifying and generative principle, namely the disposition with regard to the future, itself determined by the objective chances of reproduction of the group, i.e. by its objective future.[22]

The observable patterns in the behaviour of individuals or groups across different fields derive, in other words, not from any intrinsic homology between those fields as fields, but from the fact that the strategies available to people reflect in similar ways in all fields the precise point which they occupy in a temporal continuum, gauged in terms of their degree of inherited capital. Those in possession of a high degree of capital have the capacity to project strategies which can involve changing the rules of the game whereas those without capital have only limited control over their future. This introduction of the notion of degrees of future orientation as differentiating indicators of social position is a revision of ideas which Bourdieu had advanced in discussing the attitude of Algerian peasants to time and which he had elaborated in relation to class consciousness in 'Condition de classe et position de classe' (1966). The difference now, however, is that Bourdieu is saying not simply that perceived class positions are determined by objective class conditions but that these mutually reinforcing social classifications constrain the opportunities for change through history of those people (all people) who are born to internalize the strategies of the contexts within which they are nurtured.

'Les stratégies de reconversion' offers an account of the function of educational qualifications as seen from a position within an autonomizing field of business or enterprise. The twist of perspective brilliantly illuminates Bourdieu's relational approach. In the competition for supremacy within the business field, educational achievement is used in the same way as Bourdieu had on several occasions shown that extraneously acquired cultural competence is often deployed to undermine the likelihood of equal educational opportunity. Historically, industrial or commercial managers had been able to pass on the 'family business' to their sons without the interposition of educational achievement. With the collapse of the traditional mechanism for social reproduction, the old managers were forced to work the system which required the acquisition of educational qualifications. One solution, of course, was to make educational success dependent on the cultural competences which may have been the by-products of the original economic dominance of the old managers. The introduction of examinations had the same effect as the subsequent use of opinion polls by politicians and political scientists whose effects were analysed in 'Les Doxosophes'. Whereas in that article, however, Bourdieu seemed to be looking to the articulation by those without capital of a counter-problematic which would rupture the continuing historical process of social deprivation imposed on them by those with capital, 'Les stratégies de reconversion' seems to look, instead, to the exercise of limited control over the future. 'Avenir de classe et causalité du probable' (1974) elaborated this further. There are important philosophical discussions in which Bourdieu argues that his use of the future orientation of action does not lead him to a 'finalism' which might seem to be as inimical to strategic agency as the 'mechanism' of rule-governed assumptions about human behaviour. In particular, Bourdieu suggests that the explanations of economic behaviour offered by 'economists' have a social function which is similar to the imposed 'political' explanations of a-political behaviour proposed by 'political scientists'. Bourdieu argues that the concept of 'habitus' removes the difficulties inherent in either 'finalism' or 'mechanism'. For everyone, behaviour is an expression of a class ethos which is instilled by processes of 'habitus' and every class ethos has a set of objective future possibilities associated with it. The actions of individuals may seem to be determined by their future possibilities (the causality of the probable), but this is only because these actions are the unconscious expression of class dispositions which have future possibilities contained within them. It is the reintroduction here by Bourdieu of the notion of 'habitus' which allows him to show that the relations of individuals or groups in and between different fields of activity cannot be adequately understood only synchronically. By outlining the idea of a 'slope',[23] or predictable class trajectory, Bourdieu is able to explore in 'Avenir de classe' the ways in which all aspects of human behaviour are to be seen as expressions which, like art production and art appreciation, are adopted to reinforce a social trajectory.

The discussion of dress and manners within 'Avenir de classe' anticipates the detailed consideration of La Distinction (1979) in the same way as Bourdieu's references to the ethical behaviour which resists the superimposition of 'political' or 'economic' labels by intellectual specialists anticipates the account of Le Sens pratique (1980). These two texts were the products of refinements of thinking which were first advanced in the essays of the early 1970s. Many of the connections between his thoughts are most evident in the inter-relationships between these essays and in the subsequent explorations reported, mostly, in the Actes de la recherche en sciences sociales. The essays of the late 1970s are the subject of Chapter 9. The immediate concern is now with the process by which Bourdieu's adherence to the idea of strategies developed into a full account of the 'sens pratique'.

From the theory to the
logic of practice

Esquisse d'une théorie de la pratique, précédé de trois études d'ethnologie kabyle (1972) was an attempt to re-state the epistemological ideas of *Le Métier de sociologue* (1968) in terms which were pertinent to the practice of anthropologists. In order to get behind the language in which social agents conceptualize themselves and their situations and to avoid either accepting the views which agents have of themselves at face value or imposing explanations which say more about the explainers than the explained, sociologists must systematically reflect on the social positions from which they produce their social interpretations. The structure of *Esquisse* seemed to suggest that Bourdieu was, in 1971–2, offering just such a reflection on the interpretations which he had earlier given of his Algerian observations, but the text actually emphasized the changes in his interpretations rather than the changing social positions from which Bourdieu had produced them. The substance of Bourdieu's re-interpretation was that he argued that agents do not act in conformity with established and formulated 'rules' but, instead, adopt strategies of behaviour which are based on their perceptions of their objective situation and are influenced also by their objective situation itself which expresses itself through their dispositions to act in ways to which they have been already habituated. This re-interpretation involved, in other words, the introduction of the idea of 'habitus' to explain the way in which the behaviour of agents is adopted in relation to structures which are inherent in their situations rather than to explain it artificially by reference to the supposed regulation enforced by structures artificially constructed by observers. The re-interpretation entailed a full rejection of 'structuralism' but, increasingly, Bourdieu saw 'structuralism' as only a particular case of 'objectivism'. The problem posed in *Le Métier de sociologue* had seemed to be resolvable by advocating reflexive observation of practice, but the work of the 1970s wrestled rather more with the problem of how practice might be liberated from the tyranny of being observed – how it might be understood for itself without, in the process, being constituted as something different. The notion of 'strategy' was not wholly satisfactory for Bourdieu's purposes because it still seemed to sustain the dominant standpoint of the privileged observer. There was still the sense that the 'strategies' identified by observers might be as artificial as 'rules' because the actions of agents might be placed in a framework which could be known in detachment by observers but could not be known by participants. Had, for instance, an observer been able to have an aerial view of the Battle of Waterloo from a helicopter, he might have produced interpretations of the 'strategies' of the various military commanders on the assumption that they all possessed his own synoptic vision of the whole battle whereas the actual 'strategies' deployed by Napoleon and Wellington were based upon their limited intelligences of the whole position and on their differently constituted dispositions to act.

In moving from an outline of a 'theory of practice' to the articulation of a logic of practice, or a practical logic, Bourdieu was, therefore, trying to produce an account of practice which would identify the immanent strategies of agents. He did not want to 'empathize' with Napoleon or endorse Napoleon's primary experience of the battle. He did not want to assert that the aerial observer knew what was really happening, but it was clearly not sufficient to suggest that in this situation the best procedure would be for the helicopter pilot simply to reflect on the interpretative consequences of his privileged aerial perspective. The prescription of *Esquisse* was in danger of being only negative in this unsatisfactory way. The challenge for Bourdieu was to use the synoptic vision offered by detachment as an instrument for understanding the structures in force within societies in the context of which agents actually generate their own strategies.

The textual sequence of the progress of Bourdieu's thinking is as follows. For Part I of *Esquisse* (1972), Bourdieu reproduced three earlier analyses of traditional Algerian behaviour – the first two of which were specifically placed as 'structuralist'. In Part II, Bourdieu offered a critique of 'structuralism' in favour of a third mode of knowledge which he called 'praxeology', but the focus of the discussion was mainly on the deficiencies of 'structuralism' as evidenced in his earlier articles rather than on the attempt to give substance positively to a 'science of practices'. 'Les stratégies matrimoniales dans le système de reproduction' (1972) offered an explicit revision of the earlier 'Célibat et condition paysanne' (1962), substituting, as the title suggests, the framework of strategic action for the original one of structuralist rule-dominated behaviour. It was only in an article published in 1976 in *Actes de la recherche en sciences sociales* – 'Le sens pratique' – that Bourdieu 'prolonged', as he put it in a footnote, 'the analysis of the specific logic of practice'[1] presented in *Esquisse*. In 1977, Bourdieu published *Algérie 60* which became the basis of an English publication of 1979 entitled *Algeria 1960*. Between these two publications had appeared the English version of *Esquisse*, rendered as *Outline of a Theory of Practice* (1977). The structure of *Outline*, however, is completely different from that of *Esquisse*.

Bourdieu's intention was clearly to remedy the deficiencies of *Esquisse* in such a way that *Outline* would emerge as positively praxeological rather than negatively structuralist. *Outline* is not preceded by the 'passé' Kabyle studies. Instead, *Outline* specifically revisits the earlier analyses, overtly reconsiders them and uses this reconsideration to clarify the nature of the transition from 'rules' to 'strategies' to the 'logic of practice'. The first two of the studies offered in *Esquisse* were made available in *Algeria 1960* where they supplemented the text of *Algérie 60* which had offered only a slightly edited re-publication of most of the second part of *Travail et travailleurs* (1963). The third part of *Outline* is a translation of the 1976 article entitled 'Le sens pratique' and the fourth part incorporates a second article of 1976 entitled 'Les modes de domination'.[2] It is important to realize, therefore, that *Outline* is to be regarded as a new text rather than simply as a translation of *Esquisse*. *Outline* was the text in which Bourdieu consolidated the changes in his thinking during the mid-1970s and it was the mid-point between *Esquisse* and the further consolidation of his position advanced in the book entitled *Le Sens pratique* (1980).

The discussion which follows justifiably works from the English texts of *Outline* and *Algeria 1960*, but it will constantly try to clarify the modifications which Bourdieu made to his French texts. In this way the discussion will endeavour to summarize both Bourdieu's explicit modifications through which he tried to clarify the development of his thinking and also those tacit ones which lie somewhere between the French and English texts by which the changes in Bourdieu's position are additionally revealed.

The new emphasis of *Outline* is apparent in the re-formulation and re-ordering of its sub-titles and sub-headings. The second part of *Esquisse* had begun with a discussion of the 'observer observed' which had been followed by a further sub-section entitled 'the three kinds of theoretical knowledge'. By contrast, the first of the four major sections of *Outline* is called 'The objective limits of objectivism' within which the text of 'the three kinds of theoretical knowledge' is closely reproduced under the new sub-title of 'From the mechanics of the model to the dialectic of strategies'. Whereas *Esquisse* had been content to cast doubt on the validity of 'participant observation' and to recommend that observation should systematically be observed, *Outline* is anxious to expose the threat posed to the understanding of practice as much by the objective representation of it as by observing it. Whereas *Esquisse* had been prepared to identify three kinds of knowledge of the behaviour of social agents, *Outline*, instead, tries to undermine the apparently objectivist supposition of that formulation by signalling a transition from a way of thinking in which the 'model'-making of observers generated a 'mechanical', 'rule'-dominated interpretation of practice to one in which a 'dialectic' is suggested not just between the 'strategic' practice of agents and the social structures within which those strategies are deployed, but also – which may amount to the same thing – between the practice of agents and the strategic practice of 'scientific' observers. Although the words in which the third kind of knowledge is explained in both *Esquisse* and *Outline* are almost exactly the same, a significant change of emphasis is secured by a re-ordering of the statements. A strict translation of the version presented in *Esquisse* is as follows:

> Finally, the knowledge which can be called praxeological has as its object not only the system of objective relations which the objectivist kind of knowledge constructs, but the dialectical relations between these objective structures and the structured dispositions within which they are actualized and which tend to reproduce them – that is to say the double process of internalizing the external and externalizing the internal. This knowledge implies a break with the objectivist kind of knowledge, that is to say a questioning of the conditions of possibility and, through that, of the limits of the objective and objectifying standpoint which grasps practices from outside, as a fait accompli, instead of constructing their generative principle by situating itself within the very movement of their accomplishment.[3]

It is worth lingering over a direct comparison between the organization of this passage and that of the version offered only in English in *Outline*:

> Finally, it is only by means of a second break, which is needed in order to grasp the limits of objectivist knowledge – an inevitable moment in scientific knowledge – and to bring to light the theory of theory and the theory of practice inscribed (in its practical state) in this mode of knowledge, that we can integrate the gains from it into an adequate science of practices. The critical break with objectivist abstraction ensuing from inquiry into the conditions of possibility, and thereby, into the limits of the objective and objectifying standpoint which grasps practices from outside, as a fait accompli, instead of constructing their generative principle by situating itself within the very movement of their accomplishment, has no other aim than to make possible a science of the dialectical relations between the objective structures to which the objectivist mode of knowledge gives access and the structured dispositions within which those structures are actualized and which tend to reproduce them.[4]

Several important points emerge from this comparison. The insertion into the first sentence in *Outline* of the comment that the understanding of the limits of objectivist knowledge is 'an inevitable moment in scientific knowledge' is interesting. It articulates a continuity between the approach recommended here and that previously outlined in *Le Métier de sociologue* – the introduction of the third kind of knowledge is represented as an example of the way in which any science has to constitute itself as science. This backward-looking nuance is confirmed by the change from the adjectival form of 'praxeological knowledge' in *Esquisse* to the rendition as 'science of practices'. The effect of this insertion, therefore, is that the *Outline* passage seeks to differentiate 'science' from 'knowledge'. At the same time, however, the continuation of the first sentence points forward to Bourdieu's increasing awareness that objectivist, or abstract or theoretical knowledge is itself to be understood as practice rather than as theory. The parenthetical 'in its practical state' acknowledges that the exercise of theoretical knowledge is a particular form of practical logic and thus tacitly removes any gap between the observer and the observed which might have been thought still to adhere to the *Esquisse* formulation. Similarly, the critical break with objectivism is now presented as having 'no other aim' than to make possible a science of dialectical relations whereas *Esquisse* had ambivalently made the point that praxeological knowledge had these relations as its object ('pour objet') in addition to the system of relations constructed by objectivism. Whereas, finally, the passage from *Esquisse* suggests here that praxeological knowledge offers something extra to objectivist analysis, the *Outline* passage is much more explicit in indicating that the science of practices goes beyond objectivism by using it – by using the knowledge of structures to which it 'gives access' and by then integrating 'the gains from it' into an account of phenomena which becomes more 'adequate'.

This is certainly the orientation of the whole argument of *Outline* – that the new way of thinking does not replace the old but is, on the contrary, only made possible by assimilating and then going beyond the old. Bourdieu proceeds to offer several specific examples of the way in which the restitution of the practice of agents is both dependent on and enriched by the accommodation of earlier structuralist analyses. Whereas the momentum of the account of 'praxeology' in *Esquisse* was immediately lost as Bourdieu entered into a digressive critique of the 'objectivism' of Saussurean linguistics,[5] *Outline* at once gives, instead, an example 'to show how this sort of third-order knowledge does not cancel out the gains from objectivist knowledge but conserves and transcends them . . . '.[6] This example is a reproduction of a passage which was positioned late in the text of *Esquisse* under the sub-title: 'The action of time and the time of action'. In that context, it had been used to expose 'the reificatory effect of the theory produced by the conversion of the polythetic into the mono-thetic'.[7] Although the mention of 'polythesis' is characteristic of Bourdieu's developing thought about the logic of practice, the emphasis in *Esquisse* is negatively on the inadequacies of reification. In giving the example which was differently contexted in *Esquisse* and *Outline*, Bourdieu invited the reader to recall the criticism made by Lévi-Strauss of Mauss's approach to gift exchange. Mauss is offered as the representative of the 'ethnomethodological' or 'pheno-menological' approach whilst Lévi-Strauss is made to stand for structuralism. In opposition to Mauss, Lévi-Strauss had contended that there are structural patterns in gift exchange which amount to rules which govern the behaviour of the participants in exchanges. Bourdieu's contention is that the structuralist approach which correctly questioned the validity of the 'native experience' of events was, however, wrong in proposing a synchronic model in which exchange might be thought to be comparable to a static equation or calculation. Bourdieu argues that the temporal dimension has to be restored to exchange. Actions which take place over a period of time may appear to abide by a fixed formula of action and counter-action when viewed retrospectively and from outside the process, but the imposition of such a formula flattens out the context within which the actions occur and removes from analysis the possibility that agents within the process might actually be involved in a series of *ad hoc* corrective strategies to salvage miscalculations or misjudgements.

The temporal dimension is crucial to the next reinterpretation offered by Bourdieu in *Outline*. 'Honour' is taken as a particular case-study for the analysis of exchange behaviour, and the variations in Bourdieu's presentation of his argument clarify the nature of the changes in his thinking between 1965 and 1979. 'The sentiment of honour in Kabyle society' had been published only in English in 1965.[8] With a new title – 'Le sens de l'honneur' – it was the first of the three studies of the Kabyle which formed the first part of *Esquisse*. The change in the title is significant, and the significance was implicitly suggested by the quotation offered on the title page of the first part of *Esquisse*. The quotation selectively reproduces aspects of a French dictionary definition of 'sens'. The primary meaning – 'borrowed from the Latin *sensus*' – is given as 'action, manner of feeling; sentiment; thought; meaning'. A subordinate meaning – 'by analogy' – is given as 'faculty of knowing in an immediate and intuitive manner (like that which the properly called sensations appear to manifest)'.[9] It is clear that the change in title from 'The sentiment' to 'Le sens' of honour linguistically registers a change in conceptual emphasis. 'Sentiment' is a static, passive feeling, whereas 'le sens' is a dynamic disposition to act. The last paragraph of Bourdieu's original article seems to confirm that he was already dissatisfied with the adequacy of 'sentiment' to do justice to the phenomena which he observed:

> The sentiment of honour is the common and intimate code with reference to which the Kabyle judges his actions and those of others. But are the values of honour really the ideal norms that everyone accepts and feels bound to respect? Or are they on the contrary unconscious models of behaviour that govern one's conduct and regulate one's attitudes without clearly rising to consciousness, and which colour one's attitudes without ever being formulated?[10]

Bourdieu is suggesting rhetorically here, in other words, that the 'sentiment' of honour should not be thought to have an 'ideal' or 'objective' existence but as being an immanent, self-regulating system of values deployed by agents who follow dispositions with which they have been inculcated. In short, Bourdieu's interpretation was in need of the concept of 'habitus' which, in 1965, he had not yet articulated. We can observe the introduction of the concept of 'habitus' by following the transformations of one short passage of 'The sentiment of honour'.

'Honour' and 'dishonour' are socially defined in the exchange of 'offence' and 'riposte'. The problem is to know within what time-scale actions and 'counter'-actions can be said to be structurally related. In a passage written in 1965, Bourdieu wrote:

> Dishonour remains virtual as long as the possibility of riposte remains; but it becomes more and more real the longer vengeance is delayed. Thus honour requires that the time lapse between the offence and its reparation should be as short as possible. . . . Doubtless the reply is sometimes delayed for a very long time. . . . But revenge taken after a long delay is only praised in retrospect: before taken, it is all the more doubtful and uncertain; once it is taken, it is all the more meritorious.[11]

This last sentence is replaced in *Esquisse* by a new commentary of some 25 lines in which Bourdieu acknowledges that events which are retrospectively rationalized by agents as much as by observers are not, therefore, to be thought to have been predictable within the process of the 'exchange', but the main emphasis is to insert the notion of 'habitus' to explain the relationship between the strategies of agents and perceived patterns of behaviour:

> Although every matter of honour, considered from outside and as a fait accompli, that is to say from the point of view of the foreign observer, presents itself as a regulated and rigorously necessary sequence of obligatory acts which can therefore be described as a ritual, it remains the case that each of these moments, whose necessity is revealed post festum, is, objectively, the result of a choice and the expression of a strategy. What is called the sentiment of honour[12] is nothing other than the cultivated disposition, the habitus which enables each agent to engender, arising from a small number of implicit principles, all the practices consistent with the logic of challenge and riposte, and only such practices, by means of countless inventions, which the stereotyped unfolding of a ritual would in no way demand.[13]

This is typical of *Esquisse* in highlighting the negative aspect of 'objectivism' and in insisting on the need to recapture the strategies of agents. *Outline* adds a further interpolation before the first sentence above, omits that sentence, slightly revises the second sentence, and then offers more commentary on the parables which had been cited in the 1965 article. In the first new interpolation, Bourdieu comments:

> However close it may come to the logic of practices (and to the extent that it does), the abstract diagram which has to be constructed in order to account for that logic is liable to obscure the fact that the driving force of the whole mechanism is not some abstract principle (the principle of isotimy, equality in honour), still less the set of rules which can be derived from it, but the sense of honour, a disposition inculcated in the earliest years of life and constantly reinforced by calls to order from the group, that is to say, from the aggregate of the individuals endowed with the same dispositions, to whom each is linked by his dispositions and interests.[14]

Bourdieu answers the rhetorical question which he had posed at the end of his 1965 article and explicitly rejects any suggestion that equality in honour might constitute some abstract 'ideal norm', but his attention has shifted away from the task of negating 'objectivism' towards that of deciding how it might be possible to represent practices diagrammatically in a positive way which might avoid the imposition of an artificial order. Equally, there is an indication of a greater interest in the ways in which 'habitus' might operate in practice rather than in its function as a useful explanatory concept. Without mentioning 'habitus' as such, Bourdieu's new sentence suggests the way in which he regards the 'disposition to act' which it signifies as the product of a process of socialization which occurs within social groups and in which the identities of the groups and of the individuals within those groups are reciprocally constituted. A further new sentence emphasizes that this disposition is not simply 'attitudinal' but is fundamental to the relations which human beings have with the physical universe and with their own bodies. After adding that the Kabyle word for the sensitivity and determination needed to exact reprisal for dishonours suffered – 'nif' – literally means 'nose' and is, therefore, associated in meaning with virility, Bourdieu writes:

> This is sufficient to remind us that the point of honour is a permanent disposition, embedded in the agents' very bodies in the form of mental dispositions, schemes of perception and thought, extremely general in their application, such as those which divide up the world in accordance with the oppositions between the male and the female, east and west, future and past, top and bottom, right and left, etc., and also, at a deeper level, in the form of bodily postures and stances, ways of standing, sitting, looking, speaking, or walking.[15]

Although there is here the one phrase which is reminiscent of the article of the mid-1960s on 'systems of education and systems of thought',[16] 'habitus' is now being assigned a function much greater than the one which it had then fulfilled in modifying structuralism. 'Habitus' is now seen as the mechanism by which meanings of the cosmos are internalized and incorporated. It is no surprise, then, that the version of the sentence beginning 'What is called the sentiment of honour . . . ' substitutes, in *Outline*, 'inscribed in the body schema and in the schemes of thought' for the one word 'habitus' of *Esquisse*, and, equally, that it removes the brief remark of *Esquisse* that 'habitus' engenders practices 'arising from a small number of implicit principles'. It was the positive achievement of *Outline* to begin to offer some suggestions concerning the ways in which these principles which seemed to be only 'logical' in *Esquisse* should be understood as examples of 'practical logic'.[17]

The distinction between 'logic' and 'practical logic' is a difficult one. Bourdieu had argued in abstract in *Esquisse* that in societies where no autonomous educational system has been instituted, individuals acquire their dispositions to act by imitating the actions of others rather than by following models. Having discredited the relevance of objectivist models to the situations in which people act, Bourdieu invoked the function of 'habitus' to describe the ways in which the models of behaviour in societies are unconsciously imbibed. 'The incorporation of structures' was the sub-title of a section towards the end of *Esquisse* in which he emphasized that the acquisition of the capacity to act strategically was not dependent on the rational awareness of agents of the structures inherent in their situations. Nevertheless, there was still the sense that the disposition to act was the product of processes of non-conceptual imitation. Every society organized 'structural exercises'[18] by which the appropriate dispositions were transmitted. Whereas Bourdieu's reflections on his early 'The sentiment of honour' focused, in *Esquisse* and in *Outline*, on the de-temporalizing effect of 'objectivism', his re-interpretation of 'The Kabyle house or the world reversed' transforms an article which had been an exercise in spatial structuralism by presenting the structures which had originally been objectively identified as, instead, 'structural exercises' which provided a dispositional apprenticeship for individuals. The original article was a 'structuralist' tour de force which, significantly, had been written for a collection of essays produced in honour of Lévi-Strauss. It describes the way in which a Kabyle house is spatially organized internally by a series of oppositions such as fire/water, cooked/raw, high/low and light/shadow, which correspond with the way in which the universe is similarly organized dialectically. More importantly, however, it describes the way in which the house which is itself homologous with the universe is, nevertheless, also part of an opposition, that of the internal in opposition to the external, of the private to the public, and of the world of women to the world of men. Bourdieu was intrigued by the fact that the operation of the same principle of division both within a divided component and within the universe of which it was a divided component seemed to function in practice without confusion, but this was not the main theme of the original article. His initial conclusion was that the internal world of the house should be seen as the inverse or reverse of the external world – reflecting the different functions of women and men in the world outside the house. The structure of *Esquisse* had meant that the original article had been reproduced without specific comment, but it was incorporated into *Outline* precisely so as to illustrate the way in which methodologically the praxeological approach could surpass structuralism to offer an account of how observed structures practically functioned as exercises. Introducing an excerpt from the original article, Bourdieu comments:

> This analysis of the relationship between the objectified schemes and the schemes incorporated or being incorporated presupposes a structural analysis of the social organization of the internal space of the house and the relation of this internal space to external space, an analysis which is not an end in itself but which, precisely on account of the (dangerous) affinity between objectivism and all that is already objectified, is the only means of fully grasping the structuring structures which, remaining obscure to themselves, are revealed only in the objects they structure. The house, an opus operatum, lends itself as such to a deciphering, but only to a deciphering which does not forget

that the 'book' from which the children learn their vision of the world is read with the body, in and through the movements and displacements which make the space within which they are enacted as much as they are made by it.[19]

Bourdieu's discussion of 'The Kabyle house or the world reversed' is the climax of the second section of *Outline*, devoted to the consideration of 'Structures and the habitus'. The first section had re-considered 'The sentiment of honour' and had reproduced without further comment the third of the Kabyle studies included in *Esquisse*. The third section is not in *Esquisse* at all. It is a translation of an article of 1976 entitled 'Le sens pratique' which is given the general title: 'Generative schemes and practical logic: invention within limits'. There is no longer the sense, therefore, that Bourdieu is defining his new position in continuity with the old through revisions of earlier analyses. The object of the analysis is still Kabyle society, but that analysis is to be seen in the context of the 'field'-studies of the first half of the 1970s. Crudely, the spatial movements within the Kabyle house which constituted 'structural exercises' are to be seen as equivalent to the position-taking within autonomous fields which is designed to safeguard the reproduction of those fields. Certainly by the mid-1970s, Bourdieu was no longer simply interested in the strategies of reconversion adopted by individuals and groups within fields to maintain their capital and power, but also in the genesis of those fields. As its title suggests, 'Genèse et structure du champ religieux' (1971) had explored both in respect of religion. Basing its theoretical reflection largely on the secondary material provided by Weber's work in the sociology of religion, the earlier article had considered the social procedures by which the religious field had established itself by differentiating itself from mythical and magical practices and beliefs and had then sustained itself by constructing and institutionally reinforcing an exclusion of the 'profane' from the privileges of the 'sacred'. At both stages, a principle of division had been at work. The world of autonomous fields stands in relation to the world within which fields are generated in the same relation as does the internal world of the Kabyle house to the external world. Basing his thinking now on his immediate knowledge of traditional Kabyle society, Bourdieu was able to move towards a consideration of how the dispositions which he had called by the term 'habitus' might have been generated instead of clarifying by repetition his understanding of the mechanisms by which that 'habitus' fostered practice.

The object of Bourdieu's analysis was the agrarian calendar. As before, he is concerned with the problem of how to represent diagrammatically a temporal dimension. Having reached an understanding of the dynamics of practices, or having divested himself of the last remnants of an objectivist comprehension of immanent practice, Bourdieu is concerned to avoid reinserting objectivism through his mode of expressing his new understanding. The text offers several linear representations of the seasons and their characteristics but Bourdieu is anxious to insist that the symbolic organization of the temporal sequence for agents is not only a function of a continuous chronology but also a function of the practical significance of events which might seem to be objectively and chronologically random. As Bourdieu succinctly puts it:

> The problem is that the calendar cannot be understood unless it is set down on paper, and that it is impossible to understand how it works unless one fully realizes that it exists only on paper.[20]

It was particularly important for Bourdieu to wrestle with this problem because he was aware of finding himself in a position similar to that of the political scientists whom he had attacked in 'Les Doxosophes'. By constituting analytically a linear calendar, the anthropologist would be in danger of imposing a definition of time which might suppress the counter-definition of practical logic and, therefore, contribute to the strategic exclusion of dominated modes of thinking and dominated people. There would then be no difference between the effect of this analysis and the political consequences of the rejection of the 'no responses' in political surveys, and, in the present, the same result would be achieved by the anthropologist as had been secured historically by the Catholic and the Islamic attempts to standardize the calendar. Because these thematic connections with Bourdieu's other articles of the period relating to other fields are mainly only made explicit in the footnotes to the 'Le sens pratique'[21] article rather than in the version reproduced in *Outline*, the English text loses some of the sense of political urgency which Bourdieu clearly felt in seeking to allow practical logic to manifest itself. In seeking to state clearly in what ways 'practical logic' was different from ordinary logic, Bourdieu successfully reached a new level of explanation of the phenomena which he had first described in 'The Kabyle house or the world reversed'. The defining characteristic of practical logic is that it is 'polythetic'[22] – that is to say that practical logic is capable of sustaining simultaneously a multiplicity of confused and logically (in terms of formal logic) contradictory meanings or theses because the overriding context of its operation is practical. This kind of logic stands in the same relation to formal logic as engineering science might to physical science in the sense that the concern of the engineer might typically be with the application rather than the truth of a concept. Practical logic is polythetic rather than monothetic or synthetic because it is prepared to accrete meanings in response to the require-ments of practical situations without needing to consider whether these meanings have any intrinsic stability. In one master stroke, Bourdieu succeeded in offering an explanation of the apparently contradictory use of the 'same' symbols in different social contexts – inside or outside the Kabyle house, for instance, and in placing himself in alliance with philosophers of language, such as Austin, for whom the 'meanings' of words are defined by their deployment in different contexts, and, finally, in tacitly offering an account of his own intellectual practice.

An understanding of what Bourdieu means by 'polythetic' is crucial. In describing Bourdieu's attempt to restore to actors the logic which actually motivates them in their actions, it has been tempting to think of this as an attempt to define the essence of human behaviour – some intrinsic quality of human nature. This has always had to be resisted linguistically because nothing could be further from the truth of Bourdieu's conception. His enquiry has taken the form of a quest for underlying dispositions, but it has never rested with any form of essentialism and has always insisted not just on relativity but, more accurately, on the primacy of relations. 'Habitus' does not transmit fixed structures or norms to fixed recipients. Individual 'selves' are polythetic. They deploy identities in 'contradictory' ways because these identities are the product of involvement in contradictory situations rather than the expressions of anything which could be said to be unchanging or to possess an intrinsic nature in isolation from the processes which actually constitute it. Similarly, language operates polythetically. Since there are no realities behind words to which they refer in unchanging certainty, it is foolish, for instance, to search for a systematic meaning in the symbols deployed in mythico-ritualistic practice when the explanation for logically 'fuzzy'[23] practice is to be found in the fact that the participants in rites or rituals are engaged in improvisatory practice where any word or object which comes to hand is endowed with a temporary significance (which then may accrete other significances) without reference to any controlling, objective meaning.

Bourdieu's account is richly supported with detailed examples. It has to be read directly rather than through any paraphrase to be fully appreciated, but, for the purposes of this discussion, one major problem must be raised. If practical logic is totally non-referential, are there any controls which are able to ensure that outrageously ridiculous events or words do not acquire symbolic currency? Bourdieu's answer, of course, is that the social conditions within which practical logic operates provide a self-regulating mechanism. Polythetic practice is possible within the kinds of social contexts which it is itself partly responsible for constituting. In raising the question of the social conditions within which practical logic applies, Bourdieu was, inevitably, posing the question whether or not it was a form of thinking and behaviour that was limited to a 'pre-logical' state or might be deployed within 'differentiated' societies. The problem can be put differently. The main purpose of *Esquisse* had been to expose the inadequacies of objectivist analysis. Bourdieu's revisions of his earlier work demonstrated that objectivist analysis could not properly represent what was actually happening in traditional Algerian society. The more that Bourdieu identified the characteristics of the practical logic which objectivism necessarily failed to observe, the more Bourdieu himself seems to have become attracted to that form of practical thinking. He found himself describing the ways in which institutionalized pedagogy had historically destroyed practical logic whilst, at the same time, he was tacitly advocating a return to practical logic in preference to the kind of cultural domination which he had already exposed within the French higher education system. The discussion which was contained in the section of *Esquisse* entitled 'The embodiment of structures' and in the section of *Outline* called 'The dialectic of objectification and embodiment' itemized some of the losses incurred as a result of the rational domination or suppression of practical logic. 'Pedagogic reason' and literacy colluded in perverting practices which were fundamentally corporal and oral. The notion of ethics or of codes of ethical behaviour distorted that of behaviour emanating naturally from an 'ethos'. Precisely those kinds of procedures to which Bourdieu had objected in relation to contemporary political participation in 'Les Doxosophes' were typical of the domination which had consigned practical logic to the past of traditional society. What remains unresolved in the discussion, however, is whether Bourdieu is positing a historical progression from 'traditional' to 'modern' modes of thinking or whether he is arguing that, given the appropriate social conditions, either mode of thinking is realizable at any period in history. The text of *Outline* explores these issues further than did that of *Esquisse* and, significantly, introduces the notion of 'power' into the title of the final section: 'Structures, habitus, power: basis for a theory of symbolic power'. This section offers a translation of 'symbolic capital' from *Esquisse* and adds 'Modes of domination' which had been published as a separate article in 1976. Here the objectivist target is the kind of economism which, working with capitalist assumptions, can only see the practical economics of practical logic as a form of pre-capitalist or non-capitalist activity rather than as a form of economic organization possessing its own practical meanings in its own context. What economic objectivism misses by thinking monothetically are the strategies of reconversion in operation within practical contexts whereby symbolic capital constantly conceals its material base.

The publication of *Algérie 60* in 1977 was the product of Bourdieu's reflection on his earlier analysis of the economic process of transition from traditionalism to modernity in Algeria. The essay entitled 'The disenchantment of the world' mainly reproduces large parts of the text of Part II of *Travail et travailleurs en Algérie* (1963). The only significant insertion to the text comes in the second section of the essay in which Bourdieu attacks Lerner's *The Passing of Traditional Society: Modernizing the Middle East* (1958) on the grounds that it tacitly reads into traditional thinking a psychological yearning for modern society – 'that is to say, American society in its capitalist form'.[24] Bourdieu's opposition, in other words, is to the impositions on practical logic of capitalist assumptions on the part of objectivist analysts. As he puts it in his preface:

> In situations of transition between a pre-capitalist economy and a capitalist economy, the objectivist abstraction in which neo-marginalists join hands with structural-Marxists is so flagrantly inadequate that one has to be blind to reality to reduce the economic agents to mere reflections of the economic structures and to fail to pose the problem of the genesis of economic dispositions and of the economic and social conditions of their genesis.[25]

This prefatory comment is at the same stage of reflection vis-à-vis *Travail et travailleurs* as *Esquisse* had been vis-à-vis the early anthropological studies. Bourdieu was himself aware, however, that he should ideally review *Travail et travailleurs* in the light of the approach to practical logic developed in *Outline*.[26] The inclusion of 'Modes of domination' within *Outline* came close to supplying such a revision because it recognized that the kind of economic objectivism that Bourdieu had attacked in *Algérie 60* as a 'modern' analytical imposition was a pre-condition within the immanent historical process for the emergence of modern society from out of the remains of the traditional. The first paragraph of 'Modes of domination' boldly states that, in general, in undifferentiated societies or 'societies which have no "self-regulatory market" (in Karl Polanyi's sense), no educational system, no juridical apparatus, and no State . . . ',[27] the personal strategies of agents have to be constantly renewed, whereas in differentiated societies objectified fields exist within which and between which power is deployed. To put this in the language of 'field'-studies: the genesis of autonomous and institutionalized 'fields' such as that of religion – a genesis which in origin is itself the product of a strategy of differentiation and a mode of domination – has the effect of consigning personal strategies and the power of 'personality' exercised in primary contact to a secondary position. The mode of domination which is most effective in any given society depends on whether that society has established institutions which make personal power almost redundant, which, by definition that 'society' could only have done if the objectivist thinking of one section within that society had become dominant. In short, 'The modes of domination' makes it clear that the relationship between practical logic and objectivist thinking is one which is to be explained sociologically within history rather than by reference to any assumed progress from one form of social organization to another. The general contention is then elaborated in relation to economic development and the field of economics. Within traditional society where practical logic dominates, actions are neither intrinsically 'economic', 'religious' or 'political' or anything. Actions have no intrinsic or essential character. Symbolic meanings and significances are attached to these neutral actions in ways which may be mutually contradictory depending on context. Bourdieu argues that properly economic behaviour (as much as properly religious or political behaviour) can only come into existence as such – become constituted rather than lived – when a field of economic discourse is established supported by an institutionalized field of economic activity (equivalent to the discourse of theology and the establishment of the Church). Until this happens, Bourdieu insists, 'economic wealth cannot function as capital'.[28] This means that in relation to capitalism and to all aspects of the 'modern' world, the struggles for domination within and between established fields are merely the etiolated enactments of the primary, pre-emptive struggles out of which the coming into existence of any field at all sealed the first disenchantment of the world.

Towards the end of 'Modes of domination', Bourdieu drives home his conception of the difference between the traditional and the modern by reference to an example drawn from modern social behaviour. He writes:

> The greater the extent to which the task of reproducing the relations of
> domination is taken over by objective mechanisms, which serve the interests

of the dominant group without any conscious effort on the latter's part, the more indirect and, in a sense, impersonal, become the strategies objectively oriented towards reproduction: it is not by lavishing generosity, kindness, or politeness on his charwoman (or on any other 'socially inferior' agent), but by choosing the best investment for his money, or the best school for his son, that the possessor of economic or cultural capital perpetuates the relationship of domination which objectively links him with his charwoman and even her descendants.[29]

Once fields exist which owe their existence to the fact that they embody the inclination of sections of society to dominate and exclude other sections, these fields operate automatically to preserve the status of those who are included quite regardless of the relative personal power or qualities of the included and the excluded. In the above example, the best schooling or the possession of economic or cultural capital are tokens of differentiation which relate to no intrinsic merit or worth. We are, therefore, led into a new way of thinking about the relations between educational, cultural and economic practices. The significance of a piece of knowledge or of the kind of school or college within which that knowledge was acquired, and the significance of the possession of an item of furniture or of a perception of a work of art, are both as fluidly independent of any absolute, fixed point of reference as are the significances of the moon or cooked food or the hearth in the polythetic constellation of Kabyle symbolic expressions.

'Modes of domination' was positioned in *Outline* as the final section. Its last pages are devoted to an analysis of the ways in which the established economic field exercises economic power by concealing its economic nature under the guise of other indicators. The function of symbolic capital is to help to sustain economic power by enabling it to present itself as something economically neutral. The very last paragraph of *Outline* suggests that one of the methods of accumulating symbolic capital is to embark on the 'collection of luxury goods attesting the taste and distinction of their owner'.[30] The end of *Outline* leads, in other words, directly into the huge study of 'distinction' which was published in French in 1979. In the context of the discussion of *Outline*, it is important to remember that the action of making 'distinctions' is seen as one method adopted by the dominant sections of society to reinforce institutionalized fields which owed their original existence to the suppression of practical logic. The question posed by the relationship between *La Distinction* (1979) and *Le Sens pratique* (1980), therefore, is whether the social conditions can be recreated to make possible a revival of practical logic and polythetic thinking – whether, in short, practical logic might constitute a counter-problematic by which the revolution could be introduced which is necessary to overthrow the tyranny of 'distinction'.

'Distinction'

Bourdieu has not revisited his early cultural researches in the same kind of public manner as in the overt reinterpretations of his Algerian work offered in *Esquisse* and in *Outline*, but an imposed recapitulation of his previous studies forms a necessary background to the text of *La Distinction* (1979). This summary autonomizes one field of Bourdieu's activities over a period of 20 years in the same way as his own reviews of his Algerian fieldwork autonomized a field of anthropological enquiry. In both cases, the summaries have to be seen in the context of the autonomization necessarily effected in seeking to represent the progress in the totality of the work of 'Bourdieu' within this historical period.

In his first publication – *Sociologie de l'Algérie* (1958) – Bourdieu had been perplexed methodologically by the problem of how to avoid imposing a social identity on the object of his analysis – 'Algeria' – where no actual social identity existed. He satisfied himself that the 'diversity' which he perceived was, in part, really a deliberate 'diversification'[1] whereby tribes differentiated themselves from others and, at the same time, constructed an over-arching sense of identity or community within which 'differences' could be appreciated and effective. What might appear to be diverse to the objectivist observer – to use Bourdieu's language of the 1970s – was the product of active strategies of differentiation. The feeling of Bourdieu's account of 1958 was that differentiation was a mechanism by which tribes secured their group identities.

In 1958 there was still a philosophical, perhaps Sartrean, nuance which seemed to suggest that differentiation was part of a process of constructing a societal 'self', but, by the time of *Travail et travailleurs* Bourdieu was already clearly interested in the ways in which differences of life-style functioned in the process of transition from traditional to modern society. In a section entitled 'From the pressure of necessity to the contagion of needs', Bourdieu had sought to show that the process of adapting to a colonially imposed capitalism was different in kind from the process of becoming capitalist as it had been traditionally understood by theorists. The adoption of capitalism was different from the rise of capitalism because Algerians were beginning to imitate the life-styles of capitalism without ever needing to generate for themselves the puritanical ethos which had been traditionally associated with capitalist behaviour. Bourdieu was already arguing that possessions such as houses or furniture fulfilled their functions in the modernizing process because 'needs have their own logic and dynamism'.[2] Although the capacity to enter into the needs market is economically determined, the differentiation of groups secured by the possession of luxury goods performs a semi-autonomous function.

In 'Célibat et condition paysanne' (1962), Bourdieu similarly accepted that status differences were already enshrined in the objective structure of peasant societies. In discussing, first, the traditional peasant society of the Béarn, Bourdieu had argued that what seemed like a rigid system of rules of matrimonial exchange was based on 'the principle of differentiation used by the inhabitants of Lesquire themselves'[3] – between 'great houses' and 'little houses' or between 'great peasants' and 'little peasants'.[4] As we have seen, Bourdieu was subsequently to develop his sense that the perceived system of rules was, in fact, the basis of sophisticated improvisatory 'games' or 'strategies', but, in 'Célibat et condition paysanne' itself he was more interested in asking whether the basis of the differentiation which was a crucial stake in the matrimonial game was entirely determined economically. Even in traditional society, difference of status – often manifested in an opposition between houses of two storeys or one[5] – was independent of wealth to a quite significant degree. 'Great families' were characterized by their 'noblesse' as much as their wealth and this social quality was an important factor in the calculations surrounding marriage partnerships. As Bourdieu proceeded to analyse the breakdown of the traditional rural society, he then argued that non-economic factors contributed strongly to the separation of the town from the country. Urban language and urban body language were both cited as examples of symbolic practices which were homologous and solidary in effecting a differentiation of the 'citadin' from the 'paysan'.[6] This was, however, still presented as Bourdieu's perception, from outside, of patterns which operated practically but whose immanent modes of operation remained unexplored. There was still, indeed, the sense that the immanent situation was to be seen in terms of 'self-definition' for Bourdieu commented that it was only as a consequence of being labelled a peasant by the town-dweller that the peasant came to experience himself as such.[7]

It was only in *Un Art moyen* (1965) that Bourdieu shifted explicitly from the language of 'difference' to the language of 'distinction'. The shift registers the point which Bourdieu had made in insisting that the relations between Algerian tribes indicated diversification rather than diversity, and it also anticipates Bourdieu's inclination to substitute 'sens' for 'sentiment' in relation to the concept of honour. The exploration of the social uses of photography gave access to the way in which a cultural practice which might be thought to have affinities with 'art' functioned itself – as a 'form' – as a non-economic register of social position between the rural/traditional and urban/modern poles. In the first of the two long sections specifically written by Bourdieu himself, the discussion of photography is related closely to the issues already considered in 'Célibat et condition paysanne'. Within the traditional context, formal photographs taken of social groups at special occasions – such as weddings or baptisms – help to consolidate the objectified social organization which is visually caught. But to become involved in taking photographs, Bourdieu argues in a section entitled 'Distinctions de classe et classe distinguée', is to 'play at' being a town-dweller.[8] It is an attempt to adhere to a social practice which differentiates the practitioner from traditional values and tends to be undertaken by those – like celibates, unmarried men – who find themselves deprived of a meaningful place in a society in transition from the traditional to the modern.

In order to function as mechanisms for social differentiation, non-economic tokens have to be assigned a weighting. Objects or activities have no natural or intrinsic value. The status of an article or activity which confers social distinction must first have the capacity to confer that distinction conferred upon itself socially. The capacity of photographic activity to consolidate the distinction of town-dwellers from peasants was, in the first instance, determined by the economic means of town-dwellers which made them more able to purchase cameras and expensive equipment, but, additionally, its success as a strategy was dependent on the social status assigned to photography within a hierarchy of cultural legitimacy. It followed that Bourdieu should want to analyse the relevance of the aesthetic criteria of artistic judgement to photographs. In his second long contribution to *Un Art moyen*, Bourdieu attacked the simple notion that photography was 'realistic'. There is no sense in which the use of a camera implies a technical, automatic reproduction of any objective reality. The photographer creates as much as any artist in his selection of subjects and in his composition, and his photographs only seem 'real' because he imitates the pre-notion of reality which has been already socially constructed by artists. Within a hierarchy of legitimate culture, photography is, as the title of the book suggests, a 'middling art', which is situated half-way between 'the "vulgar" practices which are apparently abandoned to the anarchy of tastes and colours and the noble cultural practices which are submissive to strict rules.'[9] Photography is in the process of legitimating itself, in generating its own rules, and, as a result, Bourdieu claimed, both the practice of photography and the judgements made of photographs were particularly amenable to sociological analysis because both were the expressions of the class ethos of those involved.

In retrospect, it now appears as if the educational research of the 1960s, as first revealed in the major text – *Les Héritiers* (1964), and the research on museums which was published as *L'Amour de l'art* (1966) both diverted attention from the issues which were raised by *Un Art moyen*. In the terms which Bourdieu himself developed in the mid-1970s, the questions posed to students on which the analyses of *Les Héritiers* were based were 'culturological' in the way in which he argued that political surveys are 'politicological'.[10] *Les Héritiers* showed that working-class students – particularly the children of parents from rural areas – did not possess the kind of culture which educational institutions esteemed. Because Bourdieu was at the same time taking the view that educational institutions are the neutral agencies by which differentiated societies have the possibility of enabling the ethos of component 'classes' to encounter each other, he became preoccupied, certainly within the field of his educational thinking, with the inadequacies of these institutions. Until he became clearer, in *La Reproduction* (1970), that educational institutions were themselves instruments of symbolic violence in which pedagogic work generated an artificial 'habitus' which might be in conflict with an authentic class disposition, Bourdieu seemed to be more inclined to investigate how people might be introduced to a proper appreciation of established works of art rather than how their own practical, cultural activities, such as photography, might be legitimated.

The thinking of *Le Métier de sociologue* (1968) was applied to art appreciation in an article published the same year: 'Éléments d'une théorie sociologique de la perception artistique'.[11] *L'Amour de l'art* had already argued against the view that the capacity to appreciate great art is a 'gift' – an 'eye'[12] comparable to the 'ear' for music – in favour of the view that this capacity can be acquired, through education, in such a way that the acquired seems to be 'natural'. 'Éléments d'une théorie' attempted to show how education can do this. Art appreciation involves the confrontation between an observer who has been constituted in his social context and a work of art which is the product of the artist's own understanding of the stylistic possibilities open to him and of the likely framework of understanding of the people for whom the picture was directly painted. An immediate 'comprehension' of a work of art is only possible in the special case where the codes of the producers and of the observers happen to coincide. Without education, the codes of most observers are unlikely to be in accord with those of the producers with the result that most works of art are naturally miscomprehended. Those people who present themselves as being capable of spontaneously appreciating works of art – as in possession of an enabling 'gift' – are in fact taking advantage of attitudes to those works which are not conscious responses to the works themselves. They are responses to which they have become familiarized by the 'habitus' of their class. Bourdieu argues that it is in the interest of the bourgeoisie to conceal the fact that its artistic competence had been learned so that familiarity with the cultural products of the past exibited in museums and art galleries can be used as a basis of social distinction which thrives on a partition of society into those who are culturally included and those of 'barbarous' taste who are excluded.

This was the framework of thinking that was dominant in *Les Héritiers* and *L'Amour de l'art* but it was becoming clearer to Bourdieu by the end of the 1960s that the educational system would not introduce to the popular classes, by rational pedagogical methods, the science of art appreciation with which the dominant classes were already unconsciously familiar. The educational system colluded in the exclusiveness of class distinction. 'Éléments d'une théorie' outlined the basis of the necessary science but, increasingly, Bourdieu presented his thinking directly without reference to any possibility that it might be functional in the practice of educational institutions. The development of Bourdieu's theory of art perception was based upon a tacit analogy between a society – Algeria, for instance – and a painting. Both are social constructs which objectively contain within themselves the principles of their own generation without reference to any extraneously guiding intention or purpose. For Bourdieu, this analogy held good because artists are not to be thought of as autonomous, creative 'selves' so much as amanuenses by whom the generative principles of creativity of their historical period are conveyed to canvas. Following Panofsky, Bourdieu suggested three kinds of response to paintings of the past. These kinds were equivalent to the modes of knowledge to be outlined in *Esquisse*. 'Naive beholders' of paintings only observe the 'phenomenal meaning' which can, for instance, be apprehended as simply an affective response to the apparent texture of an object. To reach the secondary meaning of paintings involves either the understanding of the explicit iconography within the visual representation – that a painting is 'of' the fall of Troy, or an understanding of the iconography generally available to the artist on the basis of which one particular representation was strategically deployed. If these alternative versions of Panofsky's secondary meaning are separated, the three categories of art perception closely adhere to the 'phenomenological', 'structuralist' and 'praxeological' modes of knowledge developed in *Esquisse* in relation to anthropological observation.[13] In extremely condensed form, 'Éléments d'une théorie' anticipated the development in Bourdieu's thinking which was fully articulated in his representation of the process which led him, in anthropology, from structuralism to the science of practices. It argues that the full development of the science of art appreciation entails, first of all, a critical awareness of both phenomenological and structuralist responses to paintings. It is only by understanding the way in which we ourselves categorize paintings, the way in which we deploy the analytical tools which are at our disposal in our society to construct an objectivist response to them, that we can begin to comprehend these paintings as the constructs emanating from the range of possibilities open to the artist. In short, it is only when we understand the meaning of the aesthetic distinctions current in our own society – between, perhaps 'impressionist' and 'expressionist' – which constitute our objectivist classificatory code, that we can begin to understand the distinctions which were immanently constitutive of historical paintings.

The 'science' of art appreciation, then, involves the capacity to comprehend the distinctions immanent in the production of works of art. The difficulty with Bourdieu's thinking is that the scientificity of art appreciation which is recommended in opposition to the social use of art as an instrument of social distinction can only be developed when people recognize the hidden, distinguishing function of non-scientific appreciation in their own society and are, thereby, enabled to comprehend the way in which the same hidden function was also in operation in the original production of the work that is now the

object of sanctified attention. In effect, this means that Bourdieu's aesthetic
and sociological analyses are mutually reinforcing and it follows that his analyses
of 'fields' of aesthetic production and consumption are both to be seen as his
own strategies to oppose cultural domination within the field of French culture
by recommending scientificity.

The emphasis on 'science' was the platform in the period following *Le Métier
de sociologue*. The studies of the early 1970s explored ways to understand the
relationship between the production and consumption of art objects in history
and, simultaneously, to understand the social uses of those objects in the present.
'Le marché des biens symboliques' (1971) was an important essay in integrating
Bourdieu's theory of art perception with the conceptual framework of 'fields'
that he had developed, in the first instance, by reflecting on Weber's sociology
of religion. As early as 'Champ intellectuel et projet créateur' (1966), Bourdieu
had argued that there had gradually emerged in France by the nineteenth century
an autonomous intellectual field in which the thinking of writers was, for the
first time, freed from the control of the Church or the State. 'Le marché' suggested
that one correlative of this new freedom was that artistic activity established
itself as an economic activity. Art became a commodity which was produced
and consumed, but, paradoxically, the more the autonomous art market
developed, the more there developed an ideology of art as non-commodity.
Bourdieu then elaborated a distinction between the field of 'large-scale' production
and the field of 'restricted' production. The more the art market became itself
an independent economy, the more it became essential for artists to distinguish
themselves within that market in order to make their works marketable within
the closed shop of people who shared the same general esoteric values. Equally,
the success of the restricted field was dependent on the initiation of consumers
into the value of the products. The products generated within the restricted
field could only be accessible to those who were capable of understanding their
underlying codes. By contrast, Bourdieu commented that 'consumption in
the field of large-scale cultural production is more or less independent of the
educational level of consumers'.[14] The effect of Bourdieu's separation of the
two fields of production was, in other words, to contextualize socially the attitude
towards art perception which he had outlined in 'Éléments d'une théorie'. The
acquisition of an educated appreciation of artistic products was only necessary
in relation to those products which had specifically generated the demand for
that kind of response. Bourdieu had succeeded in placing his aesthetic analysis
in a wider, sociological perspective, and, by putting his own mastery of the
codes of society to work he had been able to 'place' the aesthetic mastery of
artefacts within present society as simply one mark of social distinction. The
changed attitude towards educational institutions was, again, crucial here. It
became clear that the educational system was only an accomplice in reinforcing
the minute stylistic distinctions adopted by artists to sustain the distinctiveness
of the restricted from the large-scale field of production. The scientific art
appreciation which Bourdieu wanted to recommend had to be applied to all

cultural products, however aesthetically 'trivial', and this kind of cultural analysis could not be expected within an institution which was partisan in maintaining the distinction of consecrated art.

Bourdieu's rejection of the neutral, social function of the schooling system had the effect of enabling him to develop fully a sociology of symbolic production alongside a sociology of the social uses of symbolic products. There had always lingered the feeling that schooling might neutralize the different cultural dispositions of students from different class backgrounds so that everyone would be able to appreciate works of art equally and would, therefore, be equally disposed to take advantage of those institutions, like museums, where these works were displayed. This democratic ideal which envisaged a society which might become culturally homogeneous gave way to an equally democratic celebration of cultural pluralism. If it can be said that the original motivation behind Bourdieu's consideration of aesthetic theories had been to articulate a scientific approach to art which could be conveyed to everyone, then the consequence of this consideration was that the original motivation had to be revised. The artefacts of the past had only been the tangible products of the strategies adopted by artists as social agents to define and consolidate their class positions. That process of consolidation had always involved the simultaneous production of products and of consumers disposed to appreciate those products. In turn, the dispositions of consumers to appreciate some products rather than others – either, for instance, 'dead' works of art where the market of consumption might now be completely different from the market of production or, on the other hand, 'modern' art where the two markets might be virtually the same – depended on the different class positions of those consumers. Art consumption is a token in the game of social distinction for consumers in the same way as is production for producers. To know all this, Bourdieu originally argued, would enable people to appreciate works of art properly – neither naively, nor objectively, but 'praxeologically' – but knowing it all sociologically had the effect of inserting people into what was known rather than of using it. Bourdieu's developing science of social practices offered, in other words, simultaneously a model for properly appreciating art and a basis for understanding that the range of ways of appreciating art, of which the 'proper' appreciation is one, all constitute different strategies of social distinction which owe their differences to different class origins.

It followed, of course, that the 'sociology of art' necessarily collapsed into a general sociology of symbolic forms of which those things which are socially labelled 'art' are particular cases in just the same way as are furniture or food. 'Styles' of furniture and 'tastes' in food require the same kind of analysis as 'styles' and 'tastes' in painting. By a circuitous route, Bourdieu's thinking had reached the point which was emergent in his consideration of the 'social uses' of photography. Photography was a 'middling art' which, in 1965, could be said to be situated half way between the restricted field of cultural production and the large-scale field. Bourdieu's analysis at that date had suggested that photographic activity was still partly embedded in traditional social practice where it fulfilled a practical function, but was also partly imitating the behaviour associated with an 'art' form by establishing 'genres' and other tokens of restrictive distinction. The transitional status of photography corresponded with the transitional social status of its practitioners.

By the mid-1970s, therefore, the stage was set for a full-scale treatment of the relations between the distinguishing judgements made of all cultural products and the social distinctiveness of those people or groups making the judgements. From the very beginning of the journal *Actes de la recherche en sciences sociales* which Bourdieu launched in January 1975, and in the very first contribution made to it by Bourdieu – 'Méthode scientifique et hiérarchie sociale des objets'[15] – it was clear that the task of the sociologist was thought to be the scrutiny of all social phenomena, however much they might be regarded as menial or trivial by the sociological establishment. Bourdieu had apparently developed his thinking about 'fields' in respect of consecrated culture – art and literature – and in respect of religion, and was about to extend it into the respectable field of the sociology of science in 'The specificity of the scientific field and the social conditions of the progress of reason' (1975),[16] but the catholic intention of the journal was aggressively confirmed in 'Le couturier et sa griffe' (1975)[17] which applied the same mode of analysis to the field of fashion production and consumption. At this time, two features of Bourdieu's thought which have been considered in earlier chapters impinged on his elaboration of the full implications of the workings of 'distinction'. As we have seen, first, Bourdieu's analyses of the operations of 'fields' gradually incorporated the temporal dimension so that he was able to suggest that, over time, the dominant classes were able to deploy strategies of reconversion which adjusted the relative weighting of dominance in different fields in ways which could not be understood through a synchronic 'snap-shot' of the state of power relations at any one time. The study of the fashion industry offered a potent analogy for the whole of society in this respect because, as an industry, it depends on producing clothes in any one season which satisfy the demand for social distinctiveness synchronically but, equally, its survival depends on the capacity in each season to produce clothes which are distinguished diachronically from those of previous seasons. The fashion industry manufactures temporal distinction. In parallel with this increased awareness of the importance of the strategic use of time which was a theme which was central to Bourdieu's revision of 'The sentiment of honour' there was, also, an increased attention to the problem of representing this dimension of social phenomena. Bourdieu's discussion of the immanent status of an objectified version of the agrarian calendar and of the status of his own objectified representation of that dubious objectification was at the core of 'Le sens pratique' (1976) which became the third section of *Outline of a Theory of Practice* (1977).

These two features imposed themselves on the consideration of all symbolic forms or, to put this differently, on the task which now confronted Bourdieu of trying to apply an approach derived from the sociological analysis of 'high' culture (already 'aesthetically' pre-selected) to the analysis of all culture (understood anthropologically) in which the social definition of 'culture' constituted part of what was to be analysed. The first attempt was 'Anatomie du goût' (1976).

Published in *Actes de la recherche en sciences sociales*, 'Anatomie du goût' affirms from the outset that it is in accord with the journal's policy in that the intention to 'anatomize taste' is in itself an attempt to de-consecrate both the art objects and the 'criticism' of those objects which is normally undertaken so as to consolidate the distinction of the critics by association only with works of distinction. As Bourdieu puts this himself:

> Scientific discourse on art and on the social uses of the work of art is destined to appear at once vulgar and terrorist: vulgar, because it transgresses the sacred border which distinguishes the pure kingdom of art and culture from the inferior territory of politics, a distinction which is at the very heart of the effects of symbolic domination exercised by culture or in its name; terrorist, because it claims to reduce to 'uniform' classes everything which is 'fragmented' (éclaté) and 'disengaged' (libéré), 'multiple' and 'different' . . .[18]

By clarifying the social uses of the work of art, in other words, Bourdieu is hoping to expose the ways in which aesthetic distinctions are constructed so as to sustain social differentiation. The text was based on empirical research originally undertaken in 1963 at the same time as the work which was separately used for the analysis of the social uses of photography – *Un Art moyen* (1965) – and complemented by further researches carried out in 1967–8. In an initial section entitled 'The operations of the research', Bourdieu comments that in an earlier version of the text he had attempted to represent the interactions between research and interpretation in the period between 1963 and 1976 but had finally settled on a presentation which offers a summation.[19] Bourdieu had wanted to recapture the process of his own research in *Esquisse* but had, finally, presented some old essays alongside a theoretical discussion which revised their findings. In 'Anatomie du goût', by contrast, Bourdieu is prepared to venture a synoptic presentation which is his static, and therefore transient, account of a situation which he knows to be objectively dynamic. In this essay Bourdieu was more interested in registering the dynamism of objective events than in registering the dynamism of his own perception of those events. This was because the basis of his own reflection on his own past research was precisely that he had failed to come to terms with the 'modality of practices'[20] which were concealed in standardized and standardizing questionnaires. In 1963 Bourdieu had been mainly interested in tastes as reflections of inherited or acquired cultural capital set in an observed canvas of structural relations, whereas in 1976 he was more interested in considering the earlier questionnaire responses as themselves examples of practical logic in action rather than as signs of social positions possessing some kind of separate existence. In the language of 'Le sens pratique', Bourdieu was wanting to analyse the old questionnaire responses as polythetic practice, as non-referential words, or, to use a distinction used by Bourdieu himself, to analyse them 'socio-logically' rather than sociologically.

Bourdieu's reflections on his past research at the beginning of 'Anatomie du goût' carried him further than the representation which he offered in the rest of the text. There he tackles the problem of the diagrammatic display of systems of relations by superimposing a map of the social space of life-styles over a corresponding map of the space of social positions by means of transparent, flimsy paper. Each page is organized to present a high volume of capital at the top of the page and a low volume at the bottom; and to the left represents high cultural capital whereas to the right represents high economic capital. Looking through the flimsy paper it is, for instance, possible to read a series of correspondences. The life-style corresponding with the farmers at the bottom of the centre of the page, with an income of 13,000 francs, includes football and the consumption of ordinary red wine; whereas the life-style corresponding with the liberal professions at the top of the centre of the page, with an income of 83,000 francs, includes golf and whisky. To the top left where higher education teachers are situated (possessing, that is, a high volume of capital of a cultural kind), a typical life-style correspondence is the music of Boulez, whereas at an equivalent level on the top right where industrialists and commercial employers are situated (possessing, that is, economic capital), a typical life-style correspondence is, comparably, the Hungarian Rhapsody. In order to try to indicate the temporal dimension, Bourdieu suggests, with an arrow, a declining, rising, or static social trajectory for each of the groups situated in the map of social positions.

The plotting of positions and correspondences on these maps was the result of Bourdieu's analysis of questionnaire responses which he undertook in conjunction with the scrutiny of a range of official statistical investigations, all of which are cited and evaluated. Bourdieu was fully aware – and anxious to insist – that the diagrammatic representation was a device, an exemplifying paradigm, which would be in need of constant revision and adjustment. It was certainly not to be understood as anything more definitive than a transitory systematisation of society. The device helped to clarify visually many of the arguments which Bourdieu had been trying to advance in linear logic in the 'field'-studies of the earlier 1970s. Whereas 'Champ du pouvoir, champ intellectuel et habitus de classe' (1971) had tried to talk about the relationship between the autonomous logics of the fields of power and intellect and had tried to use the concept of 'habitus' to explain the way in which the temporal dimension was itself a determinant within this fluctuating relationship; or whereas 'La défense du corps' (1971) had tried to explore the reciprocity between changes of status within the academic profession and changes in the labour market; or whereas 'Reproduction culturelle et reproduction sociale' (1971) had explored the relations between these variables; or whereas 'Les stratégies de reconversion' (1973) had tried to ascribe the relative weight assigned to educational qualifications at any time to the constantly shifting significance of the position held on the economic/cultural capital axis as a basis for maintaining dominance at the top of the vertical, volume of capital axis; the importance of 'Anatomie du goût' was that it enabled readers to perceive these points by looking around something which approached a three-dimensional model. In the remainder of the essay, Bourdieu proceeded to read off interpretations by, as it were, taking soundings within his own model. These interpretations were presented systematically in class terms. Bourdieu elaborated on the nuances of the variations of the dominant taste, of the 'petit-bourgeois' taste, and, especially, of the different tastes within the 'petite-bourgeoisie' depending on whether it was a fraction of that class which was in decline, aspiring, or to be defined as a 'new petite-bourgeoisie'. In spite of the fact that this form of interpretation might seem to imply a willingness on Bourdieu's part to regard classes as 'real', his concentration on the temporal shifts in the very classification of the petite-bourgeoisie suggests his actual position. He spelt out that position in a postscript to the whole article which was offered as a 'caution'.[21] He acknowledged that one of the inadequacies of the synchronic representation which he had attempted was that it fixed as a structure of class relations a situation which is only a transient moment in an ongoing historical class struggle – a 'class' struggle, however, which is not 'substantial', 'real' or 'material' but one in which the act of classification (including the class classification used in sociological research) itself is a potent force in the struggle. In spite of the use made of 'class' classifications to interpret the maps, Bourdieu used the arguments advanced in 'Classes et classement' (1973) to disown any possible reading of his intentions in terms of stratification theory or Marxism.[22]

The text of *La Distinction* (1979) is divided into three parts and contains several appendices. A substantial proportion of this text re-uses material contained within 'Anatomie du goût' (particularly, for instance, the reproduction of the three-dimensional space diagram in Part II, its interpretation in Part III, and the reproduction of the methodological discussion as Appendix 1) and it also uses articles which had already been published – Chapter 8 corresponds partly with 'Les Doxosophes' (1972) and Appendix 4 corresponds with 'Un jeu chinois' (1976). Bourdieu was trying to pull together into one statement the strands of his thinking which have just been, in this brief summary, re-inserted into a developmental sequence. By attempting a synoptic statement, Bourdieu was himself imposing an intellectual synchronicity on his own work. Many of the themes which are presented in *La Distinction* are re-statements of earlier positions which do not need to be re-discussed here. In summarizing the organization of the new text, the purpose of the discussion which follows will be to consider how both the form and the content of Bourdieu's 'summa' relates to his previous work and to the work which has followed since.

Bourdieu begins Part I – 'A social critique of the judgement of taste' (which, in English, reproduces the sub-title of the book, but which, in French, is only a particular case of a proposed general social critique of 'jugement') – with

an immediate disclaimer of his own 'objectivity' and an invitation to readers
to recognize their own non-objectivity. Nevertheless, the book is not to be
taken to be a 'subjective' statement nor to be read 'subjectively'. Bourdieu
re-states his conviction that the false polarization of 'subjective' versus 'objective'
must be avoided by adopting a reflexive approach:

> There is no way out of the game of culture; and one's only chance of
> objectifying the true nature of the game is to objectify as fully as possible
> the very operations which one is obliged to use in order to achieve that
> objectification.[23]

This reminder, Bourdieu says, 'is meant for the reader as well as the
sociologist'.[24] It is a reminder for both of the inadequacy of the objectivist
position which had been criticized in *Esquisse*, but it is a reminder which is
itself inadequate. *Outline* had explored in some detail the consequences of trying
to restore to agents, in a science of practices, the immanent logic of their actions.
However sophisticated might have been Bourdieu's attempted exclusion of
presentational interference in this task of restitution, it inevitably remained
the case that, writing in Paris in the late 1970s, he was involved in constructing
the 'immanence' of actions which had taken place in Algeria in the early 1960s.
The logic of Bourdieu's developing methodological position meant that he needed
to attempt, in *La Distinction*, scientifically to re-create the practical logic which
generated the cultural behaviour of his readers. The content of *La Distinction* – the
cultural practices of contemporary, fellow French citizens – necessarily exposed
the 'objectivism' of the accounts of Algerian practical logic. Rather than pursue
the development of the science of practices to its logical extreme within the
contemporary French context, Bourdieu was prepared to suggest to readers
that they should critically use his own objectified account to make their own
objectifications, and to insist that he was eager himself to be critical, in relation
to his own social position, of the objectification that he offered for their use.
In spite of Bourdieu's reservations and qualifications, however, this suggestion
that the book had been written, and should be read, reflexively, was clearly
not able to prevent the fact of the text from having unintended consequences.
To put the issue crudely, Bourdieu had only come to terms with the problem
of the three-dimensional representation of social actions within a text which,
by definition, as a linear, intellectual offering, could occupy only a limited space
within the universe which he sought to represent. In terms of the spatial diagrams
first used in the 'Anatomie du goût' and reproduced (without transparent paper)
in *La Distinction*, the book itself would only be likely to be read by people situated
in the top left corner – as a life-style token, like the music of Boulez, of the
possession of the kind of high cultural capital associated with university professors.
In Bourdieu's own terms, the readers of the book who were invited to reflect
on their own cultural practice would be likely to be precisely those people
who would have the power to use their awareness of the mechanisms of
'distinction' to develop better strategies for preserving it. Because of the book's

likely position within the market of symbolic goods, it could not fail, therefore, to encourage a cultural voyeurism amongst the dominant classes and reinforce the cultural exclusion of non-readers. Because *La Distinction* could not possibly enable non-readers to reflect on the class disposition which ensured that they were non-readers, it could not fail to be a book about non-readers for readers.

This may seem a harsh judgement but, as will be clear from the discussion of Bourdieu's subsequent work, there is every reason to suppose that he was well aware that a text such as *La Distinction* would inevitably be politically dysfunctional and that he has taken steps to adopt personal strategies which might not be so readily self-defeating. The harshness arises from the sense which is partly suggested within the text that it was offering a consolidation of a position beyond which Bourdieu had already moved. This sense is conveyed by the concentration of much of the text on negation. Bourdieu is devastating, for instance, in opposing conventional sociological attempts to establish correlations between 'independent' and 'dependent' variables since these attempts inevitably impose a static model on those very factors which are the tokens deployed dynamically to bring about social change. For Bourdieu, conventional analyses of 'social mobility' miss the dynamics of what is actually occurring through history because they operate with an 'illusion of constancy' and suppose the 'nominal identity' of 'indicators'.[25] To take an example which, like the discussion in *La Distinction*, is reminiscent of 'Le titre et le poste' (1975), it is a fallacy to conduct an analysis of 'social mobility' on the assumption that 'being a teacher' has the 'same' social weight or meaning in 1979 as it had in 1939. The social status of a teacher is a stake within social change and not a detached indicator of it. To suppose that 'titles' or 'jobs' have constant meaning is to fall into the trap of regarding them as essences rather than constructs. This leads Bourdieu persuasively to attack forms of essentialism, such as, for instance, in the comment that 'Aristocracies are essentialist'[26] and, relatedly, to criticize the kind of artistic 'intentionalism' which he had already exposed with reference, in particular, to Sartre's reading of Flaubert. Bourdieu's discussion, therefore, is not in itself new but it is newly contexted. Consciously drawing on data acquired during the empirical research which led to the publication of *Les Héritiers* (1964) and *Un Art moyen* (1965), Bourdieu successfully re-visits that work in a way which removes the privileged social status of the educational system which had then been assumed. In the mid-1960s, the educational system had functioned as a social 'constant' in Bourdieu's cultural and sociological studies, and the discussion in the first part of *La Distinction* exposes it as such.

The positive implication of Bourdieu's negations, of course, was that accounts of social events have to be understood as representations of infinite temporal and relational variations. Following 'Anatomie du goût', this was what Parts II and III of *La Distinction* tried to demonstrate. In introducing the idea of 'social trajectory' as a way of describing the operation of the temporal dimension, Bourdieu was able to suggest that the parameters of variation between 'variables' and 'invariables' which are statically identified are functions of the potential for variation inherent in dispositions which precede that static identification. The capacity for infinite variety of any social factor is, in other words, circumscribed by the prior social conditions which generated its orientation towards the future. The concept of 'habitus' is introduced in a way which, again, is not theoretically new but which is newly exemplified. The discussion in 'The Habitus and the space of life-styles' pursues the effects of 'habitus' in areas of practice other than art where it is most obvious into practices such as food consumption or sporting activity. It is the operation of the 'habitus' which explains why tastes in food are not directly functions of income but of inherited life-style.

The insertion of the analysis of aesthetic culture into an analysis of culture understood anthropologically gradually shifts, in the consideration of eating habits and corporal bearing, into an actual anthropological analysis of contemporary French living where the distinctions in culinary taste within factions of French society are clarified with the same sort of precision as Bourdieu had shown in his minute exegesis of polythetic terminology in Kabyle practices. Whereas *Les Héritiers* had only undertaken an anthropological analysis of French students analogically – by the symbolic use of language as in the title – *La Distinction* moves to a real anthropological analysis. With the 'sens pratique' formulated in relation to Algerian phenomena in the mid-1970s now coincides the 'sens social' operative within French society. This social sense deploys signs for a practical purpose – the registering of personal distinction – in the same kind of non-referential way as does the Kabyle woman in her house:

> The social sense is guided by the system of mutually reinforcing and infinitely redundant signs of which each body is the bearer – clothing, pronunciation, bearing, posture, manners – and which, unconsciously registered, are the basis of 'antipathies' or 'sympathies' . . . [27]

These 'unconsciously registered' dispositions are transmitted pre-logically as much in modern France as in traditional Algeria. It is, therefore, in Part II of *La Distinction* – significantly entitled 'The economy of practices' – that Bourdieu's discussion comes to the brink of assimilating the strands of his Algerian anthropological studies and his French cultural studies. The unspoken and unanswered question is whether the practice of 'distinction' in differentiated societies is the same thing as the practical logic of undifferentiated societies.

Part III of *La Distinction* embellishes the account given of the homologies between life-styles and social positions offered in 'Anatomie du goût' and uses 'Les Doxosophes' to suggest that political affinity is as much a taste as fondness for kinds of food and that, equally, tastes in food are pawns in a power struggle as much as are political 'opinions'. The conclusion, finally, discusses in more detail the position on classes and classification which Bourdieu had raised in the postscript of 'Anatomie du goût', but there is a reversal. Whereas Bourdieu had there wanted to emphasize that 'class' should be thought of as a token in a historical struggle so that his three-dimensional map should not become reified, with 'class' as an 'essence', it is as if his incipient discussion of the polythetic language of 'distinction' (accentuated in the 'parlour game' offered as Appendix 4) had made him anxious to retreat from incipiently mentalist consequences. Bourdieu suddenly sees the acute danger of Berkeleyanism – of reducing 'social being to perceived being, to seeming'[28] – contained in the intellectual route on which he seemed to be embarked. As a result, he first reaffirms:

> The individual or collective classification struggles aimed at transforming the categories of perception and appreciation of the social world and, through this, the social world itself, are indeed a forgotten dimension of the class struggle.[29]

but he immediately continues:

> But one only has to realize that the classificatory schemes which underlie agents' practical relationship to their condition and the representation they have of it are themselves the product of that condition, in order to see the limits of this autonomy.[30]

In short, the argument of 'Condition de classe et position de classe' (1966) is revived to counteract the logical extreme of 'Classes et classement' (1973). Bourdieu's concluding contention is that all people of all class conditions need reflexively to consider the limits on their position-taking, and, hence, 'distinction'-making, imposed on them by their objective class conditions. The work which has followed in the 1980s has involved Bourdieu in attempting both to actualize his own position-taking in these terms as a mode of self-presentation whilst, at the same time, continuing to refine the substance of his thinking which constitutes the 'content' which his personal 'form' transmits.

· 9 ·

From practical logic to
logical practice

In the article 'Le sens pratique' – published in 1976, and in 'Anatomie du goût' – published in the same year, Bourdieu had tried to find ways of mapping social behaviour which might resolve the tensions in his analyses. 'Structuralism' had originally enabled Bourdieu to question the explanations of events provided by agents themselves (which ethnomethodology was disposed to take at face value), but it was flawed because it imposed on events the interpretative assumptions of objective observers and, relatedly, assumed that social agents acted by executing 'rules' which were hidden from them but which were, in fact, those which were disclosed by the observers. Bourdieu had sought to go beyond 'structuralism' in *Esquisse d'une théorie de la pratique* (1972) by suggesting that agents are not determined by regulating structures but, instead, have the capacity to deploy them for their strategic purposes. The intention of *Esquisse* was to show the explanatory benefits to be derived from relinquishing 'rule'-orientation in favour of acknowledging the strategic sophistication of agents, and it realized this intention principally by indicating the shortcomings of an approach which, for instance, synchronized mechanisms of exchange which only acquired their full meaning if understood as temporal strategies. The English version of *Esquisse* tried to demonstrate the advantages of the 'science of practices' more positively. It incorporated the text of 'Le sens pratique' (1976). In that article Bourdieu had discussed the limitations of the objectivist, linear representation of the social world embodied in his diagrammatic accounts of the agrarian calendar, and had, at the same time, tried to describe the peculiar features of the symbolic activity of the Kabyle which was 'pre-logical' by the standards of logical logic but was, nevertheless, informed by a practical or contextual logic which was 'polythetic' or 'polysemic'. Placed within *Outline*, it seemed as if Bourdieu was on the verge of considering the celebration of non-referential or non-signifying symbolic activity as the only remaining function for the anthropologist after the demise of objectivist structuralism. In identifying the ways in which, pre-logically, the Kabyles structured their universe by orchestrating natural phenomèna – whether of the body, of the seasons, or of the cosmos – symbolically in a manner which would seem random to cultivated logic but was meaningful in the context of their practices, Bourdieu seemed to be reaching back to the fundamental principles of the relations between human beings and the physical world. At the same time, 'Anatomie du goût' (1976) and 'Un jeu chinois' (1976) together seemed to be establishing, by juxtaposition, a similar feeling in respect of the function of 'distinction' in modern French society. 'Anatomie du goût' offered a three-dimensional model of French society which possessed a status comparable with that of the agrarian calendar of 'Le sens pratique' (1976). Even though the three-dimensional model was one in which Bourdieu tried to incorporate the notion of dynamic strategies operating, as it were, within the model, it remained the case that it was a provisional model *of* practices. It represented an idea of practice rather than practice itself. By contrast, 'Un jeu chinois' presented the findings of an enquiry which seemed to suggest that the ways in which modern French people clustered into symbolic patterns the attributes of their leading politicians, in respect of their tastes or their physical appearance and in association with the socially constructed significances of natural objects like trees, was as 'polythetic' as anything Bourdieu had observed in Algeria. It seemed possible, therefore, that the impulse to make 'distinctions' was the modern manifestation of the practical logic in operation in Kabyle society which generated, apparently randomly, series of symbolic 'couples', divisions, or oppositions.

'Le sens pratique' (1976) showed signs of Bourdieu's reading of the Pre-Socratic philosophers and of Heidegger's reading of them. There was no erosion of Bourdieu's opposition to essentialism, but his pursuit of the immanent logic of practice was certainly analogous with Heidegger's pursuit of pure being. The problem of the relationship between the science of being (ontology) and being itself was clearly analogous with the problem which Bourdieu was encountering in the mid-1970s in distinguishing between the science of practices (praxeology) which he advocated and the practice itself which he felt that he had identified and which he seemed to want to free from praxeological contamination. When, therefore, in 1975, Bourdieu attempted a sociological analysis of Heidegger's ontological philosophy, his main concern was not to 'place' Heidegger's work in its social context but, instead, to explore for his own purposes what might be the social conditions which would make possible the development of a sociology of practices rather than the 'theory of practice' he had already outlined in *Esquisse*. The title of Bourdieu's essay was very important. It was 'The political ontology of Martin Heidegger' and Bourdieu was indicating in this title that the 'form' of Heidegger's philosophizing performed a political function which shaped its content. Bourdieu proceeded to show that Heidegger's academic ontological philosophy had affinities with the 'völkisch' attitudes which had become entrenched in the common consciousness in Germany in the 1930s, but that it was, nevertheless, a philosophical formulation by which Heidegger endeavoured strategically to establish his social distinctiveness from the masses. Bourdieu's intention was to argue that a full understanding of Heidegger's work could not be gained either by ignoring the social context within which his texts had been produced or, alternatively, by suggesting that his work was nothing other than just the philosophical expression of a particular spirit of the times. Bourdieu was not being polemical in relation to debate about how texts should be read. Rather he wanted his understanding of the integral relation between 'form' and 'content' in Heidegger's work to operate as a caution in respect of his own practice.

Bourdieu realized that to imagine what Heidegger 'would have said in another form' would be to imagine an 'impossible' Heidegger.[1] It is important to follow Bourdieu's analysis of Heidegger in some detail to appreciate its reflexive implications for him – implications which were particularly pertinent as he struggled to find an appropriate 'form' for the representation of immanent practice. One of the characteristics of Heidegger's strategy, Bourdieu suggested, was that he deliberately transformed (literally, that is, put into new form) common words by seeking to invest them with a significance which was other than the practical meaning of ordinary usage. He used neologisms as well so as to separate his discourse, as sacred, from the profanity of vulgar practice. The style of writing adopted by Heidegger enabled him to establish the kind of context within which his work should be considered. It invited interpretations and commentaries which were all parts of the process of differentiation from normal discussion. In his own lifetime, Heidegger generated the sense that only certain kinds of responses to his philosophy could be legitimate and the denial, for instance, of any sociological approach to his work, is one which has remained potent to the present. It was Bourdieu's intention to challenge that particular aspect of the rejection of potential criticism which he thought was an intrinsic part of Heidegger's pre-emptive, self-authorizing strategy. Bourdieu realized that his intention involved an analysis – which he could only provide in outline – of the whole social structure of Weimar Germany and, in particular, of the place of the discipline of Philosophy within the universities and, importantly, of the place of universities and university 'mandarins' in the social system.

To summarize briefly Bourdieu's own sketch, he suggested, first of all, that social conditions in Germany between the First World War and the great depression of 1929 affected the 'vision of the social world of a whole generation of intellectuals'[2] and that it was in this context that an original 'ideological humour'[3] developed at the margins of the universities. The 'völkisch' humour gradually became a socially constructed collective consciousness which flourished within the universities so that when Heidegger sought to 'think about the social world'[4] he did so in terms which were pre-established by the writings of authors such as Karl Schmitt or Oswald Spengler. Bourdieu summarized the thinking of Spengler and showed the patterns in the thinking of the 'sub-field' of 'conservative ideologues'[5] with reference to the texts of Ernst Jünger. Bourdieu argued that Heidegger used his familiarity with the work of Jünger consciously to transform the conservative ideology which was now incorporated within society into an acceptable philosophical position. Heidegger's philosophy was the product of the socially conservative revolution of the German intellectuals between the wars, but, importantly, it was also the product of an attempt to conceal its dependence on its popular origins. Heidegger was sufficiently a master of his philosophical trade to be able to produce a 'philosophical sublimation'[6] of the popular ideas which had originally informed his thinking. Within the autonomous field of philosophical discourse, Heidegger effected a strategic victory by using Kantian arguments to defeat the dominant neo-Kantians – a strategy which Bourdieu called that of the 'distinctive re-reading', that is to say, 'the fact of thinking about texts known to everyone in a different way and of thinking something different about them'.[7]

What was it about Heidegger that enabled him to use philosophy in the way in which he did to occupy a social position? Bourdieu suggested that there was a relationship between the dispositions arising from Heidegger's peasant origins – his particular 'habitus de classe' – and the philosophical 'trade' ('métier') which he followed. Heidegger's philosophical work was a function of the social trajectory which was at his disposal and this was a specific case of the relations between the fields of philosophy and politics. Heidegger's philosophy was a token in a game by which he sustained his class position and, Bourdieu argued in conclusion, this remained the case even after his famous 'reversal' as expressed in his *Letter on Humanism*. The distinction between Heidegger I and Heidegger II was the ultimate expression of the strategy of self-authorization, whereby the post-Second World War Heidegger sustained his 'distinction' by indulging in self-interpretation and in constructing a theory of linguistic practice on the basis of his own analysis of his own previous practices.

As we have seen, Bourdieu had already made it completely clear, by 1975, that he thought that the processes here described in relation to German academic philosophy of the 1930s had been in operation within France in the post-Second World War period in the rise of 'structuralist anthropology' associated with Lévi-Strauss.[8] His own decisive break with philosophical anthropology coincided with the deliberate attempt to establish a 'science' of social phenomena and, simultaneously and necessarily, to establish a scientific institution which would not indulge in fabricating self-sustaining academic distinctions. Bourdieu's account of Heidegger's work was, therefore, an account of the systematic operation of the kind of objectivism that he had attacked theoretically in *Esquisse* (1972). After Bourdieu had lost confidence in the capacity of the educational system to become intellectually and institutionally unaligned within the French social system, he had, instead, advanced the notion that the scientificity of social enquiry might fulfil an equivalent function. In *Le Métier de sociologue* (1968) he had tried to present the sociologist as a tradesman inserted within social reality deploying its logical tools to make practical sense of it, in contrast with the trade of the philosopher, as evidenced by Heidegger, which depended on constructing an artificial discourse so as to transcend mundane social affairs.

The studies of the early 1970s were all attempts to be sociologically scientific in fields where scientific enquiry was traditionally taboo – in relation to art appreciation, religious belief or literary creativity. Bourdieu developed a schema which explained the genesis of autonomous fields and the struggles for supremacy within these fields once established, and, in 1975, he published 'La spécificité du champ scientifique et les conditions sociales du progrès de la raison' in which the schema was applied to a field – that of 'science' – where, just as in the other 'fields', it was a condition of the preservation of status and autonomy of the field that it should present itself as 'distinterested', as independent of any social existence.

In the year in which Bourdieu published 'L'ontologie politique de Martin Heidegger', therefore, he also published an article which caused him to question the autonomy or social neutrality of the sociological scientificity which, since 1968, he had placed in opposition to objectivism and intellectualism. At the very moment when he was struggling to produce a science of practices which, in an appropriate form, would express the practice of agents, Bourdieu realized, in short, that scientific discourse was itself a 'form' with its own social conditions in the same way as had been Heidegger's philosophical discourse. Significantly, 1975 was the year in which Bourdieu established and began to edit the *Actes de la recherche en sciences sociales* which was committed to research which would deliberately not try to secure status for itself by analysing only high status social issues but would be prepared to analyse strip cartoons as much as religious belief. The articles which Bourdieu published in 1975 all appeared in *Actes* rather than in established 'scientific' journals such as the *Revue française de sociologie*. 'Les catégories de l'entendement professoral' (1975) minutely analysed the terminology adopted by lecturers in marking the work of students and suggested that the terminology was a strategy designed to sustain the social distinction between teachers and learners. 'Le fétichisme de la langue' (1975) analysed the ways in which an official language sustained in French society by professors, administrators and lexicographers, systematically excluded or marginalized the ordinary usage of the majority of the population. If this essay documented the use of official language by the dominant classes to sustain their authority over the dominated classes, 'La lecture de Marx: quelques remarques critiques à propos de "Quelques remarques critiques à propos de lire *Le Capital*" ' (1975) devastatingly exposed the stylistic techniques employed by Étienne Balibar in his critique of Althusser on Marx to establish his own reputation rather than to elucidate Marxist thought – exposed, in other words, the strategies of distinction used within an academic field which is itself already strategically distinguished from the world of practice.

Although they were formally situated within Bourdieu's new journal, these articles were still discussions of, or arguments against, various 'forms' of objectivism – whether in the 'form' of official language or of academic gamesmanship – rather than themselves formal attempts to be something other than what they attacked. This was the formal context of both 'Le sens pratique'

(1976) and of 'Anatomie du goût' (1976). In the former, Bourdieu talked about the relationship between his objectivist representation of immanent practices and practices themselves, and in the latter, he experimented formally by trying to introduce a three-dimensional model into a written text in such a way that readers would be able to situate themselves within the model rather than observe it. In neither essay, however, did Bourdieu come to terms with the problem of whether the models which he superimposed on immanent practice were generally valid for all agents within his hypothesized structure or were only objective expressions of his own personal position within that same model. Bourdieu had already raised this crucial question indirectly in returning to an analysis of the work of Flaubert in 'L'invention de la vie d'artiste' (1975). His earlier reflections on Flaubert's work in 'Champ du pouvoir, champ intellectuel et habitus de classe' (1971) had concentrated on Flaubert's career – on the social trajectory of the individual author which was a matter of 'position-taking' within and between the 'structures' of the social, political and intellectual fields of mid-nineteenth-century France as constructed by Bourdieu's own objectivist social historical analysis. Bourdieu had argued that Flaubert's work and his career were mutually reinforcing strategies and that, by implication, Flaubert had devised his strategy by unconsciously inserting himself within the structuralist model of French society retrospectively created by Bourdieu over 100 years later. Flaubert had been placed analytically within a model which was not of his own making in the same way as readers of *La Distinction* (1979) were invited to locate themselves within the anatomy of taste which Bourdieu provided for their use. 'L'invention de la vie d'artiste' (1975) is an interesting turning-point in Bourdieu's thinking because he there looked at the substance of Flaubert's novel – *L'Éducation sentimentale*, published in 1869 – rather than at Flaubert's career. Flaubert had intended, as he put it, 'to write the moral history, or rather the sentimental history, of the men of my generation',[9] and, in order to do so, he had constructed a model of his society within which he had inserted 'types' as characters and within which he explored their social trajectories. Notably, he had inserted into his model a character – Frédéric Moreau – through whom he could fictively explore the parameters of his own social trajectory. Bourdieu's article challenged the facile assumption – made especially by Sartre – that the character of Frédéric was 'autobiographical'. Bourdieu argued instead that it was an extension of Flaubert's social position (as already analysed in 'Champ du pouvoir, champ intellectuel et habitus de classe') that he should seek to be unattached socially and to cast himself as an omniscient observer of social practices, particularly of the tastes and foibles of the bourgeoisie. Through the character of Frédéric, Flaubert was able to juggle with an idea of himself which was other than the self of the author capable of perceiving the fictional totality which he had created.

The reflexive significance of Bourdieu's discussion of Flaubert is evident, and it is this which makes Bourdieu's comment, in a postscript, so important. Bourdieu wrote:

Through writing Flaubert bestows on himself the gift of social ubiquity – the unreal realization of the ambition to live all lives, which itself is only an inversion of the impossibility of living, or of refusing to live, any of the lives really on offer.[10]

Taking Bourdieu's two different kinds of analysis of Flaubert together, he was saying that Flaubert's career had been dependent on the production – and marketing within a defined and prescribed field of intellectual consumption – of a literary 'form' whose content constituted a representation of French society but which derived its formal power, for Flaubert and for his readers, from the fact that it seemed to provide social involvement whilst, in fact, it was reinforcing leisured detachment. The implication for Bourdieu here is clear. There was a danger, in the mid-1970s, that he might, as an author, try to invent a logic of practice for agents, or characters, situated within a social world which was equally of his own invention, and that the 'form' of his own practice – and the market for his products – would be such that, in spite of the intention apparent in his content to restore to agents the logic of their practices, he would in fact be sustaining the detachment of himself and of his readers.

The consequences of Bourdieu's awareness of this danger were enormous in the late 1970s and his resolution of the problem in this period provides a necessary background for understanding his contemporary position. The first clue can be found in 'Questions de politique' (1977) which continued the line of enquiry which had been commenced in 'Les Doxosophes' (1972) and had also been reported in 'La production de l' idéologie dominante' (1976). Bourdieu had initially argued that political surveys construct a political 'field'. Political scientists generate a political discourse which must, in order to establish itself, deny that events and behaviours might be a-political. The strategy of generating a political discourse politically excludes those people who are not initiated into it and who have not internalized this way of thinking about their actions. The labelling of social actions as 'political' as opposed, perhaps, to 'religious' is part of the struggle for domination in the field of power. There was nothing particularly new about Bourdieu's application of his 'field' schema to politics in these articles, but, at the end of 'Questions de politique' (1977) he suggested significantly that the field of ideological production was different in kind in some important respects from the field of science:

> The field of ideological production only ever has the appearances of the autonomy of the scientific field. Political struggles do not oppose judgements of which the strongest would necessarily be the most true . . . but 'idées-forces', instruments of power which owe their particular effectiveness to the fact that they function as instruments of knowledge, of construction of the representation of the social world, whose weight depends, in relation to internal struggles, on the force which they can mobilize and demonstrate – by the mustering of the mobilized group which doubles its own force by making it visible to other groups and to itself. In short, 'idées-

forces', even when they invoke the truth of science, are never reduced, like science, to the force of their truth – the properly political force of the idea residing in the last analysis in the force of the group which it can mobilize . . .[11]

Even though 'La spécificité du champ scientifique et les conditions sociales du progrès de la raison' (1975) had exposed the extent to which the domination of scientific theories and problems should be understood as a social process, it had not challenged the assumption that natural science offered some access to objective truths which then had to be marketed within a field of scientific production and consumption. By contrast, the 'truths' of political science have no existence outside the field within which they are marketed with the result that no political theories carry any intrinsic weight or truthfulness. Bourdieu was shortly to repeat in respect of social science what he argued here in relation to political science. Bourdieu was about to suggest that the claims made by both social science and political science to be 'scientific' are really euphemized assertions of power. It was no longer possible for him to analyse political science sociologically or to suggest that political science was inadequate because it was insufficiently sociological without accepting that the identical critique had to be made of the political interventions of social scientists. Bourdieu had tried to construct the conditions within which an a-political social science of practices might flourish, but he seems to have become convinced both that the cultivation of scientific and institutional disinterest was a disguised form of political interest and also that the desire to develop a science of practices was wrongly expressed. There was a fundamental error in supposing that practices can be known or understood 'scientifically' in any way other than by living the practice of acquiring science as a practice. Bourdieu was not falling into the trap of idealizing the practice – perhaps 'primitive' – of other people, but, instead, wanting to insist on the affinities of different modes of doing in opposition to forms of detached knowing.

The passage quoted above from 'Questions de politique' (1977) indicates the main elements of Bourdieu's new thinking and acting. It is observable, analytically, that the analysis of the social world is used as a way of imposing the vision of the world preferred by social scientists. Bourdieu argued in 'Une classe objet' (1977) that

The representation of the social world is not a given or, what amounts to the same thing, a recording or a reflection, but the product of numerous acts of construction which are always already done and always to be re-done.[12]

The social scientist's representation of the social world does not dominate because of its 'truth' or because of any intrinsic scientific authority and, as a result, it is involved in a political struggle to establish its supremacy. To this end, it must take steps to establish the conditions within which its representation will be socially received as 'true' in the same way as artists have to create the conditions for the reception and appreciation of their products. This is not to say, however, that social science has to 'go commercial'. 'La production de la croyance: contribution à une économie des biens symboliques' (1977) was, ostensibly, an analysis of the art business but, by analogy, it also examined the paradoxical status of social science. In order to establish market value, art and science both have to emphasize their indifference to, or disinterest in, the market within which they are assigned value. Bourdieu argued that research which accepts the disinterestedness of the production of symbolic goods at face value or, equally, claims to expose the disinterestedness as mercenary self-interest, fails to understand the delicate balance which must be preserved within the economy of symbolic goods. As soon as science is socially perceived to be merely sponsored consultancy or merely income generation it must, at that point, lose the capacity to generate income which it derived from being thought to be 'scientific'.

It is quite clear that in this discussion of 1977 Bourdieu was reflecting on the strategy which he should adopt as a social scientist. Much of the substance of his analyses had been devoted to exposing the assumption of disinterest (in higher education teaching, for instance) because it concealed political domination, but it now seemed that those analyses were leading him to recognize that they could acquire no power or influence socially unless they were presented as the products of disinterested science. To put the paradox personally, the logic of Bourdieu's analyses of the fields of intellectual production and consumption seemed to make it inevitable that he would be able to communicate his own representation of the social world only by acting in a way which would seem to be in opposition to the purpose of the representation – by creating for himself and in himself the symbolic power which might enable him to disclose with authority the way in which he had manufactured that authority. Through 'La production de la croyance' (1977) Bourdieu was thinking about the situation of his own products within the market of symbolic goods. The article takes the perceptions reached in 'Le couturier et sa griffe' (1975) about the function of the specific hallmark or label ('griffe') in acquiring and sustaining commercial success for individual fashion houses, and applies them to the context of artistic and intellectual production. Just as established fashion houses were constantly challenged by new young designers who sought to appropriate the status of the old without destroying the hierarchy which they wished to dominate, so it might be that he, Bourdieu, might be challenging the taken-for-granted world of the dominant intellectuals by a means of production which would safely sustain what he was challenging.

In the field of intellectual production, Bourdieu's 'griffe' was becoming associated with the publishing house of Éditions de Minuit. It was significant, therefore, that Bourdieu should attempt to locate Éditions de Minuit in the field of production in comparison with the position of another house at the opposite pole of the field. Bourdieu was mastering the objective meaning of his 'griffe'. This was the kind of mastery that was necessary to ensure that his social scientific analyses would be endowed with the authority of a personal label and that, by mobilizing the collective power of the readership of the Éditions de Minuit, they would acquire the status of 'idées-forces' – able to impose themselves within the field of power rather than simply within the field of science. Although 'La production de la croyance' (1977) does not actually situate the Éditions de Minuit within a model representing the three-dimensional world of the field of publishing after the manner of 'Anatomie du goût' (1976), all the material for such a model is supplied. Whereas, however, the model which was reproduced in *La Distinction* (1979) offered Bourdieu's objectivist objectification of the social world within which readers were invited to situate themselves, the latent model of 'La production de la croyance' (1977) constitutes Bourdieu's attempt to objectify his own subjective situation.

At the same time, in 'Sur le pouvoir symbolique' (1977), it was almost as if Bourdieu was seeking to subjectify – to internalize or incorporate or, at least, to make subjectively applicable – the kind of objectivist representation of the social world which he had originally offered as science. It was as if the recognition of the social attributes of symbolic power – presented as the logical consequence of synthetically transcending the interpretative schemas of Durkheim, Weber and Marx – was no longer to be thought of as a cumulative scientific achievement but rather as itself simply a process which legitimated itself. What Bourdieu says 'objectively' of symbolic power only makes sense if it is understood that he is not offering an alternative account of symbolic systems but is, instead, using previous accounts to authorize and actualize a subjective symbolic practice. As Bourdieu wrote, this means that

> symbolic power does not reside in 'symbolic systems' in the form of an 'illocutionary force', but that it is defined in and by a determinate relationship between those who exercise this power and those who undergo it – that is to say, in the very structure of the field in which belief is produced and reproduced. What makes the power of words, the power of words to command and to order the world, is belief in the legitimacy of the words and of him who utters them, a belief which words themselves cannot produce.[13]

Bourdieu's statement here has to be taken in its form and in its content. As we shall see, Bourdieu was shortly to articulate the view that the appropriate task for the 'objective observer' of social phenomena should not be to attempt any 'participant observation' which would entail the adoption of a false subjectivity but, instead, to undertake a 'participatory objectification' which would involve making the objective subjective and the subjective objective. In 'La production de la croyance' (1977), Bourdieu had begun to situate himself within his own objectivist structure. In 'Sur le pouvoir symbolique' (1977), he had begun to subjectify the objectivist conceptual tools with which he had previously objectified observed phenomena. Formally, all that was now lacking was that Bourdieu should objectify his immanent presence – unmediated by any reference to his

own a priori, objectified model – in cultural or cognitive encounter with
something phenomenally objective which could be grasped in its own specific
subjectivity.

The content of Bourdieu's statement suggested the means by which the cross-
cultural encounter that he sought – the authentic meeting of different
authenticities – might be effected in practice. It could not be effected through
the written word which, by definition, is abstract, objective and disembodied.
It could be effected in speech where words express the whole person which
is itself a socially constructed representation of a group identity. 'L'économie
des échanges linguistiques' (1977) – which was to be the basis, and the sub-
title, of *Ce que parler veut dire* (1982) – offered the theoretical underpinning
for the elevation of speech acts over the written word which was, increasingly,
to become a significant aspect of Bourdieu's strategy to present himself as a
scientist in possession of symbolic power. Briefly, 'L'économie des échanges
linguistiques' outlines three key respects in which the sociology of language
use is superior to 'sociolinguistic' analysis. It substitutes the study of contextually
'legitimate' language for the study of 'official' or 'normalized' language; it
substitutes the notion of relations of symbolic power in place of the notion
of human 'communication' which attempts to autonomize linguistic communication without reference to the framework of power relations within which
this communication occurs; and, finally, it replaces the notion of linguistic
'competence' with the idea of symbolic capital which enables attention to be
paid to the social conditions which constitute different competences.

The articles which Bourdieu published between 1975 and 1977 seem to have
led him in two directions which can be artificially separated by distinguishing
between formal and substantive implications. One way of responding to the
work of the second half of the 1970s is to suggest that it is possible to separate
these strands analytically precisely because Bourdieu had not himself synchronised
their separate developments. He was well aware that there must be an integral
relationship between form and content, but it remained the case that the way
in which he chose to articulate that awareness was partly responsible for ensuring
that he should not actualize it in his own work. As we have seen, *Outline of
a Theory of Practice* (1977) altered the emphasis of *Esquisse d'une théorie de la
pratique* (1972). Having identified three modes of theoretical knowledge in
both works – demanding first a break from primary experience of the social
world which would enable an objectivist analysis of it and then, a second break,
this time from the objectivist analysis itself in order to liberate the possibility
of a science of the practices of agents themselves – Bourdieu had encountered,
particularly in the new parts of *Outline*, a major difficulty in trying to represent
formally the immanent practice which he thought that he had isolated
scientifically. It seemed at first that the difficulty might be removed by
experimenting with different forms of presentation within the texts, but it became
clear that the problem was much more profound. The texts themselves, as
forms, seemed to negate their contents or rather, perhaps, what Bourdieu was

wanting to express was formally censured by the field within which his texts were being produced and consumed. Bourdieu had begun to realize that the science of practices advocated in *Outline* was a refined version of objectivism. Whereas Lévi-Strauss had imposed on phenomena the universal structures to which he was personally attracted, Bourdieu realized that he had himself imposed on agents the 'liberating' view that they could themselves manipulate these structures strategically without himself relinquishing the assumption that his perception of their structures coincided with theirs. In order properly to appreciate the reciprocal relationship between structures and agents within societies, it was clear that Bourdieu had to restore the immanence of structures – to clarify that structuration, or the structuring of structures, is an aspect of the logic of practice.

The logical consequence of this development would seem to be that, in his own terms, Bourdieu's analyses were redundant. He articulated the problem fully in an aside in 'Le paradoxe du sociologue' (1977):

> I say at once that one of the fundamental problems which the theory of the perception of the social world poses is the problem of the relationship between learned and common knowledge. The act of construction – is it the fact of the learned or of the indigenous? Has the indigenous some categories of perception and from where does he gain them, and what is the relationship between the categories constructed by science and the categories which ordinary agents put into practice?[14]

As we have seen, again, *La Distinction* (1979) did not resolve the problem of the intrinsic redundancy of its own analytical model. It persisted in offering a 'scientific' model of society as if it were a true account of the structure within which all contemporary French agents would inevitably be devising their own strategies whilst, at the same time, mainly in the appendix which reproduced 'Un jeu chinois' (1976), suggesting that there might be totally different practical principles of structuration at work. It was only when Bourdieu began to articulate the view that the social scientific representation of the social world is not absolutely privileged but is only one of many possible and competing representations that he became able, as it were, to situate his own book – and himself and his publishers – within the social world which it represented. The tensions of *La Distinction* must have arisen from Bourdieu's own awareness of an uncertainty whether he was attempting to present his analysis as the 'science' which he thought it to have been when most of the research was undertaken or as the appearance of scientificity which would strengthen his symbolic power in imposing his vision of the social world on the social world.

This gloss on *La Distinction* explains, perhaps, Bourdieu's retreat, at the end of the book, from the incipient mentalism or Berkeleyanism of 'Anatomie du goût' (1976). There was clearly a danger that Bourdieu was beginning to insert his vision of the social world within a vision which was already of his own making. This was the Flaubert trap. Flaubert had projected an inauthentic self into his vision of the social world which was *L'Éducation sentimentale* and the character of Frédéric as well as the vision of the social world were both attempts on Flaubert's part to evade the social trajectory which was his inheritance. Bourdieu reaffirmed at the end of *La Distinction* that there are objective class differences which condition position-taking in society and the connected forms of distinction-making. Given Bourdieu's normal view, as expressed in 'Classes et classement' (1973), that classes have only a spurious objective existence as tokens in the classificatory dimension of the historical power struggle between dominant and dominated people, it seems likely that, self-regardingly, Bourdieu was anxious to establish that his vision of the world was not a de-contexted fantasy but, instead, the expression of his own particular position within that historical struggle.

It was simplest for Bourdieu to seem to affirm the authenticity of his vision in class terms, but, in reality, his view was that his capacity to formulate a vision of the world was a function of his personal 'habitus'. As such, it was a function of the ethos which had been his inheritance and of the symbolic power to represent that ethos which he had acquired or which had been bestowed on him. Bourdieu's vision of the social world could not, for him, be at all idiosyncratic. There was a sense in which Bourdieu had begun to internalize his own analyses in such a way that he could see himself as the delegated spokesperson for a social group sharing a similar 'habitus' who, in turn, had succeeded in using his own practical mastery of his situation to mobilize even further group support. By 1978 Bourdieu was already seeing his capacity to transform his scientific views into 'idées-forces' in terms of an inseparable combination of individual and group power. 'Sur l'objectivation participante' (1978) emphasized, in an openly reflexive manner, the view that social research is a forum for the cognitive encounters of individuals rather than for the construction of any generally valid science. 'It is by objectifying what I am', Bourdieu wrote,

> that I give myself some chance of becoming the subject of what I am; and, more, in objectifying them, I give to others the means to make themselves the subjects of what they are.[15]

but in both 'Le patronat' (1978) and 'Dialogue sur la poésie orale' (1978) – in completely different ways – Bourdieu showed that he was conscious that individuals, including himself, are never just individuals. 'Le patronat' is a detailed analysis of the economic and cultural capital possessed by a sample of major French employers. It offers a representation of the field of business which concludes the line of analysis begun in 'Les stratégies de reconversion' (1973) and 'Le titre et le poste' (1975) in a form comparable to that adopted in 'Anatomie du goût' (1976) in respect of the field of taste. Referring to the sample as of 'major French employers' highlights the particular point of the article which is of interest here. Bourdieu devoted some time in his analysis to the question whether the significance of the employers questioned in his original survey derived from their personal attributes or from the attributes of the firm which they 'represented'. He suggested that the analytical consideration of the individual social trajectories of employers was in danger of excluding from the analysis something which was itself a factor in those trajectories – namely, the symbolic power bestowed on individuals by the corporate identities or 'griffes' of the employing firms. Bourdieu's conversation with Mouloud Mammeri about oral poetry amongst the Kabyles has a similar hidden agenda. In introducing the interview, Bourdieu reflected on the common presuppositions about oral poetry – notably that

> It cannot be conceived that oral and popular poetry might be the product of learned research, as much in form as in content. It cannot be admitted that they might be made to be spoken in front of a public – and a public of ordinary people, and to enclose an esoteric meaning – destined to be meditated and commented on.[16]

This statement could be transposed slightly to read as Bourdieu's ideal for his own practice. Increasingly, his own project was that he should offer oral sociology which would be 'the product of learned research, as much in form as in content'. Bourdieu asked leading questions of Mammeri, but the nature of these questions and the answers which they secured both show the way in which Bourdieu was thinking about the process of acquiring social authority whilst, at the same time, mobilizing the authority derived from Kabyle practice to reinforce his own intentions. Three exchanges are particularly important. Bourdieu asked Mammeri how he acquired the 'tamusni' (philosophy) which was the traditional property of the 'imusnawen' (sages, poets) and Mammeri replied that

> Apprenticeship was an apprenticeship by practice. It wasn't an abstract apprenticeship. It was necessary to act in conformity with a certain number of precepts, values, without which the tamusni is nothing. A tamusni which one does not take on oneself, which one does not live, is only a code. The tamusni is an art, and an art of living, that is a practice which is learnt by practice and which has practical functions. The productions which it allows, – poems, sentences are not art for art's sake, even if their form, sometimes very recherché, very refined, makes you think so.[17]

Speaking in the present tense, Bourdieu then asks how the sage exercises his expertise. Does his practical function, for instance, involve him in knowing about the boundaries of fields or about the agrarian calendar? Replying in the past tense, Mammeri says:

> Absolutely: he was deemed to know all that better than others; he knew how jobs were distributed during the twelve months of the year, what needed to happen before, after, how one made grafts etc.[18]

Thirdly, Mammeri comments, in concluding, that

One of the names for poetry in Kabyle . . . is 'asefru' (plural, 'isefra') which
comes from 'fru' – to elucidate, clarify something which is obscure. . . .

and Bourdieu comments:

'Fru' – that's to winnow grain as well isn't it?
The poet would thus be he who knows how to distinguish and to make
distinct: he who, by his discernment, effects a diacrisis, separates the things
which are ordinarily confused?

– an interpretation which Mammeri does not deny but which he only endorses
by reiterating his own terminology:

He who elucidates obscure things. . . .
The poet is he who mobilizes the people; he is the one who
enlightens them.[19]

In the first passage, the implication for Bourdieu is that the ideal scientific
practice is a lived practice. It is the product of an apprenticeship which is in
effect a socialization within the ethos of the group which then benefits from
the practical expertise. The second passage discloses that the sage who has
been socially created by and for the group is then the person who possessses
the mastery of the group's agrarian calendar. He is, in other words, the person
within the group who possesses the knowledge of the immanent structure which
was appropriated by Bourdieu's objectivist knowledge in his account of the
agrarian calendar in 'Le sens pratique' (1976) and, again, in *Outline*. Taken
together, these two passages suggest the framework of *Le Sens pratique* (1980)
in which Bourdieu tried to draw together his recent thinking in the form of
a revision of his earlier Algerian work. Bourdieu also explicitly stated that *Le
Sens pratique* (1980) attempted to go beyond both *Esquisse* (remembering, of
course, that *Outline* had no place in the French field of reception) and *La Distinction*
(1979). The third passage from 'Dialogue sur la poésie orale en Kabylie' suggests
how this might be the case. Bourdieu was trying to convey the possibility that
the function of the practical sage – a position to which he was aspiring – might
be seen in terms of making distinctions by which the distinctions made by
others are clarified. This would vindicate *La Distinction* as practice. If Mammeri
was agreeing by embellishing Bourdieu's point, then the further and final argument
of the interview was that the efficacy of the practice of the sage was the result
of the exercise of symbolic power in simultaneously enlightening and mobilizing
the people.

The clarity of *Le Sens pratique* (1980) must be a function of the development
of Bourdieu's thinking in respect of his formal self-presentation which we have
observed in articles pre-dating the appearance of this new 'summa'. In *Esquisse*
(1972), Bourdieu had wanted to look again at his earlier Algerian researches
by capturing the process within which they were undertaken, but, instead,
he had announced the theoretical basis of an anti-structuralist mode of knowledge
and had reinterpreted his past work as a way of celebrating the explanatory
gains secured by making the second break – from objectivist as well as from

primary knowledge of the social world. In *Esquisse*, Bourdieu had talked about the need to analyse objectivism objectively, but he only exposed the inadequacies of structuralist objectivism and was not willing to explore the objective conditions in which his own objectivism had emerged. It was as if he had not had sufficient confidence that his own analyses would survive the self-exposure which he knew to be necessary. By contrast, Bourdieu had become sure enough, by 1980, of a symbolic power based upon his accumulated symbolic capital to be able to lay bare the procedures by which that accumulation was achieved. In a lucidly narrated preface, Bourdieu sketches a sociology of his own Algerian research and of his subsequent interpretations of it in a way which is reminiscent of the social history of the relations between French philosophy and sociology which he had written in 1967. Whereas the second edition of *Sociologie de l'Algérie* (1961) had largely suppressed the references to secondary authors who had been mentioned in the first edition, the preface to *Le Sens pratique* provides fascinating detail of the prevailing intellectual climate which caused Bourdieu to make use of the work of, for instance, Jacques Berque in the late 1950s.[20]

The preface functions in two ways. Bourdieu offers his own account of his intellectual development from 1958 to 1980 and, in doing so, confirms the interpretation of his work offered in this chapter. He writes, for instance, that

> It took me a long time to understand that it is not possible to grasp the logic of practice except through constructions which destroy it. . . . I never thought of moving from a critical analysis of the social and technical conditions of objectification to a 'radical' critique of all objectification and, through that, of science itself . . .[21]

At the same time, this brief critical intellectual autobiography is not an end in itself. Bourdieu's intention is to objectify the personal tradition which, in the historical or temporal dimension, has cumulatively constituted the subjectivity which now confronts those of his own old texts and notes which, in the absence of renewed fieldwork, constitute his main means of access to the objective phenomena of Algerian society. The climax of Bourdieu's account of his development is his contention that he now sees that the traditional difficulty of anthropology in seeking to understand other cultures, in seeking, as he had, to observe a foreign culture without imposing on it the assumptions of the indigenous, observing culture, is nothing other than a particular case of the relationship between knowing and doing, knowers and doers, which obtains within every culture. Bourdieu suggests that he would not have come to realize this so readily had he not himself been in touch with the peasants of the Béarn – a lived contact which had enabled him to make connections between the practices of people in Kabylia and the Béarn as well as between these and the practices about which he had read, as an academic, in the work of Plato and Montesquieu.

In so far as *Outline* had begun to celebrate primitive practice and, by extension, to disown any theoretical perception of practice, Bourdieu retreats from that self-denying ordinance in *Le Sens pratique* (1980). The first part of the book – a critique of theoretical reason – states explicitly that the intention of reflecting critically on the limits of learned understanding is 'completely alien to the intention of rehabilitation which has corrupted most of the discourses on practice'.[22] This first part offers a coherent account of the personal philosophy which is the basis of his authentic confrontation, as a knowing doer, with all forms of doing. The problem of the text is that so much of Bourdieu's indigenous stance is already constituted from the earlier interpretations of the strange culture with which he wants to confront it. *Le Sens pratique* (1980) wants to prescribe an encounter between subjective and objective or indigenous and foreign and to offer itself as a paradigmatic socio-analytical[23] confrontation, but Bourdieu is trying to illustrate an ideal interaction on the basis of 'opposed' positions which are already the product of 20 years of reciprocal modification within his mind. In his own terms, Bourdieu was trying to demonstrate his ideal *modus operandi* by artificially de-constructing the *opus operatum* which had hitherto been his life's work.

Book I has chapters which discuss the objectivizing of the objectivated; the imaginary anthropology of subjectivism; structures, 'habitus', practices; belief and the body; the logic of practice; the action of time; symbolic capital; and the objectivity of the subjective. Many of these titles are familiar. The discussions revise arguments which, in *Esquisse* or *Outline*, had been interpretations of Kabyle practices. Here, however, they are presented polemically as accounts of Bourdieu's own position. The notion of 'habitus', for instance, is used in the second chapter directly to oppose the 'rational action' views attributed to Jon Elster.[24] Through his subjective engagement with the objectivity of Kabyle society, in other words, Bourdieu has already achieved the reconciliation of opposites which, for him, has become the social purpose of social research.

There is, therefore, something slightly artificial about the supposed attention, in Book II, to the 'practical logics' of the culturally 'other'. Chapter 1 is a re-working of 'Les stratégies matrimoniales dans le système de la reproduction' (1972) and Chapter 2 re-works the third of the studies which had constituted Part I of *Esquisse* (1972) – 'Stratégie et rituel dans le mariage kabyle'. In both cases, Bourdieu's intention is to show that there were processes of structuration which were intrinsic to the practices which had earlier been thought to be strategic only in the context of an objectively imposed structure. Just as he now saw that social scientists were engaged, in their own worlds, in a struggle to impose their preferred structural model on that world, so Bourdieu contended that in the world of Algerian practice there was a struggle for domination in which the structure within which strategies were adopted was itself a token in the struggle. Chapter 3 was a re-working of the original article entitled 'Le sens pratique' of 1976, and it illustrates the general thesis of the second Part of *Le Sens pratique* (1980). As has been suggested already, Bourdieu realized that there were within Algerian society people who possessed the socially delegated authority to retain intellectual mastery over the agrarian calendar which constituted the structure within which social practices operated. His article had extrapolated an objectivist agrarian calendar. In 1976 Bourdieu had appreciated that his model was an artificial construction imposed upon immanent practices, but he had not acknowledged that a proper analysis of the Algerian situation would oblige him to analyse the ways in which the supremacy of one calendar over another within that situation was the product of a struggle between different groups seeking to establish their domination. Whereas 'Le sens pratique' (1976) had focused on the polythetic practices of the peasants and on the extent to which ritual practices could, as practices, over-rule logical logic, Bourdieu's analysis of 1980 was interested in the ways in which there were gradations of 'official' or 'unofficial' rituals which were indicative of gradations of symbolic power. Institutionalized rituals excluded the polythetic practices of individuals and functioned as mechanisms of domination.

In presenting *Le Sens pratique* (1980) in two parts, Bourdieu wanted to exemplify a socio-analytical encounter between indigenous and foreign worlds which would engender a more authentic subjectivity in both parties. The truth is, of course, that the two parts were two ways of saying the same thing, which is to say that both parts were the product of the socio-analysis which Bourdieu had already achieved rather than the raw materials which would enable it to occur. Bourdieu had already constructed his symbolic personality from out of his encounters with the otherness of the Kabyles, and it was now time for him to present that personality socio-analytically within 'real' social situations experienced in France. It is significant, therefore, that Bourdieu published *Questions de sociologie* in the same year as *Le Sens pratique* – 1980.

The cover of the first French edition of *La Distinction* (1979) showed a photograph of a Rembrandt-like picture of a gourmet,[25] whilst the cover of *Le Sens pratique* (1980) used a photograph – probably taken by Bourdieu himself – of an Algerian peasant hoeing the earth. By contrast with both of these visual messages, that of the cover photograph of *Questions de Sociologie* (1980) was significantly different. It was a photograph of Bourdieu sitting behind his office desk and gesticulating earnestly – obviously speaking. The ambiguity of the title was also important. It heralds a book which is about sociological questions but, even more, a book which asks questions of sociology – and expects answers from it. In this sense, Bourdieu was clearly offering himself as a spokesman for sociology, as a sociological respondent to the social problems experienced by other members of society. Bourdieu is dressed informally in the photograph. There is no evidence of the forms of authority – of academic robes, for instance – but he is sitting behind a desk and manifestly has things to say. The book assembled 21 talks or formal interviews which Bourdieu had given mainly in the last few years of the 1970s. There is no space here to go into any detail about the particular arguments advanced in each of the pieces, but only to spell out the formal significance of this new kind of text. First of all, the published contributions try to capture the force of the spoken word. Sometimes explicitly and almost always implicitly, Bourdieu tries to characterize the audience to whom he is speaking, whether trade unionists or teachers, or the person with whom he is conducting a dialogue. Analysis could unravel the specific detail of Bourdieu's polythetic practice in adjusting his message to his conception of its likely reception. Such an analysis would demonstrate that he was now doing what he had said should be done. He does not talk about symbolic power in this selection because it represents him as exercising it. He does talk about the need for the sociologist to be, on the one hand, not 'hors jeu'[26] – outside the game – as a detached intellectual and, on the other, not journalistic – peddling to the latest and most fashionable social self-perceptions. Whereas, presumably, it had been Bourdieu's reputation which had caused him to be invited to speak and to be listened to, such that the speaking situations had themselves been both recognitions and reinforcements of his symbolic power, nevertheless the printed text seems to insist on the scientific basis for his authority. Each transcript of the spoken words concludes with a footnote which refers the reader to the most relevant of Bourdieu's detailed discussions of the issue about which he had been speaking. It was by referring back explicitly to the scientific source of his authority that Bourdieu sustained in writing what his audiences had taken for granted – that he was not just a human speaking to others but a man of science speaking scientifically. Bourdieu's main problem during the 1980s has been to sustain his symbolic power whilst simultaneously undermining the scientificity on which it was originally founded. Some would say that he has tied the noose around his own neck and kicked away the stool from beneath his feet.

Scientifically speaking

In his Introduction to *Ce que parler veut dire* (1982) Bourdieu admits that he had at one time undertaken a scholarly piece of work – 'fortunately never published'[1] – in which he had tried to establish a 'general theory of culture'[2] on the basis of a methodical reading of Saussure's *Cours de linguistique générale*. Bourdieu whimsically suggests that this peccadillo brought home to him the danger of thinking from other people's thoughts, of accepting other people's problematics. This procedural lesson and Bourdieu's substantial disquiet about Saussure's linguistic theory were mutually reinforcing. Saussure had generated a discourse about language which supposed a separation of extraneous from internal influences on language use and his sociolinguistic discourse was a manifestation of just such an autonomous language. By attempting to start from Saussure's position, Bourdieu had been doubly denying language as practice. His inclination had been to use Saussure's work as a building block for himself – an arid form of borrowing which was made worse by the way in which Saussure's views had already imposed a framework of thinking in relation to language. Nevertheless, Bourdieu continues, the popularity of these views could not be an excuse for ignoring them:

> the work of Saussure, and then, at the moment when I realized the inadequacy of the model of the word (and of practice) as execution, that of Chomsky – who recognized the part of generative dispositions – both appeared to pose fundamental questions to sociology.[3]

Bourdieu does not give any date for his theoretical enterprise, but the first detailed reference to the work of Saussure in his texts appears in the second part of *Esquisse d'une théorie de la pratique* (1972). There, the inadequacy of Saussure's linguistics was briefly sketched in a digression which was designed to reinforce the case against the 'objectivism' of structuralist anthropology. Saussurian linguistics was described as the 'terrain par excellence'[4] of objectivism because it had created the idea of a 'langue' which had autonomous existence and regulated the ways in which words ('paroles') might be used, in exactly the same way as structuralism had created the idea of regulative social structures. Bourdieu's critique of Saussure was, therefore, a key element in his attack on philosophical structuralism and in his associated attempt to liberate practices from false impositions. By the time of *Outline of a Theory of Practice* (1977), the passage criticizing Saussure in *Esquisse* is extended to give consideration to Chomsky's theories. It is easy to see why Bourdieu might have been attracted to Chomsky's notion of a generative grammar. There was a sense in which Chomsky could be said to be attempting to give an account of immanent linguistic practice. The fundamental difficulty for Bourdieu, of course, was that Chomsky's immanence was a neuro-physiological immanence which might be regarded as essentialist or universalistic. The passage in *Outline* does not consider closely the relationship between Chomsky's 'innate' generative principles and the socially constructed and transmitted generative principle which Bourdieu was calling the 'habitus'. Instead, Bourdieu drew attention to the terminological looseness of descriptive words such as 'rules', 'norms' and 'schemes' and implied, with the assistance of a telling quotation from Wittgenstein, that all these terms were indicative of the separation of the theory or science of practice from practice itself.[5]

Ce que parler veut dire (1982) is mainly composed of pieces written by Bourdieu in the second half of the 1970s. It reinforces the understanding achieved by Bourdieu in an anthropological article such as 'Le sens pratique' (1976) that practices have to be analysed socio-logically rather than within the framework of a theory of practice. In the particular case of sociolinguistics, language practice has to be analysed in itself rather than within a pre-defined framework which has constructed a segregation between 'langue' and 'parole'. A proper sociology of language has to be saved from the falsifying effects of sociolinguistic theory. The book is divided into three parts. The first part – 'The economy of linguistic exchanges' – is dated at the summer of 1980, but it embellishes the form of the argument already presented in the article of the same title which had been published in 1977. Bourdieu does not want to deny the value of the linguistic analysis of linguistic codes, but he insists that languages should be seen as symbolic commodities in exactly the same way as, in 'Le marché des biens symboliques' (1971), he had insisted that works of art should be understood as products within a field of marketing and consumption. The language which we use involves the adjustment of the linguistic practices which we inherit from our background (our linguistic 'habitus') to suit the needs of the different contexts which constitute the market for our linguistic products. Language is powerful in itself. The competing visions of the world of sociologists or of political scientists are imposed through the medium of language but, more fundamentally, they are to be regarded as linguistic impositions. Precisely because language is non-referential, it has the capacity to create existences rather than to represent them. 'Representations' are intrinsically potent because nothing 'real' is represented. It follows that

Bourdieu's sociological analysis of languages is inseparable from a political consideration of the contexts and circumstances in which they are produced and prevail. His account of the production and reproduction of a 'legitimate language' in France, for instance, necessarily involves a short social history of the way in which the standardization of language use was an integral part, first of all, of the political strategy of the revolutionaries in seeking to dismantle the thought processes associated with the Ancien Régime and, secondly, of the bureaucratization which, by the end of the nineteenth century, had established a modern, secular State. Language use is a crucial element in the construction of group identities and, therefore, the struggle for linguistic dominance is a particular, and important, manifestation of the struggle for ideological and political domination. Debates about the value of learning Latin, it follows, are not debates about the intrinsic worth of the language but, instead, about the value to society of those people who sustain their social distinction by maintaining a closed shop of classicists.

This general discussion is followed, in Part II, by a collection of essays assembled under the title of 'Language and symbolic power'. The four chapters are entitled 'Authorized language', 'The rites of institution', 'The force of representation', and 'Describing and prescribing'. The first is 'Le langage autorisé' of 1975 whilst the second and the fourth appeared in *Actes* in 1982 and 1981 respectively. Since 'The force of representation' appears for the first time in this text, it is clear that the ideas of this part carry Bourdieu's thinking beyond the themes of 'The economy of symbolic exchanges'. The way it does so is evident in the titles. There is a concentrated interest in the political power of 'naming', in instituting by naming, in prescribing, regulating or controlling by describing or representing. As Bourdieu puts it in the short introduction:

> Social science does business with realities which are already named, already classed . . . it must take as its object the social operations of nomination and the rites of institution through which they are accomplished. But, more profoundly, it must examine the part which words play in the construction of social things; and the contribution which the classificatory struggle – the dimension of every class struggle – brings to the constitution of classes, and not just classes of age or sex or social class but also clans, tribes, ethnic groups or nations.[6]

The way in which this is phrased partly goes right back to 'Classes et classement' (1973), but there is an important difference. Whereas Bourdieu had been wrestling in the early article with the theoretical problem of the relationship between the classifications which people make and the status of the objective existence of social classes, he is here much more concerned about the processes by which all kinds of classifications secure 'objective' status. Bourdieu is here interested practically in the relationship between social perceptions and social reifications, in the political processes of symbolic power which construct the social and political units within which we tangibly live. In short, Bourdieu is interested in institutions.

This development in Bourdieu's thinking was already pre-figured in an article which was published in *Actes* in 1979: 'Les trois états du capital culturel'. Reflecting on the research which had led to the publication of *Les Héritiers* (1964), Bourdieu argues that the notion of 'cultural capital' which he had used at that time had been necessary to differentiate his position from those of both the educational psychologists and the 'human capital' economists. Although he does not explicitly say so, however, it is clear that 'cultural capital' was not wholly satisfactory because it was individualistic. The research of the early 1960s had tried to gauge the level of cultural capital possessed by students in terms, first of all, of the legacy of parental and family influence, and, secondly, in terms of their access to acquired cultural goods – whether pictures or films or records. It had tried to define cultural capital only in relation to the first two of the three states which Bourdieu now articulates. It had explored the incorporated state and the objectified state of student cultural capital, but it had not examined the 'institutionalized' state. This should have been regarded as a discrete state of cultural capital because

> as can be seen in relation to scholastic titles, it confers on the cultural capital which it is supposed to guarantee some completely original properties.[7]

La Distinction (1979) can be seen as a book which tried to document the ways in which all objects are labelled or named 'aesthetically' or in terms of 'taste'. It tried to show that the labelling which occurs within society is arbitrary by reference to any idealized criteria of pure judgement. The purpose of the labelling is to objectify status and social distinction. By illustrating the ways in which different social classes endeavoured to establish socially recognized indicators of their social distinction, *La Distinction* did, in effect, show that some groups in society try to transform, or renounce, the incorporated state of cultural capital which is their inheritance by deliberately adopting the styles of alternative, objectified states. The assumption of *La Distinction*, however, seemed to be that the temporal changes which Bourdieu tried to introduce into his structural model still depended on a manipulation of cultural objectifications. The social trajectories of agents through time seemed to be actualized by reference to the reconversion of the cultural weighting of objects. There was the sense that individuals might appropriate objects for their distinction-making purposes with infinite randomness – subject only to the control exercised by the parameters established by their particular cultural inheritance. By contrast, the second chapter of the second part of *Ce que parler veut dire* (1982) – 'The rites of insti- tution' – suggests that the process of making institutions is precisely a process of giving temporal permanence to distinctions in such a way that individuals are then seen to be doubly constrained in their choice of personal trajectory – by the ethos to which they were first habituated in the family and by the insti- tutionalized processes of socialization which they might have experienced.

Bourdieu suggests that Van Gennep's naming of the phenomenon of the 'rite de passage' may have concealed the possibility that such a rite is not just excluding people who will eventually be allowed to pass but is, more importantly, excluding those who will never pass. The rite may be a process which, superficially, controls the public transition from infancy to maturity whilst, in fact, it makes the more fundamental selection between those who will and those who will not ever make the transition at all. In this interpretation, the rite consecrates a process of social separation rather than one of general social mobility.

The substance of the chapter cross-refers to 'Épreuve scolaire et consécration sociale' which was published in *Actes* in 1981. This article offers an analysis of the élitist secondary schools (the 'classes préparatoires') which feed into the 'grandes écoles' within the French educational system. It is clear, therefore, that Bourdieu was saying that the educational system which he had originally hoped would offer a 'rite de passage' within society for all pupils from any class background actually offered only a framework for institutionally consolidating distinctions between groups. The power of institutions, therefore, is double-edged. Institutional solidarity can perpetuate social exclusion beyond the life-span of individuals but, equally, institutional power can be harnessed by individuals in order to strengthen their personal symbolic power. The third part of *Ce que parler veut dire* offers some analyses of discourses which explore the nature of the meaning which is superadded by their formal contexts. The first chapter uses much of the material of the linguistic discussion contained in 'L'ontologie politique de Martin Heidegger' (1975), and the second reproduces Bourdieu's critique of Balibar's critique of Althusser – also of 1975, but the third chapter reproduces a more recent article. 'Le Nord et le Midi. Contribution à une analyse de l'effet Montesquieu' had appeared in *Actes* in 1980 and now appears under the more general title of 'The rhetoric of scientificity'. It analyses the way in which Montesquieu's speculation about the relationship between national or regional characteristics and climate acquired a constituting mythical coherence by deploying the apparatus of science in its support. In the name of science, Montesquieu succeeded in constructing an institutionalized distinction between the regions of the north and the south – the French anticipation of the comparably potent north–south divide perceived in Europe and the world.

The ambivalent effects of institutional power of which Bourdieu was intellectually aware were forcibly actualized for him in 1982 when he was appointed to the Chair of Sociology at the Collège de France. In 1975 he had written an article – 'Les catégories de l'entendement professoral' – in which, in a manner typical of the work of that date, he had presented a taxonomy of the binary judgements used by professors in marking the work submitted by students. The second part of that article had further shown that the attitudes of professors were expressions of their particular group identity and that these could readily be traced back to their common educational 'alma mater'. Bourdieu had illustrated this point by analysing some obituaries presented in the annual report of the alumnus organization of the École Normale Supérieure. These celebrated and reinforced 'normalien' values which, Bourdieu argued, were the consequences of the shared social position of the professors constituting 'a sort of upper petty bourgeoisie committed to an ethical and intellectual aristocratism'.[8] The article made no explicit reference to the fact that Bourdieu was himself a 'normalien' and it continued to argue that the only people who manage to escape from the anomaly of the normalien's combined social and intellectual hierarchical status are those who 'realize the proclaimed ideal of intellectual excellence, but by moving outside the university field (or settling in "free territories" inside it like the Collège de France)'.[9]

Bourdieu's career can be seen as a quest for an occupational 'free territory' within a territory. This was so in Algeria. Whilst conducting his Algerian fieldwork, he sometimes was obliged to find politically 'neutral' accommodation in monasteries – to find there a kind of sanctuary. It was so in the Béarn undertaking sociological research in his native territory and it was so in the 1960s as he endeavoured to carry out educational research on his own students and with their assistance. He had, perhaps, idealized the institutional neutrality of the higher education system within which he was a teacher and, as a result, he had tried to construct his own free territory in the form of a research group in the Centre de Sociologie Européenne which was somehow in, but not of, that higher education system. 'Les catégories de l'entendement professoral' (1975) showed that Bourdieu was objectively aware both that the Collège de France possessed an objective institutional meaning which already represented what he had tried to create in 1967 and – which may amount to the same thing – that an identification of his personal identity with the public identity of that institution was the likely culmination of his social trajectory. In 1982, therefore, Bourdieu demonstrated how prescriptive had been his description of 1975.

It is not just that in 1982 Bourdieu was appointed to a new post. In the terminology of his own 'Le titre et le poste' (1975), Bourdieu had now acquired a 'title'. Several related emphases which follow from this development have characterized the work which he has subsequently produced. In *Questions de sociologie* (1980), Bourdieu presented himself as personally a man of authority speaking with authority. In so far as support for that authority was mobilized, the collection of texts, interviews, speeches and conference interventions seemed to suggest that it derived from the scientificity of Bourdieu's previous work – from the fact that he was known to be a reputable sociologist. Bourdieu has sustained the mode of formal presentation of *Questions de sociologie* (1980) – the written transcription of acts of speaking – in *Choses dites* (1987) but, as we shall see, the position from which the 'things said' are delivered has changed. From his appointment to the Chair at the Collège de France, Bourdieu's personal authority and the authority derived from his institutional position were mutually reinforcing. His symbolic power was now to be augmented by institutional power, but the anomaly was that, in the first place, his personal power was based on scientific activity which had been involved in exposing the functions of institutions in establishing social distinction and exclusion. By *Le Sens pratique* (1980) Bourdieu had lost faith in the intrinsic force of science and, as we have seen, had concluded that the only stance which was now appropriate for social science researchers was to be true to the scientists they had become and to reflect on the social processes which had generated their 'scientific' identities. Bourdieu's difficulty was that the logic of his philosophy of science was that he should use scientificity as simply formal ammunition in the struggle to impose his vision of the social world, whilst the substance of that science itself – now, perhaps, discredited as science – explored the social conditions which had generated the individuals and institutions which could adopt such a self-destructive philosophy of science. Rather than see this as a circularity, it is perhaps better to think of Bourdieu as operating simultaneously in intellectual worlds where science is differently defined and esteemed. In one perspective, *Homo academicus* (1984) and *La Noblesse d'état* (1989) have offered scientific accounts of the faculties and 'grandes écoles' of the French higher education system respectively in both of which Bourdieu has partly objectified his own subjective presence so as to refine their scientificity. In another perspective, both texts derive their power not from the refinement of their scientific content but from their presence as symbolic goods representing the personal/institutional power of Bourdieu/Collège de France within the field of contemporary intellectual exchange. The symbolic power of the texts seems to be dependent on the validity of their scientific content – not because scientific validity guarantees symbolic power but rather because the content describes and prescribes a vision of the social world within which the texts must possess power.

To put the matter less abstractly, Bourdieu was conscious in 1982 that the challenge of his new appointment would be to use his new authority to analyse the social conditions of that authority in such a way as to clarify how particular forms of authority are available to everyone. This was the challenge he took up straight away in the inaugural lecture delivered on 23 April 1982, which was published as *Leçon sur la leçon* (1982). It is easy to imagine the scene in the Collège de France – probably in one of the lecture halls presided over by busts of the great intellectuals or scientists of the third republic. Transpose the scene to any formal academic ceremony in almost any academic community to get a diminished sense of the weight of austere tradition which Bourdieu must have experienced as he began:

One ought to be able to give a lecture, even an inaugural one, without asking oneself with what right one does so. The institution exists to avoid this question and to remove the anxiety linked with the arbitrariness which comes to mind again when making a start. A rite of admission and of investiture, the inaugural lecture, the inceptio, symbolically realizes the act of delegation in terms of which the new master is authorised to speak with authority and which establishes his word as legitimate discourse, pronounced by someone possessing the right to do so. The properly magical effectiveness of the ritual rests on the silent and invisible exchange between the new entrant, who publicly offers his word, and the assembled clever men who attest by their presence in a body that this word should become universally acceptable, that is to say, in a literal sense, masterly, by virtue of being received in this way by the most eminent masters.[10]

The ambivalence of Bourdieu's total intellectual position is here in microcosm. He first insists that educational institutions exist so as to remove the need for individual lecturers to have to justify constantly their personal authority. Inaugural lectures exist to ensure that the whole academic community accepts that the individual is worthy to receive the community's delegated authority. They are ritual processes which ensure that the authority which is afterwards assumed has been explicitly and consciously bestowed. Bourdieu began his lecture by making sure that his audience were aware of the formal social function of their presence – that they were there to authorize his future words and work by receiving his present words. By describing to his audience the underlying social purpose of their presence, Bourdieu was articulating what might otherwise have been unthought and, in doing so, he was prescribing his own institution. Much of *Leçon sur la leçon* is a defence of sociology. It reads almost as if Bourdieu was conscious that many in his audience would regard social science as inferior science, but, quite apart from the substantial discussion contained within the lecture, the important microcosmic point is that Bourdieu pre-emptively imposed a vision of the situation in the lecture hall which would ensure that his authority would be endorsed whatever he might say.

The substantial argument of *Leçon sur la leçon* followed the main contention of *Le Métier de sociologue* (1968) – that the sociology of science is the means to securing an epistemological and social criticism of all science. Bourdieu was quick to point out, however, that although this critical stance may be the product of changes to the educational system which had once assumed that it could enclose and contain all knowledge, it did not imply that he thought that society could be de-institutionalized. The essence of Bourdieu's argument was, indeed, that institutions – such as the Collège de France itself – needed to achieve or revive authority precisely because it could no longer be assumed. Scientific self-criticism is, for Bourdieu, the most certain way to ensure that institutions and individuals only operate with an authority which is socially legitimate and are, therefore, restrained from the temptation to acquire a 'sovereign vision'[11] and a sovereign control over the social world. Drawing on his recent articles, Bourdieu argued that the construction of 'regions' was an example of just such an exercise of prescriptive control operating as a form of 'censorship'.[12] The exposure of the social world as the locus of struggles amongst different factions to impose a dominant vision of that world does, Bourdieu admits, bring about a certain 'disenchantment' by revealing the social and political forces in operation beneath 'science' but, in a powerful comment, Bourdieu says that those who deplore the revelation of the power interests of science achieved by the sociology of science have as little grounds for doing so as 'those who reproached Galileo for having discouraged the dream of flight by constructing the law of falling bodies'.[13] So far from discouraging flight, it could be said that Galileo's act of disenchantment was the precondition for the realization of the dream. In just the same way, the act of de-mystifying scientific attitudes which have become culturally pretentious and imperialistic by association with socially dominant groups and institutions should be the precondition for the fruitful exercise of proper scientific practice. It is not surprising that sociology is unpopular because everyone has a stake in maintaining the mystery of their positions, in sustaining the denial which, by definition, sociology must deny – that intellectual positions do not have absolute value but derive their meanings only within a network of social and political relations. Sociology threatens the established order not because it is subversive within the established order but because it introduces the possibility of exploding the fictitiously ordered network of relations by which the dominant classes sustain their domination. It is not a licensed maverick which, in fact, upholds what it challenges. It offers some scope for freedom because it acknowledges that everything, without exception, is socially determined. It was in expressing his conviction that a liberty which might not be false is only attainable if social determinism is relentlessly recognized that Bourdieu brought his lecture to a conclusion by returning to his opening statement. The deliberate exposure of the nature of the situation within which he was lecturing was an exemplification of the broader social function of the sociologist. By making explicit that his authority was being socially determined as he spoke, he had run the risk that his authority might, as a consequence, be rejected because it had become disenchanted. Taking Bourdieu's action at face value and in the terms in which he presented it, he had provided a perception of the situation which might have enabled any participant in it to have rejected the magical web in which everyone seemed to be enmeshed. He had introduced the means to overturn the mutually reinforcing network of relations in which all the participants were participating and had endangered the consensus upon which the institution was itself dependent – 'the belief which is the usual condition for the happy functioning of the institution'.[14] He had threatened the institution in the same way as sociology threatens the social consensus which is society, but he had done this for the institution to give its institutional freedom a sure foundation and, by extension, to enable his practice as a sociologist of the institution to manufacture opportunities for freedom within society by threatening its self-perceptions. As Bourdieu concluded:

> There is no sociologist who would take the risk of destroying the thin veil of faith or bad faith which generates all the charm of institutional pieties, if he did not have faith in the possibility and the necessity of universalizing the liberty in relation to the institution which sociology procures; if he did not believe in the liberating virtues of what is doubtless the least illegitimate of the symbolic powers, that of science, especially when it takes the form

of a science of symbolic powers which is capable of restoring to all social subjects the mastery over the false transcendencies which misrecognition does not cease to create and recreate.[15]

In this eloquently expressed credo, Bourdieu makes the link between *Le Sens pratique* (1980) in which he had advocated the liberation of practice from theory and the two major publications which have followed his appointment to the Chair at the Collège de France – *Homo academicus* (1984) and *La Noblesse d'état* (1989). By outlining the social conditions which create the educational institutions which socially condition our thinking, Bourdieu has tried, both reflexively and objectively, to create the conditions within which people can transcend those conditions precisely because he has enabled them to recognize them as such. In this spirit, Bourdieu has most notably analysed the French episcopacy in 'La sainte famille. L'épiscopat français dans le champ du pouvoir' (1982) and the French judiciary in 'La force du droit. Éléments pour une sociologie du champ juridique' (1986), but the analysis offered in *Homo academicus* (1984) was fundamental to these two secondary analyses and to all other possible secondary studies still to come because, as Bourdieu said in his inaugural lecture, the field of educational institutions had a 'primordial'[16] status.

The educational research which Bourdieu had undertaken in Lille in the early 1960s was in the vanguard of the developing sociology of education which had questioned the post-Second World War legacy of 1930s thinking. That legacy had been to suppose that equal provision had to be made educationally to ensure that the natural talent which was randomly distributed genetically throughout the population could be efficiently exploited. Bourdieu's view at that time was that, in the absence of there being any 'innate' abilities lodged within people, pedagogical practice had to become sociologically aware so that the process of teaching could engage with people's actual, culturally determined, capacities to learn. As we have seen, the intended transformation of pedagogical practice was, however, to take place within an educational system which was to remain unchanged. Bourdieu took for granted the functionalist view that educational systems perform a fixed function within societies. By anthropomorphizing 'society' and by applying to it the explanation of behaviour which he was developing in relation to human agents in the anthropological context, it was as if Bourdieu was able to regard the 'educational system' as the 'habitus' of 'society'. Schools were the repository of the cultural dispositions of previous generations and were the mechanism whereby these were conveyed to young people, shaping their future disposition to act. Schools were agencies for processing historical change, the catalysts of some collective purpose. Part of that processing function was to conserve preceding attitudes and values before sanctioning and supporting modifications. It was because of these views that there was no contradiction in the author of *Les Héritiers* (1964) accepting in 'L'école conservatrice, les inégalités devant l'école et devant la culture' (1966) that the school is a 'conservative force'. The idea of the educational system as a societal 'habitus' functioned for Bourdieu at this time as a means by which, in opposition to structuralism, he could explain how societies structured themselves. Similarly, 'Systèmes d'enseignement et systèmes de pensée' (1967) exemplified the way in which Bourdieu was able to use the idea of a neutral educational system as a way of explaining how the homologous structures of thinking within societies perceived by structuralists had been actively constructed within those societies themselves.

It was at about this time that the functionalist edifice crumbled in the same sort of way as had the structuralist one before it. The thinking which had been applied to an ideal, functional social sub-system – the 'educational system' – was now potentially applicable to any situation of symbolic exchange or violence which might care to call itself educational and to institutions of any kind which might seek to impose their arbitrary world views. *La Reproduction* (1970) provided the framework for analysing not the educational system's unitary reproduction of society but, instead, the plural processes of reproduction in society. The published work of the early 1970s continued the critique of functionalism, but it did not develop the incipient pluralism of *La Reproduction* (1970). 'La défense du corps' (1971) and 'Les stratégies de reconversion' (1973) both showed how inadequate was the functionalist assumption that there was a static relationship between the educational and the occupational sub-systems, between qualifications and jobs. Although Bourdieu's idea that social agents effect strategic reconversions between fields could certainly explain why there could not be any absolutely fixed relationship between the educational system and the labour market, it did nothing to undermine the status of these systems as stakes in the relational game. At the time when, in *Esquisse d'une théorie de la pratique* (1972), Bourdieu was arguing for the need to develop an objective critique of objectivist structuralism, it was equally necessary for him to develop an objective critique of objectivist functionalism. The progression in thinking which Bourdieu articulated in relation to his Algerian studies was occurring more quietly in relation to his sociological work. *Esquisse* advocated a critique of objectivism in order to emphasize the strategic action of agents but then proceeded to assume that agents operated strategically within the structure identified by objectivists. After passing through an intermediate stage expressed in English in *Outline of a Theory of Practice* (1977), Bourdieu's view crystallized in *Le Sens pratique* (1980). The most appropriate theoretical endeavour should be to comprehend the strategies adopted by other people in the light of the ways in which they structure their own worlds – to develop a science of their practices. Given, however, that it is not possible to know other people's lives, the even more appropriate endeavour is to know one's own life as practice and to juxtapose it with those other lives known to those other people.

Le Sens pratique (1980) went beyond *La Distinction* (1979) because Bourdieu explicitly accepted in the later work that it was an act of theoretical detachment to assume that other people acted within the model of the social world that he had constructed. *La Distinction* was incorrigibly objectivist. It imposed

Bourdieu's subjective objectification of the social world on that world without offering any objective analysis of the originating subjectivity. *Le Sens pratique* indicated what now should be attempted. Social agents do not juggle strategically with the functionally fixed characteristics of educational or occupational systems imposed by social 'scientists' but, instead, create for themselves the characteristics of institutions – whether teaching or employing institutions – which suit their needs. There is no single educational system fulfilling a single function within society but, rather, a multiplicity of educational institutions satisfying the social requirements of the groups which sponsor them and are sponsored by them. An appropriate theoretical endeavour here might be to understand the ways in which other people construct institutions and harness their symbolic power, but an even more appropriate endeavour might simply be for Bourdieu to objectify his own personal and institutional situation.

This was the intention of *Homo academicus* (1984) but its achievement was by no means as straightforward as it might sound. Bourdieu does not, for instance, analyse his position within the field of the French university at the time of writing – in the post-1982 period after his appointment to the Chair at the Collège de France. Bourdieu had argued in *Le Métier de sociologue* (1968) that it was necessary for sociological researchers to analyse sociologically the social and intellectual bases of their research activities. Although nothing was published at the time, it is clear that Bourdieu started to carry out that exercise in 1967 with the result that, fortuitously, he had undertaken an analysis of Parisian higher education on the eve of the events of May 1968. Appendices 1 and 4 of *Homo academicus* document meticulously the sources of information used in the enquiry, but they are less clear about the chronology of the empirical process. It would seem that information was acquired about staff in the four faculties of the University of Paris – Law, Science, Arts and Medicine – according to variables specified in Appendix 4.1, whilst more detailed information of the same kind was gathered in relation to the staff of the Faculty of Arts and Social Sciences (within which Bourdieu was situated at that time as a member of staff in the sixth section of the École Pratique des Hautes Études) – according to variables specified in Appendix 4.2. Appendix 1 describes the categories of information under seven headings. The enquiry correlated 'demographic indicators and indicators of economic and social capital, inherited and acquired'; 'indicators of cultural capital, inherited or acquired'; 'indicators of capital of university power'; 'indicators of capital of scientific power and prestige'; 'indicators of intellectual celebrity'; 'indicators of capital of political or economic power'; and 'indicators of political dispositions'. It is possible to tell from these categories that Bourdieu had attempted to carry out on staff the same kind of analysis that he had already undertaken for students in *Les Étudiants et leurs études* (1964). But there were important extensions. The work summarized in *Les Héritiers* (1964) had concentrated on correlating the cultural capital already possessed by students with their social backgrounds. The questions asked of the source material in respect of staff were certainly still concerned with the incorporated and the objectified states of cultural capital, but they were also interested in the accumulated capital of the staff which might be the aggregate of personal symbolic power, of cultural capital in its institutional state, or of political power reconverted into academic capital. The third chapter of *Homo academicus* proposes a fundamental polarity between staff who acquire academic power through involvement in committees and those who acquire scientific power by the strength of their intellectual achievements. Positions are plotted on a chart in which, for instance, the most pure form of academic power is situated in the bottom right whilst the most pure form of scientific power is situated in the top left. Two other charts are provided which then correlate the positions in the chart with homologous characteristics identified from amongst the different variables.

The plotting is characteristic of the style of representation adopted by Bourdieu in the mid-1970s and used in *La Distinction* (1979). The second chapter of *Homo academicus* carries out the same exercise in respect of the four faculties. Whereas in Chapter 3 it is the nuances of attitude between staff within the Faculty of Arts and Social Sciences which are correlated with the range of indicative variables, in Chapter 2 it is the nuances between staff of different faculties. The discipline of an individual within the chart has an impersonal correspondence with that same individual's position in respect of the polarity between academic and scientific power. The movement from Chapter 3 to Chapter 2 reflects the historical sequence of Bourdieu's research. He had originally sought to situate himself within his own intellectual field – that of the Faculty of Arts and Social Sciences – and had only gradually developed the capacity to situate the field of academic distinctions within the field of economic and cultural power in the way in which aesthetic tastes were similarly situated in *La Distinction*. Bourdieu reversed the direction of thinking in the presentation of *Homo academicus* because, in 1984, he was able to think of himself as situated within the field of power. It was, therefore, necessary now to define the political status of the intellectual field itself before returning to his earlier analysis of the power factors in operation within the field. Bourdieu is explicit that a return to Chapter 3 can only be allowed when (in Chapter 2)

> we have better defined the position of the initial object inside the interlocking social spaces and, thereby, the position of the researcher who himself participates in these different spaces with the insights and blind spots they imply.[17]

Bourdieu's current political reflexivity, in other words, now enables him to put in context the methodological reflexivity of the 1967 sociologist which autonomized the field of the Arts and Social Sciences.

Homo academicus is not a book to be summarized, but one to be used. The persona of Bourdieu was inserted in his analysis – somewhere down at the bottom left of the chart – but it was not meant to set off a biographical guessing game. The appendices were invitations to imitation. The fourth chapter reproduces 'La défense du corps' (1971) and the second appendix offers, in abbreviated form, the statistical detail about staff and student numbers, by discipline, in French higher education from 1949 to 1969 which had informed the discussion of the article. The English edition of 1988 adds, as a postscript, 'Les catégories de l'entendement professoral' of 1975 which, in this new context, fits in well with Bourdieu's reflexive orientation towards his text, but Bourdieu's interesting preface to the English edition makes it clear that, in the trans-cultural context, he regards his text as an objectified and objective statement for which he awaits a comparably socio-analytic English response.

The relationship between Chapters 2 and 3 of *Homo academicus* can be described in two further ways. In 1967, Bourdieu had carried out a sociology of science from a position within the field of higher education. It was a sociology of science which plotted the relationship between scientific positions and social or political positions but it was, nevertheless, a sociology of science which took for granted the social function of the higher education system within which that science was practised. In the 1980s, Bourdieu has reasserted the primacy of the sociology of education – no longer as the sociology of a social sub-system possessing a priori objectivist functions but as the sociology of educational institutions all of which are differently constructed and sustained to fulfil partisan purposes within the field of power. Chapter 2 of *Homo academicus* was trying to offer this kind of sociology of education analysis of the original sociology of science analysis by simultaneously re-using and situating the findings from the early research. Again, the relationship between the two chapters can be put in methodological terms. From his post-*Le Sens pratique* position in which he was dissatisfied with the objectivist mode of presenting a three-dimensional social model which he had adopted in *La Distinction*, Bourdieu was now wanting to objectify his position within Parisian higher education with the use of information which had been gathered in the context of a structuralist endeavour. What Bourdieu now calls a 'constructivist' interpretative framework was superimposed on material which had originally been interpreted structurally. This is why it makes sense to try to read *Homo academicus* – with some craning of the neck – as if Chapter 3 were inserted diagrammatically within Chapter 2.

The prologue to *La Noblesse d'état* (1989) touches explicitly on these two points which have arisen in responding analytically to *Homo academicus*. Sub-titled 'Social and mental structures', the prologue argues that the analysis of objective social structures is, at the same time, 'an exploration of the cognitive structures which agents use in their practical knowledge of the social worlds which are already structured in this way'.[18] The analysis of social structures (structuralism) is inseparable from the analysis of the processes of construction (constructivism). Bourdieu was able to reach this point because he had finally exorcized any notion that he, or any other thinker, might be outside society, observing it from some privileged vantage point. It was as if he could now renounce the original sequence of the three modes of theoretical knowledge first outlined in *Esquisse d'une théorie de la pratique* (1972). Although Bourdieu had then mentioned that the three approaches should be regarded as dialectically rather than diachronically related, his work of the 1970s had given the impression of a methodological progression in which one mode of theoretical knowing cumulatively superseded the previous one. Concentrating on his position within French society rather than on his observation of Algerian society, Bourdieu could easily see that the modes of knowledge are synchronic and inseparable. Depending on the amount of personal or institutional power that he could mobilize, his structuralist descriptions were, simultaneously, constructivist prescriptions. Since this is true for all visions of the social world, the sociology of social structures must also be a sociology of the institutions which add their power to acts of constructive thinking. Bourdieu assumes that, primarily, it is within competing types of educational institution that competing visions of the social world are fostered, and this is why

> the sociology of education is a chapter, and not the least significant, in the sociology of knowledge and also in the sociology of power – not to speak of the sociology of the philosophies of power. Far from being that kind of applied, and, therefore, inferior science – only good for the peda- gogists – which we have come to consider it, it is situated at the base of a general anthropology of power and of legitimacy.[19]

Homo academicus presented an analysis of the institutional basis of the visions of the social world emergent from the university of Paris. *La Noblesse d'état* offers an account of the group identity of the 'grandes écoles' – the élite institutions in relation to which, it must be remembered, the faculties of the French university have traditionally been second-class citizens. The first part – 'The scholastic forms of classification' – again uses material accumulated in the late 1960s. Recognizing that structuralist and constructivist analyses are logically inseparable, Bourdieu makes a presentational separation in offering a constructivist account of the grandes écoles. The first chapter shows how the process of student selection constructs the institution, and the second chapter uses again (for the second time only in French) 'Les catégories de l'entendement professoral' (1975) to demonstrate the ways in which the judgements which staff make of the work of students contribute to the constitution of the ethos of the institution. The second part looks at the anticipatory socialization which is effected before selection to the grandes écoles in the 'classes préparatoires' or preparatory institutions. Again, it is a constructivist analysis. It is a reproduction of 'Épreuve scolaire et consécration sociale' (1981), and Bourdieu demonstrates that the private educational sector inculcates values, frames of thinking, and attitudes towards intellectual labour which are solidary with the expectations and requirements of the grandes écoles. The preparatory institutions adopt strategies to distinguish themselves from the state sector and these bases for distinction have little to do with the technical or intellectual competence which they instil. As the title of the first chapter of this part implies, what is at stake is the 'production of a nobility'. Having described some of the mechanisms by which the distinctive features of the grandes écoles are socially constructed,

La Noblesse d'état offers, in its third part, a structuralist analysis of the field of the French grandes écoles. The first chapter reproduces 'Agrégation et ségrégation. Le champ des grandes écoles et le champ du pouvoir' (1987), and charts the status distinctions amongst 84 institutions, ranging from the École Normale Supérieure in the rue d'Ulm in Paris to, for instance, the École Nationale des Arts et Industries Textiles at Roubaix. The status distinctions are measured, partly, by reference to the social origins of students. In other words – to make explicit the internal, implicit cross-reference in the text – the institutions are objectively located in a structural map on the basis of the self-constructions which they had effected in their selection procedures. The second chapter – 'A structural history' – reproduces 'Variations et invariants. Éléments pour une histoire structurale du champ des grandes écoles'. As the title implies, it compares the state of the field of institutions in 1984–5 with the state already analysed in respect of 1966–70.

In the fourth part of *La Noblesse d'état*, Bourdieu tries to tackle the relationship between the fields of education and power both from a structuralist and a constructivist perspective. In the first chapter – 'Powers and their reproduction' – Bourdieu correlates the chart of institutional positions with a simplified version of the chart of social space on which the chart of tastes had been superimposed in *La Distinction* (1979). Bourdieu deliberately treats the institutional capital of educational institutions as a mark of distinction in a way which is equivalent to the distinctiveness of the forms of objectified capital, such as artistic or gastronomic taste, which had been presented in *La Distinction*. He then discusses the strategies of reproduction which have been adopted historically to generate this multiplicity of educational distinctions. One of the factors in the historical construction of educational distinctions has been the changing reproductive function of the family and the school. Which mechanism would be strategically more appropriate for sustaining economic power and patronage? Quite simply, social groups have wanted to choose the strategy for reproducing themselves and for maintaining their capital inter-generationally. It was natural that Bourdieu should reproduce 'Le patronat' (1978) at this point because the earlier article had argued that, historically, employers have strategically secured the continuation of their businesses either by reproducing a 'family' business or by attracting educationally qualified successors. The impetus for change in the structures of the fields of education and economic power and in their inter-relations has been the process whereby agents have constructed the structures which will secure their self-reproduction or succession.

On several occasions in *La Noblesse d'état* Bourdieu reflects on the relevance of research findings of the late 1960s for 1989. But quite apart from the response which Bourdieu gives to his own question in considering the validity of historical comparisons, the book was a book of 1989 in a quite different and important respect. It was Bourdieu's book for the bi-centenary of the French Revolution. The final section contains a discussion of 'State power and power over the state' which sets the notion of the 'state nobility' of the book's title in the context of the 'noblesse de robe' and 'noblesse d'épéé' of the Ancien Régime. Just as significantly, the title of the book suggests that it was conceived as an 'occasional' publication, or, at least, that Bourdieu was prepared to market it on the occasion of the bi-centenary celebrations. It was a formal intervention in the same way as the re-issue of *L'Ontologie politique de Martin Heidegger* in 1988 had also been, perhaps, indicative of the conscious exercise within the market of symbolic goods of a symbolic power which Bourdieu had not possessed when he wrote the article on Heidegger in 1975. These suggestions, maybe, are too speculative. At the beginning of 'Le sens pratique' (1976), Bourdieu had written:

> It is possible to abandon the sovereign point of view from which the objectivist idealism orders the world, without being forced to relinquish the 'active aspect' of apprehension of the world by reducing cognition to a mere recording: it suffices to situate oneself within 'real activity as such', i.e. in the practical relation to the world, the quasi-bodily 'aiming' which entails no representation of either the body or the world, still less of their relationship, that active presence in the world through which the world imposes its presence, with its urgencies, its things to be done or said, things 'made' to be said and said 'to be done', which directly command words and deeds without ever deploying themselves as a spectacle.[20]

He was recommending for himself the way of thinking which, in the article, he was to perceive in the thinking of the Kabyles and which he was to call 'polythetic'. He was recommending a practical logic which would enable him to engage with the urgent impositions of the world with its 'choses faites pour être dites et dites pour être faites'. This was a presentational style which Bourdieu tried to adopt in *Questions de sociologie* (1980) and it was repeated in the aptly named *Choses dites* (1987). This is Bourdieu at his most lucid and most accessible best. The text contains 15 articles and interviews, most of which discuss 'one-off' issues in an illuminating way. There is less inclination than in *Questions de sociologie* to speak for sociology but rather an inclination simply to speak. The first two interviews of the book in particular – ' "Fieldwork in philosophy" ' and 'repères' – provided Bourdieu with the opportunity to explain some of the complexity of his thinking. They are valuable in the same way as are others of Bourdieu's clarifications of his meaning, such as, notably, 'The genesis of the concepts of habitus and field' (1985), but it is not possible to suggest that Bourdieu is in any way retreating to mere self-presentation or self-clarification in his recent work. The truth is, rather, that Bourdieu was attracted to practical logic in a more fundamental way than might be thought by assuming that *Choses dites* is representing it. *Choses dites* does not encapsulate the way in which Bourdieu operates polythetically. Instead, *Choses dites* is just one practical action amongst the many polythetic procedures at his disposal. Catching Bourdieu now *in medias res*, in the midst of work in progress, there is no question of imposing on the present situation an ordered schema comparable with the one imposed on Bourdieu's development from 1958. He would claim that his work has always had a certain randomness or contingency and that the present situation is no exception. In conformity with his own theories, he would claim that his career has never been calculated but has rather been the consequence of his dispositions. The combined work and writing associated with the position as editor of the new European journal – *Liber* – published simultaneously in England, France, Italy, Spain and Germany – is an exciting indication of Bourdieu's desire to counter 'sovereign visions' of a new Europe by speaking scientifically so as to encourage, instead, the emergence of participant visions, but this is only one string to his contemporary bow. It is not for me to anticipate any future retrospective ordering of his present experience.

Ways of recognizing

III

The blackbird whirled in the autumn winds.
It was a small part of the pantomime.
    from Wallace Stevens, 'Thirteen ways of looking at a blackbird'.[1]

My first way arises from my personal disposition habituated by the study of English literature and, in particular, of the English Romantic poets. Bourdieu's quotation of a dictionary definition of 'sens' in *Esquisse* reinforced my disposition. Permutations of meaning of 'sense', 'sentiment', 'sensation', 'sensibility', 'sentimental' and 'sensible' – registered, partly, by Jane Austen in *Sense and Sensibility* – were key factors in a 'post-Enlightenment' awakening in Western Europe towards the end of the eighteenth century. The linguistic confusion was heightened trans-culturally in the English reception of the ideas of Rousseau. How were French 'sentiments' – feelings – related to English 'sentiments' – rationally based attitudes or opinions? Locke's theory of knowledge had argued that 'ideas' are based on 'sense impressions' and David Hartley had pushed this further to suggest that thoughts are the products of physical or physiological sensations.[2] For the generation of early English Romantic poets, 'Hartleian associationism' represented the equivalent of Skinnerian behaviourism. William Paley worked out a popular compromise which sought to rescue rational moral obligation from the threat posed by the unregulated sensationalism or emotionalism which seemed to be the ethical consequence of Hartley's determinism. 'Man is a bundle of habits'[3] wrote Paley in his influential *The Principles of Moral and Political Philosophy* (1785). People do not regulate their behaviour by explicit reference to any formulated code of morals, but the ways in which they behave 'naturally', 'unconsciously' or 'instinctively' are the products of a process of prior habituation whereby rational injunctions are transformed into feelings. The moralist has to create the conditions within which, as it were, the processes of social determinism can be harnessed to ensure that people experience imposed obligations as feelings.

Coleridge and Wordsworth both wrote under the influence of Hartley and Paley. In the early 1790s, Coleridge planned to establish a 'pantisocracy'[4] on the banks of the Susquehanna river. The intention was that conditions of complete material equality would necessarily induce inter-personal attitudes of unconditional regard by fixing the right 'habits' of behaviour. Having failed to bring this scheme into operation, there is a sense in which Coleridge saw his poetry as a form of communication which would itself be habit-forming in his readers. This was also true of Wordsworth whose poetic intention had, perhaps, a more sustained social purpose. Within the neo-platonic framework of his 'Ode: Intimations of Immortality from Recollections of early childhood', Wordsworth suggested that

> Our birth is but a sleep and a forgetting:[5]

and that the whole of human living gradually obliterates the innate sense of the intrinsic purpose of being which we possess at birth. In the same poem, however, he celebrated his view that some sense of what has been lost does remain:

> O joy! that in our embers
> Is something that doth live,
> That nature yet remembers
> What was so fugitive![6]

Wordsworth's descriptions of figures such as 'The Old Cumberland Beggar' who were almost indistinguishable from natural objects were attempts to enable his readers to 'recollect' what it means to be a harmonious part of nature and, therefore, to be constantly aware of

> What man has made of man.[7]

Coleridge's fear was not that he would lose his capacity to stay in touch with 'nature' but that he would lose 'the shaping spirit of imagination' which enabled him to reconstruct his fleeting visions of harmonious existence. When the 'person from Porlock' interrupted the creation of 'Kubla Khan' (epitomizing, in so doing, all disruptions of the visionary), Coleridge used the recollection of a 'damsel with a dulcimer' to reflect on the difficulty of restoring past visions:

> Could I revive within me
> Her symphony and song . . .[8]

Bourdieu has insisted that he has not idealized Kabyle society. There can be no question of trying to restore the values of traditional Algerian society within Algeria, let alone of trying to transplant them to Western Europe, in abstract, but it is possible to place information at the disposal of social agents in the present. The concept of 'habitus' functions for Bourdieu in much the same way as the idea of 'habit' functioned for the early English Romantics.

In both cases, it offers the opportunity for a 'soft' determinism. 'Habitus' has enabled Bourdieu to escape from Marxist determinism and to suggest that humans inter-generationally create the conditions within which they are conditioned. By 'reviving' Kabyle social organization, Bourdieu has deliberately made available a vision of how societies might still organize themselves if human agents were to choose to be habituated by that vision.

As Shelley was to articulate the assumption which motivated Coleridge and Wordsworth, poets 'are the unacknowledged legislators of mankind'.[9] Bourdieu's works are artifices or artefacts which aim to influence the ways in which people recognize their own societies – to alter their perceptions and habits. The conventional view of the English Romantics, of course, as most cogently expressed in a manner with which Bourdieu would be sympathetic – in the work of Raymond Williams[10] – is that the poets elevated the significance of their perceptions of an ideally human existence precisely because they were alienated from all the modernizing tendencies of their societies and were cushioned by the vestiges of gentlemanly patronage from having to come to terms with industry, or commerce, or technology. Bourdieu knows this very well, and, in so far as a comparison with the English Romantics has value, an awareness of the significance of Bourdieu's reflexivity offers a salutary caution. Bourdieu's intellectual problems can be located historically alongside those of the Romantics. He has wanted to give a sociological form to Kant's accounts of pure and practical reason and of aesthetic judgement. Just as the early Romantics were seeking to reconcile reason and emotional experience before any concept of the 'unconscious' had been formulated, so Bourdieu's work is similarly resolutely pre-Freudian in its attempt to reject the language of the 'psyche'. Nevertheless, Bourdieu does not try to present himself as a grand 'legislator' surreptitiously imposing a vision of the world on others. He would argue, I think, that his own habituated views – whether Romantic or pre-Freudian or whatever – can only derive their power to legislate from the extent to which they arouse or mobilize some consensus of support.

* * *

I have heard Bourdieu's work described as 'just' a mixture of Descartes and Durkheim. The Durkheimian notion of the 'collective consciousness' was corrupted by Bergsonian 'vitalism' during his lifetime so that it has become associated with a collective unconscious operating immanently within societies without human agency. Bourdieu has certainly opposed this distortion of Durkheim's meaning by insisting that human agents construct the mechanisms of social solidarity and collective thinking which enable their specific societies to cohere. Equally, if the traditional existentialist critique of Cartesianism has been that the fact of thinking in 'cogito ergo sum' says nothing about the nature of 'being' but only proves the existence of the thinking being, Bourdieu would certainly be on the side of Descartes in wanting to argue that there is no unthought being. Bourdieu would not be Cartesian, however, if that were to imply that there is an essential self which reasons or cogitates. For Bourdieu, the mind – the 'ghost in the machine'[11] – is a cerebral mechanism for processing cognitions and does not entail a controlling 'self' in charge of the operation.

It is clear that Bourdieu has always been a thorough-going phenomenologist. He has always been consistently anti-essentialist in respect of 'objects' and of 'selves'. There are no 'realities' behind appearances. This means that he can be regarded as a philosophical sceptic. Confusingly, however, he has been taken to be a Marxist precisely because he has seemed to want to imply that there are underlying material determinants of appearances. Marxism and structuralism seemed to be united in suggesting that the real explanations of what was really happening in any society were different from what they might seem to be to participants. Bourdieu's desire to offer a radical critique of contemporary society led him, illogically, to suppose that some representations of appearance are better than others. As he has tortuously disowned the superiority of objective knowledge over primary knowledge he has, in fact, endeavoured to remove the distinction. By a process of self-habituation, it just so happens that Bourdieu's objective knowledge has become his primary experience of the world and, as such, now legitimately of equal validity with all other primary experiences.

There is no suggestion, in short, that Bourdieu might offer any support to an anti-intellectual reversion to primary, unthinking experience even though much of his work seems to celebrate it. Such a reversion would be inauthentic. The use of a key term of existentialism is appropriate here. To try to be unintellectual when one has been socialized into being intellectual would be to manifest 'bad faith' in the same way as it would be to seek to empathize with the Kabyle experience of the social world if one had been brought up in France. Bourdieu is a humanist existentialist who tries to be authentic – not to a 'self' but to the social conditions which have generated his functioning persona. This means that his persona conforms with the 'type' of his class or group ethos. He seeks to be authentic in relation to the self-image of the social group by which he has been constituted and which he also seeks to represent. This authenticity relates to the objective history of the social group with which he associates himself and also to his own personal history. His current persona affirms the process of its own production. It would be impossible to deny the social processes which had made him into an intellectual on the grounds that he had not intrinsically been intellectual. Anti-essentialism, in other words, necessitates that one must create one's own authenticity. Even though the 'self' is nothing, the persona must be at any time the sum of all its previous constructions, or, on the other hand, nothing at all – a self-presentation which is unstable and constantly re-defined according to context. This last alternative possibility is inconceivable for Bourdieu. Historically and personally, he is an organicist. The 'habitus' transmits from one generation to the next the ethos of groups and classes. Individuals who possess no self-hood, nevertheless, inherit a circumscribed set of class or group parameters within which they may live their lives. Although Bourdieu presents himself as a 'socialist', he is, therefore, a traditionalist or, perhaps, a radical conservative after the fashion of Burke (to place him again within the Romantic context). He has difficulty in explaining social or political revolutions because he believes that any revolution is dependent on the existence of anticipatory conditions which alone can bring it into actuality. He is currently working on the phenomenon of artistic revolution.[12] The gradualism which seems inevitable for Bourdieu as a theory of social change also applies in respect of individuals. Our capacity to make ourselves into different selves is a function of the ways in which social conditions have enabled us to be constituted cumulatively in the past – and all of these ways are manifestations of the 'habitus' which was the disposition to act and think which was enshrined in the ethos of the group into which we were born. There is not an infinity of selves which we are free to become. It is much more nearly the case, but, in Bourdieu's view not entirely so, that we do not choose to be authentic but are authentic by necessity. This explains why Bourdieu must be defined as a 'modernist' rather than a 'post-modernist'. As we have seen, Bourdieu identified the phenomenon of 'polythetic' thinking – which can be thought to be post-modern in character. It denies any regulative referential meaning or any meta-narrative which might ensure the logical coherence of discourse. For Bourdieu, however, the exercise of this logical practice – by himself and by others – is governed by the range of possible meaning available within the social group of language users, by the total ethos of the context of linguistic exchange. The Parisian post-modernists are 'intellectual cowboys' because they abuse the ethos from which they derive their authority. In a very real sense, Bourdieu's objections to people such as Derrida or Lyotard are not so much intellectual as ethical objections. They are intellectually dishonest and have forfeited moral integrity by indulging in a shallow form of academic journalism.

* * *

What does Bourdieu's work mean for us all as individuals? We are physical creatures, but Bourdieu has little to say about biological or genetic characteristics. Biologisms are, for him, all too often poorly concealed essentialisms. He has attacked the 'racism' of intelligence testing, which implies that both ethnicity and intelligence are unacceptably essentialist ideas.[13] He has heralded the end of 'Malthusianism' which implies a rejection of the possibility that demographic trends might be autonomously predicted without any reference to constituting social attitudes.[14] Our physical appearance is not an 'essential' part of our selves. Our corporal 'hexis' – as Bourdieu calls it – is the product of our class or group upbringing. Our size and our shape and our deportment all disclose, first of all, our social inheritance and, secondly, our early socialization. We may have acquired a small physical frame either as a result of the poor lives and working conditions of our parents which had the effect of transmitting disadvantage or as a result of our own deprivation or malnutrition. Whichever is thought to be the stronger influence, in either case our physical condition is not independent of our social position. Physical attraction between the sexes is not solely or wholly biochemical. The pressures to slim or to keep fit are social pressures which constitute shared perceptions of attractiveness. Physical appearance is no more an artificial embellishment than are opinions and attitudes. It is part of a constructed integrity which is our publicly presented identity.

We are socialized initially within the immediate group where we are physically raised. The 'nature' and 'nurture' debate has little meaning because our 'natural' characteristics are the products of the accumulated effects of the nurture received by our parents and of the naturalization of our own nurture. To a very large extent, we do not choose our identity. We receive the cultural identity which has been handed down to us from previous generations. Nevertheless, as we grow older, we proceed to modify the identity which we have inherited. The identity is not intrinsic but the scope for changing it is circumscribed by the social expectations of the group with which we are associated. By our actions, we informally reinforce our inherited group affiliation. We adhere to groups, whether clubs or political or religious organizations, and we adopt the identifying images of social groups, whether in hair-style or in clothing, so as to confirm our social identity. For the same reason, we take steps to distinguish ourselves from those who belong to different groups. Our tastes and our life-styles have no intrinsic value but serve to maintain the coherence of the group to which we belong. If we aspire to adopt the tastes of a group other than the one to which we were initially socialized, many of our unconscious habits betray our origins. We may achieve a limited mobility, but there is the possibility both that we shall feel that our adopted identity is inauthentic in relation to our original one and also that the group to which we have aspired by adopting its tastes may surreptitiously close ranks and exclude us by altering the tastes by which it defines itself. There is, in other words, a fundamental group or class ethos in all groups or classes which is reproduced historically and which fosters resistance to social mobility.

We are formally socialized – certainly in most parts of the world – by a system of education. In Western Europe at the end of the nineteenth century, states established schooling systems which would provide the specialist instruction necessary for a changing labour market and would also seek to create in the whole population an affiliation to the nation-state equivalent to group or class affiliation. State education systems were attempts to construct uniform social identities within the boundaries which were themselves artificial political constructs. We are taught things in school which are subordinate to the social purpose of the exercise, but pupils and staff and whole institutions become tokens of distinction. The transmission of arbitrary culture and knowledge within the education system does not help people to reconcile their group identity with a national identity but, instead, throughout, it distinguishes people on supposed merit or ability. The equalization of opportunity provided by state education and by the recognition of 'innate' intelligence is a sham. The system simply provides a series of awards or qualifications which, as much as hair-styles, are reinforcements of our previous group identity. The content of courses is such that only those who have already been initiated into the language of school discourses by their earlier socialization are able to demonstrate their 'ability'. Schools which, in response, alter their curricula in order to be able to recognize the merit of students who have been differently socialized, will tend to find that they become marginalized as institutions because they have 'poor standards'.

Occupational opportunities are linked to educational ones. In certain historical states of the labour market, the possession of an educational qualification may provide access to a related post, but if the economy becomes saturated with equally valid qualifications, the dominant classes preserve their positions of power by redefining the criteria for employment in order to preserve the privileged opportunities of their children. To measure 'social mobility' in terms of the access to the 'same' jobs of different social classes over a historical period, Bourdieu has insisted since the early 1970s, is to ignore the strategies of reconversion adopted by the dominant classes whereby the 'same' jobs become differently esteemed in respect of status precisely when they become accessible to the dominated classes.

In short, there seems little that we can do as individuals. The dominant classes hold all the chips in the historical game. The composition of the dominant classes may be slightly modified over time and the family tree within which we are situated may shift its social position over generations, but the most healthy course for individuals is to acquiesce in this historical process and simply to do our best to make some small contribution to historical change. There is in Bourdieu's position, undoubtedly, an element of fatalism or, perhaps of reluctant cosmic conservatism. The urge to distinguish ourselves and to think by operating a principle of division cannot be 'essential' to the human condition for Bourdieu. The dualistic mode of thinking and acting which has characterized Western European civilization is itself socially constructed. We have, as it were, programmed ourselves to be binary creatures, but Bourdieu seems to hold out little hope that the social conditions can be created which would enable us to programme ourselves differently. Such a revolution is almost logically impossible for Bourdieu because he does not adequately allow for physical change in the universe or for changes in the nature of the relationship between people and the material resources of the environment.

* * *

Bourdieu has been recently described as the 'Savonarola[15] of the French social sciences'.[16] There is certainly an element of zealous iconoclasm in his work. He exposes mercilessly the covert social functions of all institutions and their reinforcing ideologies. It is the logical consequence of his philosophical position that his work should be negative and critical. Systems of thought and social institutions are not 'real' and Bourdieu sees it to be his job to lay bare their pretensions to reality and to establish, instead, that they have only a constantly fluctuating relational meaning one to another. Bourdieu's sociological methodology involves the systematic falsification of appearances and the conscious construction of 'facts' or formulation of problems – all of which is reminiscent of Popper. But, equally, Bourdieu seems driven by a fascination in a possible totality of relationships, as if some meaning might be acquired by achieving a complete picture of all actual or possible relations. He is interested in the relational perspectives adopted by Virginia Woolf in her novels, but it needs to be remembered that Leslie Stephen's totalizing empiricism lay behind her apparent relativism.[17] Bourdieu has sometimes been accused of having undertaken insufficient empirical research. On the contrary, his desire to accumulate all possible data, whether statistical or ethnographic, could be thought to be highly positivistic were it not that, for him, data are not 'facts'. He has undertaken sophisticated statistical enquiries himself and argues that the ability to do so must be part of the battery of methods deployed by any sociological researcher, but he does not accept that statistical information has any privileged access to any reality. The findings of statistical enquiries have to be counter-checked against other findings and the basis on which information has been acquired statistically has to be scrutinized in the same way as does the information which has been secured by questionnaires or by interviews.

Bourdieu tries to destroy all the props of social misrecognition. It is not intrinsically necessary that there should be religious institutions with associated systems of dogmatic thought. Historically, the institutionalization of religious belief served to confirm the distinction acquired by individuals who claimed to have special powers. It was an early form of domination by distinction which had no substantial basis in a way of thinking about the world which could be called 'properly religious'. The firm social entrenchment of religious institutions should not cause us to misrecognize the arbitrariness of their genesis. Similarly, there is no inevitability about the development of capitalism. Capitalist economic behaviour depends on the prior construction of *Homo economicus* – that is to say, on the establishment of a socially shared view that economic exchanges have a purpose of their own autonomous kind. In traditional societies, Bourdieu has argued, exchanges which are labelled as 'economic' fulfil other more important social functions. It is only when the dominant influences within any society decide that economic exchange might be an end in itself that the preconditions exist for the development of a capitalist system. The same is true of 'politics'. Actions need to be defined as 'political' and to be reinforced by political philosophy or political science in order to generate political states to which people belong. Politicization is a form of socialization which creates distinctions as much as do educational systems.

What remains after Bourdieu's negations? The bed-rock of his critical stance seems to be a deep-seated commitment to the notion that human relationships are what living is all about and, therefore, what all social organization must be seeking to facilitate. To use Bourdieu against himself, one could argue that a *Homo socius* has to be socially constructed as much as any *Homo economicus*. Sociability comes very close to being Bourdieu's only essentialism. Bourdieu would be happy to accept that the sociological representation of people in society might be an imposition as much as the economic or political representations, but he would want to be critical of all three because they distort social relations. It can be said, I think, that Bourdieu's epistemological vigilance and his ethical fundamentalism are designed to keep alive a pre-lapsarian vision of human relations. Bourdieu operates with an unarticulated utopian vision which, consistent with his own analytical position, only has the chance of becoming actualized as long as the vision remains unarticulated. Equally, actualization can never be finally achieved. It is Bourdieu's recognition of a sense of compulsion to strive continuously to process his ideals without imposing them which must explain the fact that his career can be characterized as a restless exploration which, strictly, is without any teleological direction and without any definable ultimate goal.

* * *

My account of Bourdieu's career may have imposed a developmental pattern where none exists. I have traced the 'evolution' of Bourdieu's thinking, but I have sometimes had the sensation that I have been interpreting the manifestations of a corpus of thinking which was preformed from the start. Crucially, this raises the question whether there has genuinely been an inter-action between theory and practice in Bourdieu's work and, subordinately, whether he has been influenced in his approach by the work of other people.

Bourdieu has said very little about his own originating ethos or about the dispositions which he inherited. He has not directly placed his own family ethos within his analysis of traditional society in the Béarn. He has not directly placed himself as a student from the regions transported to the prestigious École Normale Supérieure in Paris. Only in recent interviews has Bourdieu outlined the intellectual ethos of his undergraduate days. Merleau-Ponty, Sartre and Lévi-Strauss were early 'influences' shaping his way of thinking about himself and about the social world. Bourdieu's earliest work in Algeria was philosophically phenomenological, but it sought to find the answers to philosophical questions in sociological or anthropological enquiry. The work was an amalgam of functionalism, structuralism and Marxism, and there was clear evidence of the influence of some Durkheim, some Weber and some Marcel Mauss. In Algeria, Bourdieu learnt to use rigorous statistical procedures which he used to complement systematically the transcripts from face-to-face interviews. Statistical data and verbatim conversations were cross-referenced to ensure that the research findings would be neither simply positivist nor simply ethnographic. Bourdieu was interested in how different aspects of traditional Algerian society functioned in structurally homologous ways to safeguard the solidarity of tribes. Bourdieu renounced structuralist philosophy in favour of structuralist method. This meant that he could not accept that Lévi-Strauss had identified universal structural patterns of social organization but that, nevertheless, the structural models could perform a methodological function comparable to statistical findings in questioning the primary experience of social agents. Structural patterns might disclose the underlying functions of actions which were hidden from the agents themselves. There were two routes out of philosophical structuralism. Without wanting to do so, Bourdieu proposed a social theory. In the world observed by researchers – whether in Algeria or in the past known as French social and cultural history – the structures noticed by observers are not accidental. The notion of 'habitus' was first introduced to explain how 'structures' came to be actualized. There are affinities between systems of thought and systems of education or between contemporary literary, artistic or musical styles because these are the manifestations of similar dispositions which are stored and transmitted inter-generationally by means of the 'habitus'. In the early 1970s, Bourdieu explored the genesis and structure of a range of autonomous fields all of which, in pure structuralist terms, would have been held to have been expressions of some disembodied spirit of the times. At the same time, however, Bourdieu insisted that he wanted to advance a theory of sociological knowledge rather than a theory of society. This meant that the position from which any researcher might advance an account of another society must be subjected to scrutiny within the same framework as had been that other society. The basis of the objective analyses made of other societies had to be subjected to objective analysis – on the assumption, therefore, that the objective analysis had been right in the first place and now only had to be turned on itself.

In the substance of this book, we have seen that Bourdieu then began to realize that the objective framework which he had imposed on agents and then on social researchers as themselves agents might only be a framework which was an expression of his own particular position within French society. I have followed the 'progression' in Bourdieu's thinking from the primary form of theoretical knowledge to the structuralist, on to the praxeological and, finally, to the practical, but these stages were all contained within Bourdieu's statement in *Esquisse* (1972) and should, perhaps, be seen as strategic methods which have been available to Bourdieu throughout his work. In spite of Bourdieu's commitment to an inter-connectedness between theory and practice, there has not been much sense that there has been any change in his thinking which has imposed itself upon him as a consequence of engagement with new phenomena. It is only in recent years that Bourdieu has been prepared to enter into any debate with opponents. In the period leading up to 1980, there emerges the feeling that the views of others, whether Cassirer, Panofsky or Goffman, not to mention, obviously, Marx, Durkheim and Weber, and the findings of empirical research itself have all been assimilated. Bourdieu's construction of his own intellectual identity has been a process of accretion. It is because Bourdieu's work largely presents itself as governed by an internal logic that it feels as if it does conform to his own philosophical position – that his analyses are, in the last resort, non-referential, and thus no more (or, importantly, no less) about the 'real' world than, say, Shakespeare's *King Lear*. Paradoxically, it is also this sense that his analyses are about themselves that gives them a timeless and de-contexted quality – the very reverse of his stated ideological intention.

*   *   *

How then, finally, are we to respond to Bourdieu's work to date? It seems to me, first of all, that we should assimilate his thought. There can, of course, be no obligation here. There is no reason why we should understand the way in which he wrestled with the intellectual legacy of his mentors in France in the years immediately after the war. The only ground for doing so is the contention that this legacy has become generalized and now constitutes a significant element in the conscious attitudes or unconscious assumptions which influence our daily living. In the manner of Bourdieu himself, we can show that phenomeno-logical thinking, or existentialism, or 'post-modernism' are ideological positions which reinforce the identities of social groups in our society as much as, perhaps, Islamic or Christian fundamentalisms reinforce the identities of others. Never-theless, group-specific ideologies have filtered through to the whole population and an understanding of Bourdieu's thought provides a useful introduction to some of the self-images of our age and useful ammunition against some others.

Secondly, we should endeavour to apply his thinking pragmatically. Just as Bourdieu has assimilated Marx, Durkheim and Weber, and used his own synthesis in practice, we should attempt to build Bourdieu's synthesis into our own syntheses. There seems little point in arguing whether or not to accept Bourdieu's anti-essentialism. It is even debatable whether Bourdieu 'believes' in it himself or whether he adopts an austere rejection of the self in order to try to establish a legitimate social science. Regardless of whether Bourdieu's beliefs or convictions can be said to be identical to our own, there can be no denying that his many investigations and speculations cry out to be imitated or adapted in respect of social phenomena outside France. How much healthier English society would be, for instance, if there existed an article equivalent to Bourdieu's 'La production de l'idéologie dominante' (1976) or a journal so consistently subversive as *Actes de la recherche en sciences sociales*.

Finally – and in this I openly display my admiration for Bourdieu's work and my support for his prescriptions – we should regard his integrated combination of thought and practice as paradigmatic. Knowing is a kind of doing and, as such, should not be the basis for contriving social distinction. Scepticism should be a great social leveller. There is much to be done to save authentic intellectuality from institutionalized academicism. In writing this book, I have often found myself applying two well-known quotations to Bourdieu's predicament. Through the character of Dr Pangloss in *Candide*, Voltaire explored the dilemmas of a philosopher – perhaps Leibniz – who was trapped intellectually within a system of thinking of his own making that willed that all experience would necessarily be for the good in spite of the fact that he experienced sufferings and evil which manifestly threatened the credibility of that self-contained and self-fulfilling system. Candide – the young man who witnesses the struggles of Pangloss – finally concludes that 'il faut cultiver notre jardin'.[18] I have usually thought of this as a resigned, world-weary injunction, but, if Bourdieu's situation is at all comparable in dramatically juxtaposing the claims of theory and of practice, the conclusion he offers is, perhaps, that we have a positive obligation to work hard to tend the culture which is particular to our circumstances and should not try to fabricate universal systems. The famous Voltaire dictum is impersonal but the other quotation is deeply personal. When asked to retract the Wittenberg theses in which he condemned the system of indulgences which epitomized the organized corruption of the Catholic Church, Martin Luther stated simply: 'Hier ich stehe; ich kann nicht anderes.'[19] This was a declaration of an absolute obligation to be true to himself rather than to embark on defences or disquisitions to establish the validity of his position. My reading of Bourdieu's message is that the challenge which is accessible to us all is to be as intransigently authentic in our own limited social situations.

Bibliographical note

As I have indicated in my preface, this book seeks to offer a chronological account of the development of Bourdieu's thinking. In attempting to do this, I have followed the *Bibliographie des travaux de Pierre Bourdieu* established by Yvette Delsaut, dated December 1986, and her revised *Bibliographie des travaux de Pierre Bourdieu, 1958–1988*, dated 1989, both of which are available from the Centre de Sociologie Européenne du Collège de France et de l'École des hautes études en sciences sociales, 11 Place Marcelin Berthelot, 75005 Paris. A selected version of these bibliographies is presented in the English translation of *Choses dites – In Other Words* (1990). What follows is a similar extraction from the original, complete bibliography and is offered with the kind permission of Yvette Delsaut – who has also provided me with up-to-date information for the period from the end of 1988 until March 1990. In the main, I have selected only the books and articles listed in the original bibliography, although I have listed several 'oral communications' and 'interviews' as 'articles'. I have excluded all the details of translations into other languages than English which are supplied in the full bibliography.

All English translations are listed under the date of the publication of the original French text rather than of the translation. This procedure has some awkwardness for the English reader because it emphasizes the French chronology. I have already written about the reception of Bourdieu's work in England in the period up to 1977 ('Bourdieu in England, 1964–1977', *Higher Education Policy*, vol. 2, no. 2, June 1989, pp. 40–6) and I hope to bring this analysis up to the present in a subsequent publication. The sequence of the translations into English has meant that, for the English reader who has no French, the English 'meaning' or 'significance' of Bourdieu is very different from that in France. The purpose of this book is to attempt to represent the French meaning of Bourdieu. Hence the concentration on the French chronology, but, even here, there are difficulties. As will be clear from Chapter 7 in particular, some 'translations' of Bourdieu are not simply translations but opportunities for revision. Depending on the level of control that Bourdieu has been able to exercise over the translations of his texts into other languages, the study of all the language versions of his works offers an opportunity to clarify his 'intention' quite apart from his 'meaning' in different cultures. To some extent, therefore, I try to interpret Bourdieu's Anglo-French intentions without attempting here at all to analyse his English meaning. Indeed, it could be said that my intention is to counteract the kind of appropriation of Bourdieu's texts by the English context which has occurred to date by representing as fully as possible his French meaning – accepting, of course, that this intention is a function of my particular position within the English intellectual field.

To secure the integrity of the above intention, I have normally worked from Bourdieu's French texts in the first instance. Where no translations exist in English publication at the time of writing, I have offered my own translations for the quotations in the text. Where translations into English do exist, I have normally used those translations – taking care, however, to ensure that what I use is genuinely a translation. As far as possible, I have tried not to assume any knowledge of French. I have sometimes preserved French titles where no English translation exists, but my main aim has been to direct English readers to those works which are translated in such a way that they will be able to place these works in the context of those which are untranslated. Clearly, this contextualization will have to be taken on trust as an interpretation until more translations are made which will enable readers to make their own meanings.

There is, finally, the bibliographic problem of attribution which is only thinly distinguished from the philosophical problem of authorship. Many of Bourdieu's works have been the products of collaboration. The precise details of the collaborators in every case are supplied below in the bibliography. In most cases in my text, however, I refer to Bourdieu as the sole author. The main exception here is in relation to *Les Héritiers* (1964) and *La Reproduction* (1970) where I often talk about the co-authors – Pierre Bourdieu and Jean-Claude Passeron. This exception is significant. To use one of Bourdieu's favourite distinctions, the question of attribution is integrally related to the question whether my book is a representation of his work as *opus operatum* or as *modus operandi*. From a *post hoc* perspective in 1990, the collaborative work of Bourdieu and Passeron in the 1960s can conveniently be attributed to Bourdieu, but, in 1970, there was, perhaps, little reason to suppose that in 1990 they might not equally be attributed to Passeron. I have respected the *modus operandi* perspective for the 1960s by referring to both authors and have tried to maintain that perspective subsequently by not mentioning the names of collaborators in my text. The reason for this will emerge from my account of the development of Bourdieu's thinking. The texts assigned to Bourdieu are not to be analysed as texts without author, nor are they to be analysed as the products of an autonomous self. For Bourdieu, the individual is defined by the relationship with groups. These group affiliations are similar to class affiliations simply because individuals constitute themselves as individuals in relation to the groups or classes which they also partly constitute. In the 1970s Bourdieu was the leader of a group at the Centre de Sociologie Européenne and associated with the publication of the journal, *Actes de la recherche en sciences sociales* which was both a reflection and an expression of himself. His name, therefore, can be legitimately used as the 'label' for group products. Richard Nice was right, in 1977, to append a bibliography to his translation of *La Reproduction* which gave details of the work undertaken by the group within the Centre de Sociologie Européenne rather than of the work of Bourdieu or Passeron alone. In the 1980s, however, this sense of a corporate identity nominally represented by 'Bourdieu' has diminished. As will be clear from the discussion contained in Chapter 9, Bourdieu has increasingly adopted a strategy which involves greater self-presentation and personal engagement. Bourdieu's recent texts make use of the materials deriving from the collaboration of the corporate period, but the texts no longer present themselves as collaborative products in the same way. 'Bourdieu' is now not so much a label as a persona.

1958

Book

1. *Sociologie de l'Algérie*, Paris, PUF, 'Que Sais-je?' collection, No. 802. (New edition, revised and corrected, 1961.)
1E. *The Algerians* (trans. A.C.M. Ross), Boston, Beacon Press, 1962.

1959

Articles

1. 'Tartuffe ou le drame de la foi et de la mauvaise foi', *Revue de la Méditerranée*, 4–5 (92–3), July–October, pp. 453–8.
2. 'La logique interne de la civilisation algérienne traditionnelle', in *Le Sous-développement en Algérie*, Alger, Secrétariat social, pp. 40–51.
3. 'Le choc des civilisations', in *Le Sous-développement en Algérie*, Alger, Secrétariat social, pp. 52–64.

1960

Article

1. 'Guerre et mutation sociale en Algérie', *Études méditerranéennes*, 7, spring, pp. 25–37.

1961

Article

1. 'Révolution dans la révolution', *Esprit*, 1, January, pp. 27–40.

1962

Articles

1. 'De la guerre révolutionnaire à la révolution', in F. Perroux (ed.), *L'Algérie de demain*, Paris, PUF, pp. 5–13.
2. 'Les relations entre les sexes dans la société paysanne', *Les Temps modernes*, 195, August, pp. 307–31.
3. 'Célibat et condition paysanne', *Études rurales*, 5–6, April–September, pp. 32–136.
4. 'La hantise du chômage chez l'ouvrier algérien. Prolétariat et système colonial', *Sociologie du travail*, 4, pp. 313–31.
5. 'Les sous-prolétaires algériens', *Les Temps modernes*, 199, December, pp. 1030–51.
5E. 'The Algerian subproletariate', in I.W. Zartman (ed.), *Man, State and Society in the Contemporary Maghrib*, London, Pall Mall Press, 1973.

1963

Book

1. *Travail et travailleurs en Algérie*, Paris–The Hague, Mouton (with A. Darbel, J.P. Rivet and C. Seibel).

Articles

1. 'La société traditionnelle. Attitude à l'égard du temps et conduite économique', *Sociologie du travail*, 1, January–March, pp. 24–44.
2. 'Sociologues des mythologies et mythologies de sociologues', *Les Temps modernes*, 211, December, pp. 998–1021 (with J.C. Passeron).

1964

Books

1. *Le Déracinement, la crise de l'agriculture traditionnelle en Algérie*, Paris, Éditions de Minuit (with A. Sayad).
2. *Les Héritiers, les étudiants et la culture*, Paris, Éditions de Minuit (with J.C. Passeron). (New, augmented edition, 1966.)
2E. *The Inheritors, French Students and their Relation to Culture* (trans. R. Nice), with a new epilogue, Chicago–London, The University of Chicago Press, 1979.
3. *Les Étudiants et leurs études*, Paris–The Hague, Mouton, Cahiers du Centre de Sociologie Européenne, 1 (with J.C. Passeron).

Articles

1. 'The attitude of the Algerian peasant toward time' (trans. G.E. Williams), in J. Pitt-Rivers (ed.), *Mediterranean Countrymen*, Paris–The Hague, Mouton, pp. 55–72.
2. 'Paysans déracinés, bouleversements morphologiques et changements culturels en Algérie', *Études rurales*, 12, January–March, pp. 56–94 (with A. Sayad).
3. 'Les musées et leurs publics', *L'expansion de la recherche scientifique*, 21, December, pp. 26–8.

1965

Book

1. *Un Art moyen, essai sur les usages sociaux de la photographie*, Paris, Éditions de Minuit (with L. Boltanski, R. Castel and J.C. Chamboredon). (New, revised edition, 1970.)
1E. (forthcoming) *Photography*, Oxford, Polity Press. 1990.

Articles

1. 'Le paysan et la photographie', *Revue française de sociologie*, VI, 2, April–June, pp. 164–74 (with M.C. Bourdieu).
2. 'Le musée et son public', *L'Information d'histoire de l'art*, 3, May–June, pp. 120–2.
3. 'The sentiment of honour in Kabyle society' (trans. P. Sherrard), in J.G. Peristiany (ed.), *Honour and Shame. The Values of Mediterranean Society*, London, Weidenfeld and Nicholson, pp. 191–241.
4a. 'Langage et rapport au langage dans la situation pédagogique' (with J.C. Passeron), in P. Bourdieu, J.C. Passeron and M. de Saint Martin (eds), *Rapport*

pédagogique et communication, Paris–The Hague, Mouton, Cahiers du Centre de Sociologie Europeénne, 2, pp. 9–36.

4b.   Also in *Les Temps modernes*, 232, September, pp. 435–66.

4a/bE. 'Language and pedagogical situation' (trans. R. Teese), in D. McCallum and U. Ozolins (eds), *Melbourne Working Papers 1980*, Melbourne, University of Melbourne, Department of Education, 1980, pp. 36–77.

5.   'Les étudiants et la langue d'enseignement' (with J.C. Passeron and M. de Saint Martin), in P. Bourdieu, J.C. Passeron and M. de Saint Martin (eds), *Rapport pédagogique et communication*, Paris–The Hague, Mouton, Cahiers du Centre de Sociologie Européenne, 2, pp. 37–69.

5E.   'Students and the language of teaching' (trans. R. Teese), in D. McCallum and U. Ozolins (eds), *Melbourne Working Papers 1980*, Melbourne, University of Melbourne, Department of Education, 1980, pp. 78–124.

6.   'Les utilisateurs de la bibliothèque universitaire de Lille' (with M. de Saint Martin), in P. Bourdieu, J.C. Passeron and M. de Saint Martin (eds), *Rapport pédagogique et communication*, Paris–The Hague, Mouton, Cahiers du Centre de Sociologie Européenne, 2, pp. 109–20.

1966

Book

1.   *L'Amour de l'art, les musées d'art et leur public*, Paris, Éditions de Minuit (with A. Darbel and D. Schnapper). (New, augmented edition, *L'Amour de l'art, les musées d'art européens et leur public*, 1969.)

1E.   (forthcoming) *The Love of Art*, Oxford, Polity Press, 1990.

Articles

1.   'Différences et distinctions', in Darras, *Le Partage des bénéfices, expansion et inégalités en France*, Paris, Éditions de Minuit, pp. 117–29.

2.   'La fin d'un malthusianisme?', in Darras, *Le partage des bénéfices, expansion et inégalités en France*, Paris, Éditions de Minuit, pp. 135–54 (with A. Darbel).

3.   'La transmission de l'héritage culturel', in Darras, *Le Partage des bénéfices, expansion et inégalités en France*, Paris, Éditions de Minuit, pp. 383–420.

4.   'Comment la culture vient aux paysans?', *Paysans*, 62, October–November, pp. 6–20.

5.   'Une étude sociologique d'actualité: les étudiants en sciences', *Revue de l'enseignement supérieur*, 4, pp. 199–208 (with L. Boltanski, R. Castel, M. Lemaire and M. de Saint Martin).

6.   'Condition de classe et position de classe', *Archives européennes de sociologie*, VII, 2, pp. 201–23.

7.   'L'école conservatrice, les inégalités devant l'école et devant la culture', *Revue française de sociologie*, VII, 3, July–September, pp. 325–47.

7E1.   'The school as a conservative force: scholastic and cultural inequalities' (trans. J.C. Whitehouse), in J. Eggleston (ed.), *Contemporary Research in the Sociology of Education*, London, Methuen, 1974, pp. 32–46.

7E2.   Also in R. Dale *et al.* (eds), *Schooling and Capitalism, A Sociological Reader*, London, Routledge and Kegan Paul/The Open University, 1976, pp. 192–200.

8.   'Une sociologie de l'action est-elle possible?', *Revue française de sociologie*, VII, 4, October–December, pp. 508–17 (with J.D. Reynaud).

8E.   'Is a sociology of action possible?', in A. Giddens (ed.), *Positivism and Sociology*, London, Heinemann Educational Books, 1974.

9.   'Champ intellectuel et projet créateur', *Les Temps modernes*, 246, November, pp. 865–906.

9E1.   'Intellectual field and creative project' (trans. S. France), *Social Science Information*, VIII, 2, April 1969, pp. 89–119.

9E2.   Also in M.F.D. Young (ed.), *Knowledge and Control: New Directions for the Sociology of Education*, London, Collier–Macmillan, 1971, pp. 161–88.

1967

Articles

1.   'Les paradoxes de l'automate', *Coopération technique*, 51–52–53, April, pp. 101–4.

2.   'La communication entre professeurs et étudiants', *Travail social*, Paris, Fédération Française des Travailleurs Sociaux, pp. 133–6.

3.   'La comparabilité des systèmes d'enseignement', in R. Castel and J.C. Passeron (eds), *Éducation, développement et démocratie*, Paris–The Hague, Mouton, Cahiers du Centre de Sociologie Europeénne, 4, pp. 21–58 (with J.C. Passeron).

4.   'Sociology and philosophy in France since 1945: death and resurrection of a philosophy without subject', *Social Research*, XXXIV, 1, spring, pp. 162–212 (with J.C. Passeron).

5.   'L'image de l'image', *L'Année 66, Catalogue de l'exposition Bernard Rancillac*, Paris, Galerie Blumenthal–Mommaton, February.

6.   Postface to E. Panofsky, *Architecture gothique et pensée scolastique* (trans. P. Bourdieu), Paris, Éditions de Minuit, pp. 133–67. (New, augmented edition, 1970.)

7.   'Systèmes d'enseignement et systèmes de pensée', *Revue internationale des sciences sociales*, XIX, 3, pp. 367–88.

7E1.   'Systems of education and systems of thought', *International Social Science Journal*, XIX, 3, 1967, pp. 338–58.

7E2.   Also in E. Hopper (ed.), *Readings in the Theory of Educational System*, London, Hutchinson & Co, 1971, pp. 159–83.

7E3.   Also in M.F.D. Young (ed.), *Knowledge and Control: New Directions for the Sociology of Education*, London, Collier–Macmillan, 1971, pp. 189–207.

7E4.   Also in R. Dale *et al.* (eds), *Schooling and Capitalism, A Sociological Reader*, London, Routledge and Kegan Paul/The Open University, 1976, pp. 192–200.

1968

Book

1.   *Le Métier de sociologue*, Paris, Mouton–Bordas (with J.C. Chamboredon and J.C. Passeron).

Articles

1.   'L'examen d'une illusion', *Revue française de sociologie*, IX, special number, 'Sociologie de l'éducation', II, pp. 227–53 (with J.C. Passeron).

2a.   'Éléments d'une théorie sociologique de la perception artistique', *Revue internationale des sciences sociales*, XX, 4, pp. 640–64.

2b.   Also in *Noroit*, 134, January 1969, pp. 3–14, 135, February 1969, pp. 5–14.

2a/bE.   'Outline of a sociological theory of art perception', *International Social Science Journal*, XX, winter 1968, pp. 589–612.

3.   'Structuralism and theory of sociological knowledge' (trans. A. Zanotti-Karp), *Social Research*, XXXV, 4, winter 1968, pp. 681–706.

1969

Articles

1.   'Le système des fonctions du système d'enseignement', in M.A. Mattijssen and C.E. Vervoort (eds), *Education in Europe*, The Hague, Mouton, pp. 181–9.

2.   'Sociologie de la perception esthétique', in *Les Sciences humaines et l'oeuvre d'art*, Brussels, La connaissance S.A., pp. 161–76, 251–4.

1970

Book

1.   *La Reproduction. Éléments pour une théorie du système d'enseignement*, Paris, Éditions de Minuit (with J.C. Passeron).

1E.   *Reproduction in Education, Society and Culture* (trans. R. Nice), London–Beverley Hills, Sage Publications, 1977.

Articles

1.   'La maison kabyle ou le monde renversé', in J. Pouillon and P. Maranda (eds), *Échanges et communications. Mélanges offerts à Claude Lévi-Strauss à l'occasion de son 60ème anniversaire*, Paris–The Hague, Mouton, pp. 739–58.

1E1.   'The Berber House or the World Reversed', *Social Science Information*, IX, 2, April 1970, pp. 151–70.

1E2.   Also 'The Berber House', in M. Douglas (ed.), *Rules and Meanings. The Anthropology of Everyday Knowledge. Selected Readings*, Harmondsworth, Penguin, 1973, pp. 98–110.

2.   'L'excellence scolaire et les valeurs du système d'enseignement français', *Annales*, XXV, 1, January–February, pp. 147–75 (with M. de Saint Martin).

2E.   'Scholastic excellence and the values of the educational system' (trans. J.C. Whitehouse), in J. Eggleston (ed.), *Contemporary Research in the Sociology of Education*, London, Methuen, 1974, pp. 338–71.

1971

Articles

1.   'Champ du pouvoir, champ intellectuel et habitus de classe', *Scolies*, Cahiers de recherches de l'École normale supérieure, 1, pp. 7–26.

2.   'Une interprétation de la théorie de la religion selon Max Weber', *Archives européennes de sociologie*, XII, 1, pp. 3–21.

2E.   (Modified version.) 'Legitimation and structured interests in Weber's sociology of religion' (trans. C. Turner), in S. Whimster and S. Lash (eds), *Max Weber, Rationality and Modernity*, London, Allen and Unwin, 1987, pp. 119–36.

3.   'Genèse et structure du champ religieux', *Revue française de sociologie*, XII, 3, pp. 295–334.

4.   'Disposition esthétique et compétence artistique', *Les Temps modernes*, 295, February, pp. 1345–78.

5.   'Le marché des biens symboliques', *L'année sociologique*, 22, pp. 49–126.

5E.   'The market of symbolic goods' (trans. R. Swyer), *Poetics* (Amsterdam), 14, 1/2, April 1985, pp. 13–44.

6.   'La défense du corps', *Information sur les sciences sociales*, X, 4, August, pp. 45–86 (with L. Boltanski, P. Maldidier).

7.   'The thinkable and the unthinkable', *Times Literary Supplement*, 15 October, pp. 1255–6.

8.   'Reproduction culturelle et reproduction sociale', *Information sur les sciences sociales*, X, 2, April, pp. 45–99.

8E1.   'Cultural Reproduction and Social Reproduction', in R. Brown (ed.), *Knowledge, Education, and Cultural Change*, London, Tavistock, 1973, pp. 71–112.

8E2.   Also in J. Karabel and A.H. Halsey (eds), *Power and Ideology in Education*, New York, Oxford University Press, 1977, pp. 487–511.

9a.   'L'opinion publique n'existe pas', 9b. *Noroit*, 155, February. Conference, also in *Les Temps modernes*, 318, January 1973, pp. 1292–309.

9c.   Also in P. Bourdieu, *Questions de sociologie*, Paris, Éditions de Minuit, 1980, pp. 222–35.

9aE.   'Public opinion does not exist' (trans. M.C. Axtmann), in A. Mattelart and S. Siegelaub (eds), *Communication and Class Struggle*, New York/Bagnolet, International General/IMMRC, 1979, vol. 1, 'Capitalism, Imperialism', pp. 124–30.

1972

Book

1.   *Esquisse d'une théorie de la pratique, précédé de trois études d'ethnologie kabyle*, Geneva, Droz.

1E1.   (Pp. 162–89), 'The three forms of theoretical knowledge', *Social Science Information*, XII, 1, 1973, pp. 53–80.

1E2.   *Outline of a Theory of Practice* (trans. R. Nice), Cambridge, Cambridge University Press, 1977.

1E3.   (Pp. 3–9, 72–3), 'Structures, strategies, and the habitus', in C.C. Lemert (ed.), *French Sociology, Rupture and Renewal Since 1968*, New York, Columbia University Press, 1981, pp. 86–96.

Articles

1.   'Composition sociale de la population étudiante et chances d'accès à l'enseignement supérieur', *Orientations*, 41, January, pp. 89–102 (with C. Grignon and J.C. Passeron).

2.   'Les Doxosophes', *Minuit*, 1, November, pp. 26–45.

3.   'Les stratégies matrimoniales dans le système de reproduction', *Annales*, 4–5, July–October, pp. 1105–27.

3E.   'Marriage strategies as strategies of social reproduction' (trans. E. Forster), in R. Forster and O. Ranum (eds), *Family and Society, Selections from the Annales*, Baltimore–London, The Johns Hopkins University Press, 1976, pp. 117–44.

1973

Articles
1.   'Classes et classement', *Minuit*, 5, September, pp. 22–4.
2.   'Les stratégies de reconversion. Les classes sociales et le système d'enseigne-
        ment', *Information sur les sciences sociales*, XII, 5, October, pp. 61–113 (with
        L. Boltanski and M. de Saint Martin).
2E.   'Changes in social structure and changes in the demand for education', in
        S. Giner and M. Scotford-Archer (eds), *Contemporary Europe. Social Structures
        and Cultural Patterns*, London, Routledge and Kegan Paul, 1977, pp. 197–227
        (with L. Boltanski).

1974

Articles
1.   'Avenir de classe et causalité du probable', *Revue française de sociologie*, XV,
        1, January–March, pp. 3–42.
2.   'Les fractions de la classe dominante et les modes d' appropriation des œuvres
        d'art', *Information sur les sciences sociales*, XIII, 3, June, pp. 7–32.
3a.   'Haute couture et haute culture', conference *Noroit*, 192, November, pp. 1–2,
        7–17.
3b.   Also in P. Bourdieu, *Questions de sociologie*, Paris, Éditions de Minuit, 1980,
        pp. 196–206.

1975

Articles
1.   'Méthode scientifique et hiérarchie sociale des objets', *Actes de la recherche
        en sciences sociales*, 1, January, pp. 4–6.
2.   'Le couturier et sa griffe. Contribution à une théorie de la magie', *Actes de
        la recherche en sciences sociales*, 1, January, pp. 7–36 (with Y. Delsaut).
3.   'L'invention de la vie d'artiste', *Actes de la recherche en sciences sociales*, 2, March,
        pp. 67–94.
4.   'Les catégories de l'entendement professoral', *Actes de la recherche en sciences
        sociales*, 3, May, pp. 68–93 (with M. de Saint-Martin).
4E.   'The categories of professorial judgement', in P. Bourdieu, *Homo Academicus*,
        Oxford, Polity Press, 1988, pp. 194–225.
5a.   'La spécificité du champ scientifique et les conditions sociales du progrès de
        la raison', *Sociologie et sociétés* (Montreal), VII, 1, May, pp. 91–118.
5b.   Also 'Le champ scientifique', *Actes de la recherche en sciences sociales*, 2–3, June,
        1976, pp. 88–104.
5aE1.   'The specificity of the scientific field and the social conditions of the progress
        of reason' (trans. R. Nice), *Social Science Information*, XIV, 6, December 1975,
        pp. 19–47.
5aE2.   Also in C.C. Lemert (ed.), *French Sociology, Rupture and Renewal Since 1968*,
        New York, Columbia University Press, 1981, pp. 257–92.
6.   'Le titre et le poste. Rapports entre le système de production et le système
        de reproduction', *Actes de la recherche en sciences sociales*, 2, March, pp. 95–107
        (with L. Boltanski).
6E1.   'Formal qualifications and occupational hierarchies: the relationship between

the production system and the reproduction system' (trans. R. Nice), in *Reorganizing Education*, 1, 1977, pp. 61–9.

6E2. Also 'The educational system and the economy: titles and jobs', in C.C. Lemert (ed.), *French Sociology, Rupture and Renewal Since 1968*, New York, Columbia University Press, 1981, pp. 141–51.

7. 'Le fétichisme de la langue', *Actes de la recherche en sciences sociales*, 4, July, pp. 2–32 (with L. Boltanski).

8. 'La critique du discours lettré', *Actes de la recherche en sciences sociales*, 5–6, November, pp. 4–8.

9a. 'L'ontologie politique de Martin Heidegger', *Actes de la recherche en sciences sociales*, 5–6 November, pp. 109–56.

9b. (Modified version) *L'Ontologie politique de Martin Heidegger*, Paris, Éditions de Minuit, 1988.

10. 'Le langage autorisé. Note sur les conditions sociales de l'efficacité du discours rituel', *Actes de la recherche en sciences sociales*, 5–6, November, pp. 183–90.

10E. forthcoming in *Language and Symbolic Power*, Oxford, Polity Press, 1991.

11. 'La lecture de Marx: quelques remarques critiques à propos de "Quelques remarques critiques à propos de *Lire Le Capital*" ', *Actes de la recherche en sciences sociales*, 5–6, November, pp. 65–79.

12. 'Les intellectuels dans le champ de la lutte des classes', *La nouvelle critique*, 87, October, pp. 20–6 (conversation with A. Casanova and M. Simon).

1976

Articles

1. 'Le sens pratique', *Actes de la recherche en sciences sociales*, 1, February, pp. 43–86.

2. 'Les modes de domination', *Actes de la recherche en sciences sociales*, 2–3, June, pp. 122–32.

3. 'La production de l'idéologie dominante', *Actes de la recherche en sciences sociales*, 2–3, June, pp. 3–73 (with L. Boltanski).

4. 'Un jeu chinois. Notes pour une critique sociale du jugement', *Actes de la recherche en sciences sociales*, 4, August, pp. 91–101.

5. 'Anatomie du goût', *Actes de la recherche en sciences sociales*, 5, October, pp. 2–112 (with M. de Saint-Martin).

6a. 'Les conditions sociales de la production sociologique: sociologie coloniale et décolonisation de la sociologie', Intervention at a Conference on 'Ethnology and politics in the Maghreb' (Paris, June 1975), in *Le Mal de voir*, Paris, Union Générale d'Éditions (UGE), coll. 10/18, Cahiers Jussieu 2, pp. 416–27.

6b. Also 'Pour une sociologie des sociologues', in P. Bourdieu, *Questions de sociologie*, Paris, Éditions de Minuit, 1980, pp. 79–85.

1977

Book

1. *Algérie 60, structures économiques et structures temporelles*, Paris, Éditions de Minuit.

1E. *Algeria 1960* (trans. R. Nice), Cambridge–Paris, Cambridge University Press/ Éditions de la Maison des Sciences de l'Homme, 1979, pp. 1–94.

Articles

1. 'Questions de politique', *Actes de la recherche en sciences sociales*, 16, September, pp. 55–89.
2. 'Une classe objet', *Actes de la recherche en sciences sociales*, 17–18, November, pp. 1–5.
3. 'La production de la croyance: contribution à une économie des biens symboliques', *Actes de la recherche en sciences sociales*, 13, February, pp. 3–43.
3E1. 'The production of belief: contribution to an economy of symbolic goods' (trans. R. Nice), *Media, Culture and Society*, 2, 3, July 1980, pp. 261–93.
3E2. Also in *Media, Culture and Society, a Critical Reader*, London, Sage Publications, 1986, pp. 131–63.
4. 'Remarques provisoires sur la perception sociale du corps', *Actes de la recherche en sciences sociales*, 14, April, pp. 51–4.
5. 'Sur le pouvoir symbolique', Conference (Harvard University, 1973), *Annales*, 3, May–June, pp. 405–11.
5E1. 'Symbolic power' (trans. C. Wringe), in D. Gleeson (ed.), *Identity and Structure: Issues in the Sociology of Education*, Driffield, Nafferton Books, 1977, pp. 112–19.
5E2. Also in *Critique of Anthropology* (trans. R. Nice), 4, 13/14, summer 1979, pp. 77–85.
5E3. forthcoming in *Language and Symbolic Power*, Oxford, Polity Press, 1991.
6. 'L'économie des échanges linguistiques', Seminar (Paris, EHESS, 25 November, 1976), *Langue française*, 34, May, pp. 17–34.
6E. 'The economics of linguistic exchanges' (trans. R. Nice), *Social Science Information*, XVI, 6, December, 1977, pp. 645–68.
7. 'Linguistique et sociologie du langage', Participation in a round table discussion with J.C. Chevalier, S. Delesalle, P. Encrevé, G. Fauconnier, J.C. Milner and A. Rey (Paris, Maison des Sciences de l'Homme, October 1976), *Langue française*, 34, May, pp. 35–51.
8a. 'La censure', Intervention at a Conference on the 'Science des œuvres' (Lille, May 1974), *Information sur les sciences sociales*, XVI, 3/4, pp. 385–8.
8b. Also in P. Bourdieu, *Questions de sociologie*, Paris, Éditions de Minuit, 1980, pp. 138–42.
9a. 'Le paradoxe du sociologue', Conference (Arras, Noroit, October 1977), *Noroit*, 222, November.
9b. Also in *Sociologie et sociétés* (Montreal), XI, 1, April 1979, pp. 85–94.
9c. Also in P. Bourdieu, *Questions de sociologie*, Paris, Éditions de Minuit, 1980, pp. 86–94.

1978

Articles

1. 'Capital symbolique et classes sociales', *L'Arc*, 72, pp. 13–19.
2. 'Le patronat', *Actes de la recherche en sciences sociales*, 20–1, March–April, pp. 3–82 (with M. de Saint Martin).
3. 'Sur l'objectivation participante. Réponses à quelques objections', *Actes de la recherche en sciences sociales*, 23, September, pp. 67–9.
4. 'Dialogue sur la poésie orale', *Actes de la recherche en sciences sociales*, 23, September, pp. 51–66 (with M. Mammeri).
5. 'Titres et quartiers de noblesse culturelle. Éléments d'une critique sociale du

jugement esthétique', *Ethnologie française*, VIII, 2–3, March–September, pp. 107–44 (with M. de Saint-Martin).

6.   'Classement, déclassement, reclassement', *Actes de la recherche en sciences sociales*, 24, November, pp. 2–22.

6E.   Epilogue in P. Bourdieu, *The Inheritors, French Students and their Relation to Culture*, Chicago–London, The University of Chicago Press, 1979, pp. 77–97.

7a.   'Pratiques sportives et pratiques sociales', Inaugural Conference of the International Congress of HISPA (Paris, INSEP, 28 March–2 April 1978), *Actes du VIIe Congrès International*, Paris, INSEP, 1978, 1, pp. 17–37.

7b.   Also 'Comment peut-on être sportif?', in P. Bourdieu, *Questions de sociologie*, Paris, Éditions de Minuit, 1980, pp. 173–95.

7bE.   'Sport and Social Class' (trans. R. Nice), *Social Science Information*, XVII, 6, 1978, pp. 819–40.

8a.   'Savoir ce que parler veut dire', Intervention at the Congress of AFEF (Limoges, 30 October 1977), *Le français aujourd'hui*, 41, March, pp. 4–20.

8b.   Also in P. Bourdieu, *Questions de sociologie*, Paris, Éditions de Minuit, 1980, pp. 95–112.

9a.   'Le racisme de l'intelligence', *Cahiers Droit et liberté* (Races, sociétés et aptitudes: apports et limites de la science, Colloquium of UNESCO, 27 May 1978), supplement to no. 382, pp. 67–71.

9b.   Also in *Réforme*, 1 December 1979, pp. 6–7.

9c.   Also in P. Bourdieu, *Questions de sociologie*, Paris, Éditions de Minuit, 1980, pp. 264–8.

9d.   Also in J. Belkhir, *L'Intellectuel: l'intelligentsia et les manuels*, Paris, Éditions Anthropos, 1983, pp. 187–94.

9e.   Also 'Tout racisme est un essentialisme', *Différences*, 24–5, June–July 1983, p. 44.

10a.   'Les intellectuels sont-ils hors jeu?', *La Nouvelle critique*, 111–12, February–March, pp. 56–61 (conversation with F. Hincker).

10b.   Also in P. Bourdieu, *Questions de sociologie*, Paris, Éditions de Minuit, 1980, pp. 61–6.

11a.   'Deux doigts de Ravel sec', *Le Monde de la musique*, 6 December, pp. 30–1 (conversation with C. Huvé).

11b.   Also 'L'origine et l'évolution des espèces de mélomanes', in P. Bourdieu, *Questions de sociologie*, Paris, Éditions de Minuit, 1980, pp. 155–60.

12a.   Conversation (with A.M. Métailié) in *Les jeunes et le premier emploi*, Paris, Association des Âges, pp. 520–30.

12b.   Also 'La jeunesse n'est qu'un mot', in P. Bourdieu, *Questions de sociologie*, Paris, Éditions de Minuit, 1980, pp. 143–54.

1979

Book

1.   *La Distinction. Critique sociale du jugement*, Paris, Éditions de Minuit. (New and augmented edition with an introduction, 1982.)

1E1.   Prepublications (trans. R. Nice), pp. 9–61, 'The aristocracy of culture', *Media, Culture and Society*, 2, 3, July, 1980, pp. 225–54.

1E2.   Also in *Media, Culture and Society, a Critical Reader*, London, Sage Publications, 1986, pp. 164–93.

1E3.   Pp. 139–44, 'A diagram of social position and life-style', *Media, Culture and Society*, 2, 3, July 1980, pp. 255–9.

1E4.   Complete publication: *Distinction. A Social Critique of the Judgement of Taste* (trans. R. Nice), Cambridge (Massachusetts), Harvard University Press, 1984.

1E5.   Paperback edition, London, New York, Routledge and Kegan Paul, 1986.

Articles

1.   'Les trois états du capital culturel', *Actes de la recherche en sciences sociales*, 30, November, pp. 3–6.

2a.   'Des goûts artistiques et des classes sociales', *Libération*, 3–4 November, pp. 12–13 (conversation with D. Eribon).

2b.   Also 'L'art de résister aux paroles', in P. Bourdieu, *Questions de sociologie*, Paris, Éditions de Minuit, 1980, pp. 10–18.

1980

Books

·1.   *Le Sens pratique*, Paris, Éditions de Minuit.

1E.   (forthcoming) *The Logic of Practice*, Oxford, Polity Press, 1990.

2.   *Questions de sociologie*, Paris, Éditions de Minuit.

Articles

1.   'Le capital social. Notes provisoires', *Actes de la recherche en sciences sociales*, 31, January, pp. 2–3.

2.   'Lettre à Paolo Fossati à propos de la *Storia dell'arte italiana*', *Actes de la recherche en sciences sociales*, 31, January, pp. 90–2.

3.   'Le mort saisit le vif. Les relations entre l'histoire réifiée et l'histoire incorporée', *Actes de la recherche en sciences sociales*, 32–3, April–June, pp. 3–14.

4.   'Et si on parlait de l'Afghanistan?', *Actes de la recherche en sciences sociales*, 34, September, pp. 2–16 (with P. and M. Centlivres).

5.   'Le Nord et le Midi. Contribution à une analyse de l'effet Montesquieu', *Actes de la recherche en sciences sociales*, 35, November, pp. 21–5.

6.   'L'identité et la représentation. Éléments pour une réflexion critique sur l'idée de région', *Actes de la recherche en sciences sociales*, 35, November, pp. 63–72.

7.   'Où sont les terroristes?', *Esprit*, 11–12, November–December, pp. 253–8.

8E.   'Sartre' (trans. R. Nice), *London Review of Books*, 2, 22, 20 November–3 December, pp. 11–12.

8.   Published in French as 'Sartre, l'invention de l'intellectuel total', *Libération*, 31 March 1983, pp. 20–1.

9.   'La fin des intellectuels?', Conference (Arras, Noroit, October 1980), *Noroit*, 253, November, pp. 2–8.

10.   'Des contradictions linguistiques léguées par le colonisateur', *Libération*, 19–20 April, p. 13 (conversation with D. Eribon).

11a.   'La grande illusion des intellectuels', *Le Monde dimanche*, 4 May, pp. I and XVII (conversation with D. Eribon).

11b.   Also 'Comment libérer les intellectuels libres?', in P. Bourdieu, *Questions de sociologie*, Paris, Éditions de Minuit, 1980, pp. 67–78.

12a.   'La sociologie est-elle une science?', *La Recherche*, 112, June, pp. 738–43 (conversation with P. Thuillier).

12b.   Also 'Une science qui dérange', in P. Bourdieu, *Questions de sociologie*, Paris, Éditions de Minuit, pp. 19–36.

1981

Articles

1.   'La représentation politique. Éléments pour une théorie du champ politique', *Actes de la recherche en sciences sociales*, 36–7, February–March, pp. 3–24.

1E.   forthcoming in *Language and Symbolic Power*, Oxford, Polity Press, 1991.

2.   'Décrire et prescrire. Note sur les conditions de possibilité et les limites de l'efficacité politique', *Actes de la recherche en sciences sociales*, 38, May, pp. 69–73.

2E.   forthcoming in *Language and Symbolic Power*, Oxford, Polity Press, 1991.

3.   'Épreuve scolaire et consécration sociale. Les classes préparatoires aux Grandes écoles', *Actes de la recherche en sciences sociales*, 39, September, pp. 3–70.

4.   'Pour une sociologie de la perception', *Actes de la recherche en sciences sociales*, 40, November, pp. 3–9 (with Y. Delsaut).

5.   'Men and Machines', in K. Knorr-Cetina, A.V. Cicourel (eds), *Advances in Social Theory and Methodology. Toward an Integration of Micro- and Macro-sociologies*, Boston, London, Henley, Routledge and Kegan Paul, pp. 304–17.

6a.   'Mais qui a créé les créateurs?', Conference (Paris, ENSAD, 1980), in *Art: Sur 10 ans, aujourd'hui, 1981*, Paris, Ministry of Culture, pp. 71–84.

6b.   Also in P. Bourdieu, *Questions de sociologie*, Paris, Éditions de Minuit, 1980, pp. 207–21.

7a.   'Lecture, lecteurs, lettrés, littérature', Conference (Grenoble, 1981), in *Recherches sur la philosophie et le langage*, Grenoble, University of Social Sciences, Cahier du Groupe de recherches sur la philosophie et le langage, pp. 5–16.

7b.   Also in P. Bourdieu, *Choses dites*, Paris, Éditions de Minuit, 1987, pp. 132–43.

1982

Books

1.   *Leçon sur la leçon*, Paris, Éditions de Minuit. Leçon inaugurale, no. 90, Paris, Collège de France.

1E.   forthcoming in *In Other Words*, Oxford, Polity Press, 1990.

2.   *Ce que parler veut dire. L'économie des échanges linguistiques*, Paris, Fayard.

2E.   (with the exception of Part III, Chapters 2 and 3) forthcoming in *Language and Symbolic Power*, Oxford, Polity Press, 1991.

Articles

1.   'La sainte famille. L'épiscopat français dans le champ du pouvoir', *Actes de la recherche en sciences sociales*, 44–5, November, pp. 2–53 (with M. de Saint Martin).

2.   'Zaslawsky, contre la magie des mots', *Libération*, 7 December, p. 21.

3.   'Erving Goffman est mort', *Libération*, 2 December, p. 23.

4.   'Goffman, le découvreur de l'infiniment petit', *Le Monde*, 4 December, pp. 1 and 30.

4E. 'Erving Goffman, discoverer of the infinitely small' (trans. R. Nice), *Theory, Culture and Society*, 2, 1, 1983, pp. 112–13.

5a. 'Les rites d'institution' (oral communication, Neuchâtel, October 1981), *Actes de la recherche en sciences sociales*, 43, June, pp. 58–63.

5b. Also 'Les rites comme actes d'institution', in P. Centlivres and J. Hainard (eds), *Les Rites de passage aujourd'hui*, Actes du Colloque de Neuchâtel 1981, Lausanne, Éditions L'Âge d'Homme, 1986, pp. 206–15.

5aE. forthcoming in *Language and Symbolic Power*, Oxford, Polity Press, 1991.

1983

Articles

1E. 'The Philosophical Establishment' (trans. K. McLaughlin), in A. Montefiore (ed.), *Philosophy in France Today*, Cambridge, Cambridge University Press, pp. 1–8.

2. 'Le changement linguistique', *Actes de la recherche en sciences sociales*, 46, March, pp. 67–71 (with W. Labov and P. Encrevé).

3. 'Vous avez dit "populaire"?', *Actes de la recherche en sciences sociales*, 46, March, pp. 98–105.

3E. forthcoming in *Language and Symbolic Power*, Oxford, Polity Press, 1991.

4. 'Mai 68', *Lire*, 93, May, p. 22.

5. 'La discipline', *Contact*, special number, 'Exercer l'autorité aujourd'hui', 25, June, pp. 25–6.

6. 'Les sciences sociales et la philosophie', *Actes de la recherche en sciences sociales*, 47–8, June, pp. 45–52.

7E. 'The field of cultural production or: the economic world reversed' (trans. R. Nice), *Poetics* (Amsterdam), 12, 4–5, November, pp. 311–56.

8E. 'The forms of capital' (trans. R. Nice), in J.G. Richardson (ed.), *Handbook of Theory and Research for the Sociology of Education*, New York, Westport (Connecticut), London, Greenwood Press, 1986, pp. 241–58. (Translation of 'Ökonomisches Kapital, kulturelles Kapital, soziales Kapital' (trans. R. Kreckel), *Soziale Welt* (Göttingen), special number, 'Soziale Ungleichheiten', R. Kreckel (ed.), Sonderheft 2, 1983, pp. 183–98.)

9. 'Interview met Pierre Bourdieu' (with J. Heilbron and B. Maso), *Sociologisch Tijdschrift* (Amsterdam), X, 2, October, pp. 307–34.
   French publication, 'Repères', in P. Bourdieu, *Choses dites*, Paris, Éditions de Minuit, 1987, pp. 47–71.

1984

Book

1. *Homo academicus*, Paris, Éditions de Minuit.

1E. *Homo Academicus* (trans. P. Collier), Oxford, Polity Press, 1988.

Articles

1. 'La perception du monde social: une question de mots?', *Actes de la recherche en sciences sociales*, 52–3, June, pp. 13–14.

2. 'La représentation de la position sociale', *Actes de la recherche en sciences sociales*, 52–3, June, pp. 14–15.

3.   'Le hit-parade des intellectuels français, ou qui sera juge de la légitimité des juges?', *Actes de la recherche en sciences sociales*, 52–3, June, pp. 95–100.

4.   'Le champ littéraire. Préalables critiques et principes de méthode', *Lendemains* (Berlin–Cologne), IX, 36, pp. 5–20.

5.   'Capital et marché linguistiques', *Linguistische Berichte* (Constance), 90, pp. 3–24.

6.   'La dernière instance', in *Le Siècle de Kafka*, Paris, Centre Georges Pompidou, pp. 268–70.

7.   'Consommation culturelle', in *Encyclopaedia Universalis*, new edition, vol. 2, 'Art', pp. 779–82.

8.   'Le plaisir de savoir' (about Michel Foucault), *Le Monde*, 27 June, pp. 1 and 10.

9.   'Espace social et genèse des "classes"' (oral communication, Frankfurt University, February 1984), *Actes de la recherche en sciences sociales*, 52–3, June, pp. 3–12.

9E1.   'The social space and the genesis of groups' (trans. R. Nice), *Social Science Information*, 24, 2, 1985, pp. 195–220.

9E2.   Also in *Theory and Society* (trans. R. Nice), 14, 1985, pp. 723–44.

9E3.   forthcoming in *Language and Symbolic Power*, Oxford, Polity Press, 1991.

10.   'Pour une critique de la lecture' (oral communication, Strasbourg, Centre de documentation en histoire de la philosophie, 1984), *La lecture II*, Cahiers du Seminaire de philosophie, 2, pp. 13–17.

11a.   'La délégation et le fétichisme politique' (oral communication Paris, Association des étudiants protestants, June 1983), *Actes de la recherche en sciences sociales*, 52–3, June, pp. 49–55.

11b.   Also in P. Bourdieu, *Choses dites*, Paris, Éditions de Minuit, 1987, pp. 185–202.

11aE1. 'Delegation and political fetichism' (trans. K. Robinson), *Thesis Eleven*, 10–11, November 1984–March 1985, pp. 56–70.

11aE2. forthcoming in *Language and Symbolic Power*, Oxford, Polity Press, 1991.

12a.   'Réponse aux économistes' (intervention at a conference on 'Le modèle économique dans les sciences sociales', Paris I University, April 1981), *Économies et sociétés*, XVIII, 10, October, pp. 23–32.

12b.   Also 'L'interêt du sociologue', in P. Bourdieu, *Choses dites*, Paris, Éditions de Minuit, 1987, pp. 124–31.

1985

Articles

1a.   'Remarques à propos de la valeur scientifique et des effets politiques des enquêtes d'opinion', *Pouvoirs*, 'Les sondages', 33, April, pp. 131–9.

1b.   Also 'Le sondage, une "science" sans savant', in P. Bourdieu, *Choses dites*, Paris, Éditions de Minuit, 1987, pp. 217–24.

2.   'Quand les Canaques prennent la parole', *Actes de la recherche en sciences sociales*, 56, March, pp. 69–83 (with A. Bensa).

3.   'Effet de champ et effet de corps', *Actes de la recherche en sciences sociales*, 59, September, p. 73.

4.   'Dialogue à propos de l'histoire culturelle' (with R. Chartier and R. Darnton), *Actes de la recherche en sciences sociales*, 59, September, pp. 86–93.

5.   'Existe-t-il une littérature belge? Limites d'un champ et frontières politiques', *Études de lettres* (Lausanne), 4, October–December, pp. 3–6.

6E.   'The genesis of the concepts of habitus and field' (trans. C. Newman), *Sociocriticism* (Pittsburgh–Pa–, Montpellier) 2, December, pp. 11–24.

7.   'Les intellectuels et les pouvoirs', in *Michel Foucault, une histoire de la vérité*, Paris, Syros, pp. 93–4.

8.   'A free thinker: "Do not ask me who I am"' (trans. R. Nice), *Paragraph*, London, 5, March, pp. 80–7.

9a.   'Le champ religieux dans le champ de production symbolique' (oral communication, Strasbourg, October 1982), postface, in *Les Nouveaux Clercs*, Geneva, Labor et fides, pp. 255–61.

9b.   Also 'La dissolution du religieux', in P. Bourdieu, *Choses dites*, Paris, Éditions de Minuit, 1987, pp. 117–23.

10.   'Les professeurs de l'Université de Paris à la veille de Mai 68' (Paris, Colloquium organized by the Institut d'Histoire Moderne et Contemporaine and the EHESS, June 1984), in *Le Personnel de l'enseignement supérieur en France aux XIXe et XXe siècles*, Paris, Éditions du CNRS, pp. 177–84.

11.   'La lecture: une pratique culturelle' in *Pratiques de la lecture*, Paris, Rivages, pp. 218–39 (conversation with R. Chartier).

12a.   'De la règle aux stratégies', *Terrains*, 4, March, pp. 93–100 (conversation with P. Lamaison).

12b.   Also in P. Bourdieu, *Choses dites*, Paris, Éditions de Minuit, 1987, pp. 75–93.

12E.   'From Rules to Strategies' (trans. R. Hurley), *Cultural Anthropology*, 1, 1, February 1986, pp. 110–20.

13.   'Du bon usage de l'ethnologie', *Awal*, Cahiers d'études berbères, 1, pp. 7–29 (conversation with M. Mammeri).

14.   'Le rapport du Collège de France: Pierre Bourdieu s'explique', *La Quinzaine littéraire*, 445, 1–31 August, pp. 8–10 (conversation with J.P. Salgas).

1986

Articles

1.   'La science et l'actualité', *Actes de la recherche en sciences sociales*, 61, March, pp. 2–3.

2.   'L'illusion biographique', *Actes de la recherche en sciences sociales*, 62–3, June, pp. 69–72.

2E.   'The biographical illusion' (trans. Y. Winkin and W. Leeds-Hurwitz), *Working Papers and Proceedings of the Center for Psychosocial Studies* (Chicago), 14, 1987, pp. 1–7.

3.   'Nécessiter', *L'Herne*, Cahier Francis Ponge, Paris, Éditions de l'Herne, June, pp. 434–7.

4.   'La force du droit. Éléments pour une sociologie du champ juridique', *Actes de la recherche en sciences sociales*, 64, September, pp. 5–19.

4E.   'The force of law: toward a sociology of the juridical field' (trans. R. Terdiman), *Hastings Law Journal*, 38, 5, July 1987, pp. 814–53.

5.   'Les mésaventures de l'amateur', in R. Samuel (ed.), *Éclats/Boulez*, Paris, Éditions du Centre Georges Pompidou, pp. 74–5.

6.   'An antimony in the notion of collective protest', in A. Foxley, M.S. McPherson, G. O'Donnell (eds), *Development, Democracy, and the Art of Trespassing: Essays*

in Honor of Albert O. Hirschman, Notre Dame (Indiana), University of Notre Dame Press, pp. 301–2.

7a.   'Habitus, code et codification', Conference (Neuchâtel, May 1983), *Actes de la recherche en sciences sociales*, 64, September, pp. 40–4.

7b.   Also 'La codification', in P. Bourdieu, *Choses dites*, Paris, Éditions de Minuit, 1987, pp. 94–105.

8.   'De quoi parle-t-on quand on parle du "problème de la jeunesse"?' (Paris, Colloquium organized by the Programme mobilisateur Technologie, Emploi, Travail, du Ministère de la recherche et de la technologie, December 1985), in *Les Jeunes et les autres. Contributions des sciences de l'homme à la question des jeunes*, Vaucresson, CRIV (Centre de recherche Interdisciplinaire de Vaucresson), Vol. II, pp. 229–34.

9a.   'Der Kampf um die symbolische Ordnung', *Ästhetik und Kommunikation* (Frankfurt), 16, 61–2, pp. 142–63 (conversation with A. Honneth, H. Kocyba, B. Schwibs).

9b.   Published in French as '"Fieldwork in philosophy"', in P. Bourdieu, *Choses dites*, Paris, Éditions de Minuit, 1987, pp. 13–46.

9E.   'The struggle for symbolic order' (trans. J. Bleicher), *Theory, Culture and Society*, 3, 3, 1986, pp. 35–51.

10.   'D'abord défendre les intellectuels', *Le Nouvel Observateur*, 12–18 September, p. 82 (conversation with D. Eribon).

11.   'A quand un lycée Bernard Tapie?', *Libération*, 4 December, p. 4 (conversation with A. de Gaudemar).

11E.   'Revolt of the spirit' (trans. C. Turner), *New Socialist*, 46, February 1987, pp. 9–11.

1987

Books

1.   *Choses dites*, Paris, Éditions de Minuit.

1E1.   (Pp. 203–16), 'Program for a sociology of sport' (trans J. McAloon and A.D. Savage), *Sociology of Sport Journal*, 5, 1988, pp. 153–61.

1E2.   (forthcoming) *In Other Words*, Oxford, Polity Press, 1990.

2.   'L'institutionnalisation de l'anomie', *Les Cahiers du Musée National d'Art Moderne*, 19–20, June, pp. 6–19.

3.   'Agrégation et ségrégation. Le champ des grandes écoles et le champ du pouvoir', *Actes de la recherche en sciences sociales*, 69, September, pp. 2–50 (with M. de Saint Martin).

4.   'Variations et invariants. Éléments pour une histoire structurale du champ des grandes écoles', *Actes de la recherche en sciences sociales*, 70, November, pp. 3–30.

5a.   'The historical genesis of a pure aesthetic' (trans. C. Newman), *The Journal of Aesthetics and Art Criticism*, XLVI, special issue, pp. 201–10.

5b.   Also in R. Shusterman (ed.), *Analytic Aesthetics*, Oxford, New York, Basil Blackwell, 1989.

6.   'L'assassinat de Maurice Halbwachs', *La Liberté de l'esprit*, 16, autumn, pp. 161–8.

7a.   'Sociologues de la croyance et croyance de sociologues' (Paris, Congrès de l'Association française de sociologie religieuse, December 1982), *Archives de sciences sociales des religions*, 63, 1, January–March, pp. 155–61.

7b.   Also in P. Bourdieu, *Choses dites*, Paris, Éditions de Minuit, pp. 106–11.
8.   'La révolution impressionniste' (conference, Arras, Noroit, January), *Noroit*, 303, September–October, pp. 3–18.
9.   'What makes a social class? On the theoretical and practical existence of groups' (conference, Chicago, The University of Chicago, April; trans. L.J.D. Wacquant and D. Young), *Berkeley Journal of Sociology*, XXXII, pp. 1–17.
10.   'Esquisse d'un projet intellectuel: un entretien avec Pierre Bourdieu', *The French Review*, 61, 2, December, pp. 194–205 (conversation with C. Duverlie).

1988

Book
1.   *L'ontologie politique de Martin Heidegger* (new, revised edition), Paris, Éditions de Minuit.
1E.   (forthcoming) *The Political Ontology of Martin Heidegger*, Oxford, Polity Press, 1991.

Articles
1.   'Flaubert's point of view' (trans. P. Parkhurst Ferguson), *Critical Inquiry*, 14, 3, spring, pp. 539–62.
2.   'Penser la politique', *Actes de la recherche en sciences sociales*, 71–2, March, pp. 2–3.
3.   'La vertu civile', *Le Monde*, 16 September, pp. 1–2.
4.   'A long trend of change' (review of M. Lewin, *The Gorbachev Phenomenon: A Historical Interpretation*), *Times Literary Supplement*, August 12–18, pp. 875–6.
5.   'On interest and the relative autonomy of symbolic power: a rejoinder to some objections' (conference, trans. L.J.D. Wacquant and M. Lawson), *Working Papers and Proceedings of the Center for Psychosocial Studies* (Chicago), 20, pp. 1–11.
6.   'The crumbling of orthodoxy and its legacy' (conference, University of Chicago, April 1987; trans. L.J.D. Wacquant), *Theory and Society*, 17, pp. 773–87.
7.   'Heidegger par Pierre Bourdieu: le krach de la philosophie' (conversation with R. Maggiori), *Libération*, 10 March, Book Supplement, pp. vi–vii.

1989

Book
1.   *La Noblesse d'état, Grandes écoles et esprit de corps*, Paris, Éditions de Minuit.

Articles
1.   'Naître à Normale', *Le Monde de la Révolution française*, 3, March, *Journal des droits de l'homme*, p. 25.
2.   'The Corporatism of the Universal: the role of intellectuals in the modern world' (trans. C. Betensky), *Telos*, no. 81, Fall, pp. 99–110.
3.   'L'opinion publique', in *50 idées qui ébranlent le monde. Dictionnaire de la glasnost*, Y. Afanassiev, M. Ferro (eds), Paris/Moscow, Éditions Payot/Éditions Progress, pp. 204–6 (with P. Champagne).
4.   'Reproduction interdite. La dimension symbolique de la domination économique', *Études rurales*, no. 113–14, January–June, pp. 15–36.
5.   'Le beau rôle', *Liber* (supplement of *Le Monde*, 11 October), 1, October, pp. 60–1.

5E.   'He whose word is law', *Liber* (supplement to the *Times Literary Supplement* of 11 October), 1, October, pp. 12–13.

6.   'Scientific Field and Scientific Thought, Marginal Notes' (trans. L.J.D. Wacquant), in 'Author Meets Critics: reactions to "Theory in Anthropology since the Sixties"', *CSST Working Papers*, Ann Arbor, University of Michigan, November, pp. 84–94.

7.   'L'histoire se lève à l'Est', *Liber* (supplement of *Le Monde*, 16 December), 2, December, p. 3.

7E.   'History dawns in the East', *Liber* (supplement to the *Times Literary Supplement* of 16 December), 2, December, p. 3.

8.   'Le pouvoir n'est plus Rue d'Ulm mais à l'ENA' (conversation with D. Eribon), *Le nouvel observateur*, 9–15 March, pp. 80–2.

9.   'For a Socio-Analysis of Intellectuals: On *Homo Academicus*' (conversation with L.J.D. Wacquant), *Berkeley Journal of Sociology*, vol. xxxiv, pp. 1–29.

10.   'A workshop with Pierre Bourdieu' (conversation with L.J.D. Wacquant), *Sociological Theory*, vol. 7, no. 1, spring, pp. 32–55.

11.   'Entretien sur la pratique, le temps et l'histoire' (conversation with T. Yamamoto), *Iichiko intercultural* (Tokyo), no. 1, May, pp. 6–13.

1990

Articles

1.   'Un signe des temps', *Actes de la recherche en sciences sociales*, 81–2, March, pp. 2–5.

2.   'Un placement de père de famille. La maison individuelle: spécificité du produit et logique du champ de production', *Actes de la recherche en sciences sociales*, 81–2, March, pp. 6–33 (with S. Bouhedja, R. Christin, C. Givry).

3.   'Un contrat sous contrainte', *Actes de la recherche en sciences sociales*, 81–2, March, pp. 34–51 (with S. Bouhedja, C. Givry).

4.   'Le sens de la propriété. La genèse sociale des systèmes de préférences', *Actes de la recherche en sciences sociales*, 81–2, March, pp. 52–64 (with M. de Saint Martin).

5.   'La construction du marché. Le champ administratif et la production de la "politique du logement" ', *Actes de la recherche en sciences sociales*, 81–2, March, pp. 65–85 (with R. Christin).

6.   'Droit et passe-droit. Le champ des pouvoirs territoriaux et la mise en oeuvre des règlements', *Actes de la recherche en sciences sociales*, 81–2, March, pp. 86–96.

Notes

Chapter 1: Introduction

1. From 'The Windhover'. W.H. Gardner and N.H. Mackenzie, *The Poems of Gerard Manley Hopkins* (London, Oxford University Press, 1967), 4th edn, p. 69.
2. P. Bourdieu, *L'Ontologie politique de Martin Heidegger* (Paris, Éditions de Minuit, 1988), p. 7.
3. Ibid.
4. P. Bourdieu, 'L'ontologie politique de Martin Heidegger', *Actes de la recherche en sciences sociales*, 5–6 (November 1975), p. 109.
5. Ibid., pp. 148–9.
6. Ibid., p. 149.
7. Ibid.
8. Bourdieu, *L'Ontologie politique de Martin Heidegger*, p. 7.
9. Polity Press, Complete Catalogue (1990), p. 13.
10. Ibid., p. 45.
11. Bourdieu, 'L'ontologie politique de Martin Heidegger', p. 109.
12. See the account of the development of the Centre given by Stuart Hall in 'Cultural studies and the Centre: some problematics and problems', in *Culture, Media, Language. Working Papers in Cultural Studies, 1972–79* (London, Hutchinson, 1980), pp. 15–47; and in the preface to that volume.
13. North East London Polytechnic (now the Polytechnic of East London), *Cultural Studies. Sexennial Review* (1989), p. 11.
14. See P. Bourdieu, preface to the English edition of *Homo Academicus* (Oxford, Polity Press, 1988), p. xxvi. Bourdieu uses the word within the French text (*Homo academicus*, Paris, Éditions de Minuit, 1984, p. 72) which corresponds with p. 49 of the English translation for which Peter Collier provides a useful footnote: 'The original meaning of "oblate" is a child from a poor family entrusted to a religious foundation to be trained for the priesthood. Bourdieu borrows the religious term to suggest the intensity of institutional loyalty felt by the teacher of humble origins who owes his whole education, culture, training and career to the state educational system' (n. 31, p. 291).

15. For more detail of the origins and development of the BA/BSc by Independent Study, see my *The Rise of Independent Study. The Politics and the Philosophy of an Educational Innovation, 1970–87* (Milton Keynes, SRHE and Open University Press, 1988), particularly Chapters 6 and 10.

16. Taken from case-studies in Diana Robbins, *Five Projects and Poverty. Final evaluation report on five UK projects funded under the Second European Community Programme to Combat Poverty* (Centre for the Analysis of Social Policy, University of Bath, October 1989), p. 42.

Chapter 2: Algeria, 1957–64

1. See P. Bourdieu, 'The sentiment of honour in Kabyle society', in J.G. Peristiany (ed.), *Honour and Shame. The Values of Mediterranean Society* (London, Weidenfeld & Nicolson, 1965), p. 233.

2. See P. Bourdieu, 'Révolution dans la révolution', *Esprit*, 1 (January 1961), pp. 29, 31, 32.

3. See the initial acknowledgements of P. Bourdieu, *Le Déracinement*, and pp. 41 and 61 of the text for details of the enquiry. See the introductory essay of *Travail et travailleurs* (particularly, p. 13) and p. 260 where most of the named researchers coincide with those acknowledged in *Le Déracinement*. See also Bourdieu's footnote to 'La hantise du chômage chez l'ouvrier algérien', *Sociologie du travail*, 4 (1962), p. 313.

4. A. Horne, *A Savage War of Peace. Algeria 1954–1962* (London, Macmillan, 1977).

5. A flavour of the ideological context within which Bourdieu was working can be gained by considering the positions adopted by Frantz Fanon and Albert Camus. Fanon joined the FLN in 1956 and became the ambassador of the Algerian Provisional Government to Ghana. During this period he gradually articulated a philosophy which advocated world-wide violent de-colonization as a means for attaining the psychic transformation of colonized peoples. For an introduction to Fanon's thinking, see D. Caute, *Fanon* (London, Fontana, 1970). By contrast, Camus was himself a 'pied noir'. He believed himself to be a radical colonist – advocating the gradual establishment of a liberal, democratic Algérie française. His *Chroniques Algériennes, 1939–1958* which included the journalistic articles which he wrote about Kabylia in 1939 were published in Paris in 1958 as part of his campaign still to argue that his preferred anti-independence solution might be possible. For an introduction to Camus, see C. Cruise O'Brien, *Camus* (London, Fontana, 1970).

6. P. Bourdieu, *Sociologie de l'Algérie* (Paris, PUF, 1958), p. 5. This is the translation provided in P. Bourdieu, *The Algerians* (trans. A.C.M. Ross) (Boston, Beacon Press, 1962), p. xi (footnote).

7. P. Bourdieu, *Choses dites* (Paris, Éditions de Minuit, 1987), p. 16.

8. M. Merleau-Ponty, *Phénoménologie de la perception*, Paris, Gallimard, 1945. Translated as *Phenomenology of Perception*, London, Routledge and Kegan Paul, 1962.

9. J.P. Sartre, *L'Être et le néant: essai d'ontologie phénoménologique* (Paris, Gallimard, 1943). Translated as *Being and Nothingness* (New York, Philosophical Library, 1956), and first published as a University Paperback (London, Methuen, 1969).

10. Ibid. (1969), p. xxi.

11. Ibid., p. xxii.

12. Bourdieu, *Sociologie de l'Algérie*, p. 5. This passage was not retained in the second French edition and does not, therefore, feature in *The Algerians*.

13. Bourdieu, *The Algerians*, p. 1.

14. Ibid., p. 25.

15. Ibid., p. 37.

16. Ibid., p. 1.

17. Ibid., p. 25.

18. Ibid., p. 2.

19. Bourdieu, *Sociologie de l'Algérie*, p. 18. This passage is removed from the second edition as are the references to Lévi-Strauss and Mauss in the discussion which follows.

20. Bourdieu, *The Algerians*, p. 24. This is an abbreviated and modified version of *Sociologie de l'Algérie*, pp. 29–30.

21. Bourdieu, *The Algerians*, p. 38.

22. Ibid., p. 45.

23. Bourdieu, *Sociologie de l'Algérie*, p. 41. Bourdieu here cites Jacques Berque, *Les Structures sociales du Haut-Atlas*, Paris, PUF, 1955, p. 224. The passage is not retained in the second edition. See the preface to P. Bourdieu, *Le Sens pratique* (Paris, Éditions de Minuit, 1980), for Bourdieu's 'reinstatement' of Berque as an influence.

24. Ibid., p. 42.

25. P. Bourdieu, 'Révolution dans la révolution'. *Esprit*, 1 (January 1961), pp. 27–40.

26. Bourdieu, *The Algerians*, p. 155. See also the *Esprit* article, p. 32.

27. F. Perroux (ed.), *L'Algérie de demain* (Paris, PUF, 1962).

28. In 'Révolution dans la révolution', *Esprit*, 1 (January 1961), pp. 27–40. Reproduced in translation in *The Algerians*.

29. P. Bourdieu, 'De la guerre révolutionnaire à la révolution', in Perroux, *L'Algérie de demain*, p. 7.

30. Ibid., p. 7.

31. Bourdieu uses 'anomie' in a comparable context in 1962 in 'Célibat et condition paysanne' but, interestingly, he never himself applies this concept – with its Durkheimian connotations – to the condition of the Algerians.

32. In J. Pitt-Rivers (ed.), *Mediterranean Countrymen* (Paris–The Hague, Mouton, 1964), pp. 55–72.

33. In I.W. Zartman (ed.) *Man, State and Society in the Contemporary Maghrib* (London, Pall Mall Press, 1973).

34. P. Bourdieu, 'Les sous-prolétaires algériens', *Les Temps modernes*, 199 (December 1962), pp. 1030–51.

35. P. Bourdieu, *Travail et travailleurs en Algérie* (Paris–The Hague, Mouton, 1963), p. 9.

36. Appendix IX.

37. Appendix I and also in the text, particularly pp. 260–7.

38. M. Léiris, 'L'ethnographe devant le colonialisme', *Les temps modernes* (August 1950).

39. Bourdieu, *Travail et travailleurs en Algérie*, p. 303.

40. Ibid., p. 311.

41. P. Bourdieu, *Le Déracinement* (Paris, Éditions de Minuit, 1964), p. 61.

42. See, particularly, Bourdieu's reference to D. Guèrin, 'Algérie: l'autogestion menacée', *France-Observateur*, 19 (December 1963), in *Le Déracinement*, p. 169.

43. Bourdieu, *Le Déracinement*, p. 177.

Chapter 3: The early research in France

1. Bourdieu, *Choses dites*, p. 75.
2. P. Bourdieu, 'Célibat et condition paysanne', *Études rurales*, 5–6 (April–September 1962), pp. 32–136.
3. P. Bourdieu, 'Les relations entre les sexes dans la société paysanne', *Les Temps modernes*, 195 (August 1962), pp. 307–31.
4. The phrase is the one used by Bourdieu in his preface to the English edition of *Homo Academicus* (Oxford, Polity Press, 1989), p. xxvi.
5. Bourdieu, 'Célibat et condition paysanne', p. 110.
6. Ibid., p. 111.
7. P. Laslett, *The World We Have Lost* (London, Methuen, 1965).
8. See, significantly, the subsequent publication of 'Les stratégies matrimoniales dans le système de reproduction', in *Annales*, 4–5 (July–October 1972), and its translation in a selection of articles from *Annales* in 1976: R. Forster and O. Ranum (eds), *Family and Society*.
9. Bourdieu, 'Célibat et condition paysanne', p. 32.
10. Ibid., p. 33.
11. This is the essence of his retrospection in the interview already quoted which was published in *Choses dites*, entitled 'De la règle aux stratégies'.
12. See 'Les stratégies matrimoniales dans le système de reproduction' supra (n. 8).
13. Bourdieu, 'Célibat et condition paysanne', p. 38.
14. Ibid., p. 49. Note the use of the word here which has been emphasized in Bourdieu's most recent publication, *La Noblesse d'état* (Paris, Éditions de Minuit, 1989).
15. Ibid., p. 48. Notice that in French P. Bourdieu oscillates between the use of 'différenciation', 'opposition' and 'distinction' – a point which is important in relation to the theme (often misinterpreted) of *La Distinction* (Paris, Éditions de Minuit, 1979) (trans. 1984). See Chapter 8.
16. Bourdieu does not elaborate the implications or the connotations of this Durkheimian usage.
17. Bourdieu, 'Célibat et condition paysanne', p. 72.
18. Ibid., p. 80.
19. Ibid., p. 80.
20. Ibid., p. 97.
21. Ibid., p. 99. Note the use of Béarn language. Of the 12 informants to the study, six are recorded as having spoken in Béarn, three in French and three in a mixture of the two.
22. 'habitus' (Latin): 'the condition or state of a thing'; 'condition, plight, habit, deportment, appearance of the body'. Lewis and Short, *Latin Dictionary*, Oxford, Clarendon Press, 1962, p. 836. See also my summarizing comments in Chapter 11.
23. 'hexis' (Greek): 'a being in a certain state, a permanent condition or habit, of body or mind'. Abridged Liddell and Scott, *Greek–English Lexicon*, Oxford, Clarendon Press, 1953, p. 237. See also my summarizing comments in Chapter 11. Bourdieu uses 'habitus' to signify attitudinal disposition and 'hexis' to signify physical deportment, although he insists – as etymology suggests – that both are integrally related.
24. Bourdieu, 'Célibat et condition paysanne', p. 109.
25. P. Bourdieu and J.C. Passeron, *Les Étudiants et leurs études*, Cahiers du Centre de Sociologie Européenne. Sociologie de l'Éducation, 1 (Paris–The Hague, Mouton, 1964), p. 123.

26. P. Bourdieu and J.C. Passeron, *The Inheritors, French Students and their Relation to Culture* (trans. R. Nice) (Chicago, The University of Chicago Press, 1979), p. ix. All the quotations from *Les Héritiers, les étudiants et la culture* (Paris, 1964) are taken from the American edition, translated by Richard Nice. Bourdieu added a brief preface for the American edition and an epilogue. I shall not consider these here since they belong to the late 1970s. The second appendix of the American edition adds some statistical tables which are derived from Monique de Saint Martin's 'Les facteurs de l'élimination et de la sélection différentielles dans les études de sciences' (1968), *Revue française de sociologie*, 9, special number, 1968, pp. 167–84. The footnotes of the American edition are partly translations of the original footnotes and partly explanatory notes written by Nice. Although I am using the American edition, I shall only be using the material which was actually in the French text of 1964.
27. The questionnaires summarized here are presented as Appendix II of Bourdieu and Passeron, *Les Étudiants et leurs études*, pp. 135–49.
28. Bourdieu and Passeron, *Les Étudiants et leurs études*, p. 10.
29. Ibid., p. 10.
30. Ibid., p. 123.
31. M. Douglas, *Purity and Danger. An Analysis of Concepts of Pollution and Taboo* (London, Routledge and Kegan Paul, 1966).
32. M. Mead, *Continuities in Cultural Evolution* (New Haven and London, Yale University Press, 1964).
33. Bourdieu and Passeron, *The Inheritors*, p. 24.
34. Ibid., p. 43.
35. Ibid., p. 73.

Chapter 4: From *Les Héritiers* to *La Reproduction*

1. D. Pickles, *Algeria and France. From Colonialism to Cooperation* (London, Methuen, 1963).
2. D. Pickles, *Problems of Contemporary French Politics* (London, Methuen, 1982), p. 1.
3. Darras, *Le partage des bénéfices, expansion et inégalités en France* (Paris, Éditions de Minuit, 1966), p. 10.
4. M. Douglas, *Evans-Pritchard* (London, Fontana, 1980), p. 118.
5. R. Castel and J.C. Passeron (eds), *Éducation, développement et démocratie* (Paris–The Hague, Mouton 1967), p. 14.
6. G. Antoine and J.C. Passeron, *La Réforme de l'université* (Paris, Calmann-Lévy, 1966).
7. J.P. Sartre in *Le Nouvel Observateur*. This, and the following reference (note 8), were both found in the comprehensive dossier on the events of May 1968, held in the Institut d'Histoire du Temps Présent. This press cutting is filed in Box 114 of the collection under the general title of 'Fondements "théoriques" de la "contestation"'.
8. A. Touraine, *Le Mouvement de mai et le Communisme utopique* (Paris, Seuil, 1968).
9. *Le Monde*, 28 March 1969, p. 9. See Box 114 at the IHTP.
10. M.S. Archer, 'Egalitarianism in English and French Educational Sociology', *European Journal of Sociology*, XI, 1, 1970.
11. P. Bourdieu and J.C. Passeron, 'Langage et rapport au langage dans la situation pédagogique', in *Rapport pédagogique et communication*. Cahiers du CSE, Sociologie de l'Éducation. II (Paris–The Hague, Mouton, 1965), p. 30.

12. P. Bourdieu (with L. Boltanski, R. Castel and J.C. Chamboredon), *Un Art moyen, essai sur les usages sociaux de la photographie* (Paris, Éditions de Minuit, 1965), p. 11.
13. M.F.D. Young (ed.), *Knowledge and Control. New Directions in the Sociology of Education* (London, Collier–Macmillan, 1971).
14. 'Problèmes du structuralisme', *Les Temps modernes*, 246 (November 1966).
15. P. Bourdieu, 'Intellectual field and creative project', in Young (ed.), *Knowledge and Control*, pp. 166–7.
16. See Ibid., p. 184, where Bourdieu quotes these phrases from E. Panofsky, *Architecture gothique et pensée scolastique* (trans. P. Bourdieu) (Paris, Éditions de Minuit, 1967), p. 84. The English reference is E. Panofsky, *Gothic Architecture and Scholasticism* (New York, Meridian Books, 1957), p. 24.
17. P. Bourdieu and J.C. Passeron (trans. R. Nice), *Reproduction in Education, Society and Culture* (London–Beverly Hills, Sage, 1977), p. v.
18. Ibid., p. 11.
19. Ibid., p. 31.
20. Ibid., p. 54.
21. Ibid., p. 4.

Chapter 5: On practising sociology

1. Bourdieu, *Reproduction*, p. 5.
2. A. Drouard, 'Réflexions sur une chronologie: le développement des sciences sociales en France de 1945 à la fin des années soixante', *Revue française de sociologie*, xxiii (1982), pp. 55–85.
3. P. Bourdieu and J.C. Passeron, 'Sociology and philosophy in France since 1945', *Social Research*, xxxiv, 1 (spring, 1967), p. 162.
4. Ibid., p. 163.
5. T.N. Clark, *Prophets and Patrons. The French University and the emergence of the Social Sciences* (Cambridge, Massachusetts, Harvard University Press, 1973). Clark is not named but it is clear from Clark's acknowledgements (p. vii) that he had been in Paris in the spring and summer of 1965 and had encountered Bourdieu.
6. P. Bourdieu, 'Structuralism and theory of sociological knowledge', *Social Research*, xxxv, 4 (Winter 1968), p. 681.
7. Ibid., p. 682.
8. Ibid., p. 683.
9. Ibid., p. 684.
10. Ibid., p. 697.
11. P. Bourdieu, J.C. Passeron and J.C. Chamboredon, *Le Métier de sociologue* (Paris, Mouton–Bordas, 1968), p. 10 ('spécifier en préceptes pratiques le principe de vigilance épistémologique').
12. Ibid., p. 11.
13. Ibid., p. 27. This is a quote from Bachelard: 'action polémique incessante de la Raison' – from G. Bachelard, *La Formation de l'esprit scientifique*, 4th edn (Paris, Vrin, 1965).
14. Bourdieu defines 'artificialism' as 'the illusory representation of the genesis of social facts according to which the scientist would be able to understand and explain these facts "by the effort of private reflexion alone"'. (*Le Métier de sociologue*, p. 37.)
15. Bourdieu *et al.*, *Le Métier de sociologue*, p. 59.

16. Ibid., p. 103.
17. Ibid., p. 113.
18. Bourdieu, *L'Ontologie politique de Martin Heidegger*, p. 7.
19. In J.G. Peristiany (ed.), *Honour and Shame. The Values of Mediterranean Society* (London, Weidenfeld and Nicolson, 1965), pp. 191–241.
20. In J. Pouillon and P. Maranda (eds), *Échanges et communications. Mélanges offerts à Claude Lévi-Strauss à l'occasion de son 60ème anniversaire* (Paris, Mouton, 1970), pp. 739–58.
21. In J.G. Peristiany (ed.), *Mediterranean Family Structures* (Cambridge, CUP, 1972). This is the proposed place of publication which is specified, but I have found no evidence that the collection was ever published.
22. P. Bourdieu, *Esquisse d'une théorie de la pratique, précédé de trois études d'ethnologie kabyle* (Geneva, Droz, 1972) n. 1, p. 129.
23. Ibid., p. 11 ('une idéologie et une politique inhumaines').
24. Ibid.
25. Ibid., p. 155. Cf. *Le Métier de sociologue*, p. 8.
26. Ibid., p. 8.
27. Ibid., p. 155.
28. Ibid.
29. Ibid.

Chapter 6: 'Field'-studies, 1970–5

1. Bourdieu, 'Intellectual field and creative project', in Young (ed.), *Knowledge and Control*, p. 174.
2. P. Bourdieu, 'Outline of a sociological theory of art perception', *International Social Science Journal*, xx (Winter 1968), p. 595.
3. P. Bourdieu, 'Champ du pouvoir, champ intellectuel et habitus de classe', p. 15.
4. Ibid.
5. Bourdieu was responding to J.P. Sartre, 'La conscience de classe chez Flaubert', in *Les Temps modernes*, 240 (May 1966), pp. 1921–51, and 241 (June 1966), pp. 2113–53. Bourdieu gave a more detailed account of his own analysis of Flaubert in 'L'invention de la vie d'artiste' (1975) in which he there responded to Sartre's *L'Idiot de la famille, Gustave Flaubert, 1821–1857*, vol. 1 (Paris, Gallimard, 1971).
6. Sartre, 'La conscience de classe chez Flaubert', p. 1921, quoted in Bourdieu, 'Champ du pouvoir, champ intellectuel et habitus de classe', p. 13.
7. Bourdieu specifies that his analysis is based on the chapter of *Wirtschaft und Gesellschaft* which is expressly devoted to religion and on section VII of the sociology of power entitled 'Political power and hierocratic power', both of which were written between 1911 and 1913, and on some texts written after 1918. For precise details, see 'Une interprétation de la théorie de la religion selon Max Weber', *Archives européennes de sociologie*, XII: 1, n. 2, p. 4.
8. Bourdieu, 'Une interprétation de la théorie de la religion selon Max Weber', p. 3.
9. I have suggested (Chapter 5) that there was a hint of the same tendency in Bourdieu's 'Structuralism and theory of sociological knowledge' (1968), but Bourdieu's argument here in 'Genèse et structure du champ religieux', *Revue française de*

sociologie, XII: 3 (1971), pp. 296–7, suggests that he recognized and resisted the tendency.

10. Bourdieu, 'Genèse et structure du champ religieux', p. 300.
11. 'L'auto-consommation religieuse'.
12. 'La monopolisation complète'.
13. See Bourdieu, 'Genèse et structure du champ religieux', pp. 305–6.
14. This discussion is also germane to Bourdieu's attitude towards the mass media. See his early 'Sociologues des mythologies et mythologies de sociologues', *Les Temps modernes*, 211 (December 1963), pp. 998–1021.
15. Bourdieu, 'Genèse et structure du champ religieux', p. 334.
16. P. Bourdieu, 'Public opinion does not exist' (trans. M.C. Axtmann), in A. Mattelart and S. Siegelaub (eds), *Communication and Class Struggle* (New York/Bagnolet/International General/IMMRC, 1979), vol. 1, 'Capitalism, Imperialism', p. 124.
17. The Institut d'Études Politiques in Paris, nicknamed 'Sciences-Po'. See P. Bourdieu, 'Les Doxosophes', *Minuit* (November 1972), p. 28.
18. Bourdieu, 'Genèse et structure du champ religieux', p. 334.
19. Ibid.
20. The 'tacit reflection' which I am here proposing relates to the argument of 'De la guerre révolutionnaire à la révolution'.
21. 'La défense du corps' constitutes Chapter 4 of the English edition of *Homo Academicus*.
22. P. Bourdieu, 'Les stratégies de reconversion. Les classes sociales et le système d'enseignement', *Information sur les sciences sociales*, XII: 5 (October 1973), p. 61. This is re-phrased in the English translation, p. 214.
23. 'Pente'.

Chapter 7: From the theory to the logic of practice

1. P. Bourdieu, 'Le sens pratique', *Actes de la recherche en sciences sociales*, 1 (February 1976), p. 44.
2. P. Bourdieu, 'Les modes de domination' *Actes de la recherche en sciences sociales* 2–3 (June 1976).
3. Bourdieu, *Esquisse*, p. 163.
4. P. Bourdieu, *Outline of a Theory of Practice* (trans. R. Nice), Cambridge, Cambridge University Press, 1977, p. 3.
5. This critique was taken up in the section of the first part of *Outline* entitled 'The fallacies of the rule', pp. 23–30, with the addition of some discussion of Chomsky, and continued in *Ce que parler veut dire* (1982). The digression occurs in *Esquisse* between p. 166 and p. 174.
6. Bourdieu, *Outline*, p. 4.
7. Bourdieu, *Esquisse*, p. 221.
8. Bourdieu, 'The sentiment of honour'.
9. Bourdieu, *Esquisse*, p. 9. 'SENS (sanss; san jusqu'aux XIXe s.) n.m. (XIes. ROL.; empr. lat. sensus, 'action, manière de sentir; sentiment; pensée; signification.)' See my comments in Chapter 11.
10. Bourdieu, 'The sentiment of honour', p. 231.
11. Ibid., p. 214.
12. 'Le sentiment de l'honneur' – in other words, the French text still uses 'sentiment' here even though the title of the essay is changed to 'Le sens de l'honneur'. In

this passage, 'le sentiment de l'honneur' is translated in *Outline* as 'the sense of honour.'

13. Bourdieu, *Esquisse*, p. 31.
14. Bourdieu, *Outline*, p. 14.
15. Ibid., p. 15.
16. P. Bourdieu, 'Systems of education and systems of thought', in Yaug (ed.) *Knowledge and Control*.
17. To pursue Bourdieu's revision of 'The sentiment of honour' to completion, readers should see the postscriptum which he wrote for the publication of the text in *Algeria 1960*, pp. 131–2 and, in particular, n. 35 on p. 132.
18. Bourdieu, *Esquisse*, p. 191.
19. Bourdieu, *Outline*, p. 98. To pursue Bourdieu's revision of 'The Kabyle house or the world reversed' to completion, readers should see the annexe to *Le Sens pratique* (1980) pp. 441–61, and, in particular, the comment in n. 1, p. 441.
20. Bourdieu, *Outline*, p. 98.
21. See, for instance, n. 8, p. 45; nn. 24 and 25, p. 52; and n. 28, p. 53; of 'Le sens pratique' (1976). N. 20, p. 221 of *Outline* is the same as n. 24 of 'Le sens pratique' and is the only one of the four footnotes mentioned here to be reproduced in the English text.
22. The best elaboration of 'polythesis' is found on p. 110 of *Outline*.
23. Bourdieu borrows this expression from George Lakoff. See *Outline*, n. 25, p. 221.
24. Bourdieu, *Algeria 1960*, p. 32. There are minor alterations to the original text. Readers interested in taking the textual exploration further than space allows here could, for instance, compare *Algeria 1960*, pp. 4–5 with *Travail et travailleurs*, pp. 314–15 – the concept of 'habitus' is added to the earlier account. Bourdieu has wanted to suggest that the concept of 'habitus' arose directly out of his Algerian field-work – see his preface to *Algeria 1960*, p. vii – but the evidence is rather that the idea of using the concept came from his reading of Panofsky. See Chapter 4, and see, also, Bourdieu's retrospective account of the origin of his use of the concept in 'The genesis of the concepts of habitus and field' (1985).
25. Bourdieu, *Algeria 1960*, p. vii.
26. See his comment, ibid., p. viii.
27. Bourdieu, *Outline*, p. 183.
28. Ibid., p. 186.
29. Ibid., p. 189.
30. Ibid., p. 197.

Chapter 8: 'Distinction'

1. Bourdieu, *Sociologie de l'Algérie*, p. 10. (*The Algerians* (1962), p. xiii.)
2. Bourdieu, *Travail et travailleurs*, p. 372. (For the whole discussion, see pp. 368–75. Bourdieu revisits this passage in *Algeria 1960*, pp. 75–90. The version of 1979 imposes an economic conditioning on the original argument – modern housing generates malaise for those who have not adapted culturally.)
3. Bourdieu, 'Célibat et condition paysanne', p. 48.
4. Ibid.
5. Ibid., p. 49.
6. Ibid., pp. 81ff.
7. Ibid., p. 95.

8. Bourdieu, *Un Art moyen*, p. 77 ('jouer au citadin').

9. Ibid., p. 137. (Compare the terminology here with the postscript to *La Distinction* – 'Towards a "Vulgar" Critique of "Pure" Critiques'.)

10. I have coined 'culturological' to be analogous with Bourdieu's use of 'politicological' in 'Les Doxosophes' (1972), p. 31, which is rendered as 'political–scientific' in *Distinction*, p. 405.

11. P. Bourdieu, 'Éléments d'une théorie sociologique de la perception artistique', *Revue internationale des sciences sociales* (1968).

12. P. Bourdieu, *L'Amour de l'art* (Paris, Éditions de Minuit, 1966). See the forward: 'L'air du temps'.

13. Bourdieu, 'Outline of a sociological theory of art perception', p. 592. Bourdieu's presentation follows E. Panofsky, *Meaning in the Visual Arts* (Garden City, New York, Doubleday, 1955).

14. P. Bourdieu, 'The market of symbolic goods' (trans. R. Swyer) *Poetics*, 14: 1/2 (April 1985), p. 23.

15. P. Bourdieu, 'Méthode scientifique et hiérarchie sociale des objets', *Actes de la recherche en sciences sociales*, 1 (January 1975).

16. P. Bourdieu, 'The specificity of the scientific field and the social conditions of the progress of reason', (trans. R. Nice), *Social Science Information*, XIV, 6, December 1975.

17. P. Bourdieu, 'Le couturier et sa griffe. Contribution à une théorie de la magie', *Actes de la recherche en sciences sociales*, 1 (January 1975).

18. P. Bourdieu, 'Anatomie du goût', *Actes de la recherche en sciences sociales*, 4 (August 1976), p. 4.

19. Ibid., p. 5.

20. Ibid., p. 6.

21. 'Une mise en garde' – ibid., p. 81.

22. Ibid., pp. 81–2.

23. Bourdieu, *La Distinction*, p. 10; *Distinction*, p. 12.

24. Ibid.

25. Ibid., p. 17 and p. 18.

26. Ibid., p. 23 and p. 22.

27. Ibid., pp. 267–8 and p. 241.

28. Ibid., p. 564 and p. 483.

29. Ibid.

30. Ibid.

Chapter 9: From practical logic to logical practice

1. Bourdieu, 'L'ontologie politique de Martin Heidegger', p. 110.

2. Ibid., p. 124.

3. Ibid.

4. Ibid., p. 130.

5. Ibid., p. 136.

6. Ibid., p. 139.

7. Ibid., p. 143. Bourdieu says that, following Jean Bollack, this could also be called 'l'allégorie'.

8. See Bourdieu and Passeron, 'Sociology and philosophy in France since 1945'.

9. From a letter written to Mademoiselle Leroyer de Chantepie in October 1864, quoted in the introduction to G. Flaubert, *Sentimental Education* (trans. with an introduction by R. Baldick) (London, Penguin Books, 1969), p. 7. Notice the affinity between Flaubert's intention and Bourdieu's retrospective comment that he was attempting to establish a phenomenology of affective relations in his Algerian fieldwork – see Chapter 2.

10. P. Bourdieu, 'L'invention de la vie d'artiste', *Actes de la recherche en sciences sociales*, 2 (March 1975), pp. 91–2.

11. P. Bourdieu, 'Questions de politique', *Actes de la recherche en sciences sociales*, 16 (September 1977), p. 88.

12. P. Bourdieu, 'Une classe objet', *Actes de la recherche en sciences sociales*, 17–18 (November 1977), p. 2.

13. P. Bourdieu, 'Sur le pouvoir symbolique', *Annales*, 3 (May–June 1977). English translation: 'Symbolic Power', in D. Gleeson (ed.), *Identity and Structure* (Driffield, Nafferton Books, 1977), p. 117.

14. P. Bourdieu, 'Le paradoxe du sociologue', in P. Bourdieu, *Questions de sociologie*, (Paris, Éditions de Minuit, 1980), p. 86.

15. P. Bourdieu, 'Sur l'objectivation participante. Réponses à quelques objections', *Actes de la recherche en sciences sociales*, 23 (September 1978), p. 69. It is worth noting that the 'objections' to which Bourdieu responds are what might be called human queries rather than objections raised by social scientists. Compare, however, the significantly different kind of response of the late 1980s in 'A reply to some objections' in *In Other Words*, Oxford, Polity Press, 1990.

16. P. Bourdieu, 'Dialogue sur la poésie orale', *Actes de la recherche en sciences sociales*, 23 (September 1978), p. 51.

17. Ibid., p. 52.

18. Ibid., p. 53.

19. Ibid., pp. 65–6.

20. See P. Bourdieu, *Le Sens pratique* (Paris, Éditions de Minuit, 1980), pp. 9–10.

21. Bourdieu, *Le Sens pratique* (1980), p. 24.

22. Ibid., p. 47.

23. '. . . every truly sociological undertaking is, inseparably, a socio-analysis . . .' – Bourdieu, *Le Sens pratique* (1980), p. 40.

24. See Bourdieu, *Le Sens pratique* (1980), nn. 20 and 21, p. 79.

25. G. Schalken, 'Le gourmet', in the Prague National Gallery.

26. See P. Bourdieu, 'Les intellectuels sont-ils hors jeu?', in Bourdieu, *Questions de sociologie*, pp. 61–6.

Chapter 10: Scientifically speaking

1. P. Bourdieu, *Ce que parler veut dire. L'économie des échanges linguistiques* (Paris, Fayard, 1982), p. 7.

2. Ibid., p. 8.

3. Ibid.

4. Bourdieu, *Esquisse d'une théorie de la pratique*, p. 164.

5. See Bourdieu, *Outline of a Theory of Practice*, pp. 22–9.

6. Bourdieu, *Ce que parler veut dire*, p. 99.

7. P. Bourdieu, 'Les trois états du capital culturel', *Actes de la recherche en sciences sociales*, 30 (November 1979), p. 3.
8. P. Bourdieu, 'Les catégories de l'entendement professoral', *Actes de la recherche en sciences sociales*, 3 (May 1975), p. 92; and in P. Bourdieu, *Homo Academicus* (Oxford, Polity Press, 1988), p. 222.
9. Ibid.; and in Bourdieu, *Homo Academicus*, p. 223. The French is 'lieux francs'.
10. P. Bourdieu, *Leçon sur la leçon* (Paris, Éditions de Minuit, 1982), pp. 7–8.
11. Ibid., p. 12.
12. See ibid., p. 13 for Bourdieu's discussion of the meaning of the word 'censor'.
13. Ibid., pp. 19–20.
14. Ibid., p. 55.
15. Ibid., p. 56.
16. Ibid., p. 10.
17. P. Bourdieu, *Homo academicus* (Paris, Éditions de Minuit, 1984), p. 48; and Bourdieu, *Homo Academicus* (English edn), p. 32.
18. P. Bourdieu, *La Noblesse d'état. Grandes écoles et esprit de corps* (Paris, Éditions de Minuit, 1989), p. 7.
19. Ibid., p. 13.
20. Bourdieu, 'Le sens pratique' (1976), p. 43; and in Bourdieu, *Outline of a Theory of Practice*, pp. 96–7.

Chapter 11: Ways of recognizing

1. W. Stevens, *Selected Poems* (London, Faber & Faber, 1953), p. 44.
2. D. Hartley, *Observations on Man, his Frame, his Duty, and his Expectations. In Two Parts* (1749).
3. W. Paley, *The Principles of Moral and Political Philosophy*, Book I, Chapter VII, 'Virtue' in *Works*, a new edition in seven volumes (London, 1825), vol. IV, p. 32.
4. A community in which all would have equality of power.
5. W. Wordsworth, 'Ode. Intimations of immortality from recollections of early childhood' (composed 1803 (?1802)–1806; published 1807), line 58, E. de Selincourt (ed.), *The Poetical Works of William Wordsworth* (Oxford, Oxford University Press, 1960), p. 460.
6. Ibid., lines 133–6, in de Selincourt (ed.), *The Poetical Works of William Wordsworth*, p. 461.
7. W. Wordsworth, 'Lines written in early spring' (composed 1798; published 1798), line 8, in de Selincourt (ed.), *The Poetical Works of William Wordsworth*, p. 377.
8. S.T. Coleridge, 'Kubla Khan: Or, A vision in a dream. A fragment' (composed 1798; published 1816), lines 42–3, in E.H. Coleridge (ed.), *The Poems of Samuel Taylor Coleridge* (Oxford, Oxford University Press, 1957), p. 298.
9. P.B. Shelley, *Defence of Poetry* (1821).
10. See R. Williams, *Culture and Society 1780–1950* (London, Penguin Books, 1961), especially Chapter 2, 'The Romantic Artist', pp. 48–64.
11. The phrase is Gilbert Ryle's from his *The Concept of Mind*. Bourdieu refers to Ryle's words in his 'Structuralism and theory of Sociological Knowledge', *Social Research*, 35: 4 (Winter 1968), p. 690.
12. The notes on contributors for the second number of *Liber*, of which Bourdieu is the Chairman of the editorial board, comments: 'He [Bourdieu] is working on

an economy of symbolic exchanges and on a social history of the great revolutions in art.' *Liber* – A European Review of Books, Year 1, No. 2 (December 1989), p. 3.

13. See P. Bourdieu, 'Le racisme de l'intelligence', in Bourdieu, *Questions de sociologie*, pp. 264–8.

14. See Bourdieu, 'La fin d'un malthusianisme?', in Darras, *Le partage des bénéfices, expansion et inégalités en France*, pp. 135–54.

15. 'Fra Girolamo Savonarola (1452–98), Dominican monk, an eloquent preacher whose sermons at Florence gave expression to the religious reaction against the artistic licence and social corruption of the Renaissance. Savonarola was leader of the democratic party in Florence after the expulsion of the Medici, and aroused the hostility of Pope Alexander VI by his political attitude in favour of Charles VIII of France. His influence was gradually undermined, and he was tried, condemned, and executed as a heretic. There is a careful study of his character in G. Eliot's *Romola*.' P. Harvey (ed.), *The Oxford Companion to English Literature*, 3rd edn (Oxford, Clarendon Press, 1946), p. 699.

16. In a review by Tony Judt of *La Noblesse d'état* in the *Times Literary Supplement* of 18 August 1989, p. 889.

17. See, for instance, the relationship between Virginia Woolf's first novel – *The Voyage Out* (1915) – and the views expressed by her father in an essay called 'What is Materialism?' in L. Stephen (ed.), *An Agnostic's Apology, and Other Essays* (London, 1893).

18. 'It is necessary to cultivate our garden'. Voltaire, *Candide, ou l'optimisme* (1759), in H. Bénac (ed.), *Voltaire. Romans et Contes* (Paris, Éditions Garnier, 1960), p. 221.

19. 'Here I stand: I cannot do otherwise.' This may be an apocryphal version of part of the speech which Luther gave at the Diet of Worms in 1521.

Index of references to the works of Bourdieu

Index